ARCHIVAL COMMUNITIES

FROM PAMPHLETS TO PODCASTS
An Institute for Thomas Paine Studies Series
Nora Slonimsky and Mark Boonshoft, Editors

Archival Communities

Constructing the Past in the Early United States

DEREK KANE O'LEARY

University of Virginia Press
Charlottesville and London

Published in association with the
Institute for Thomas Paine Studies at Iona University

The University of Virginia Press is situated on the traditional lands of the Monacan Nation, and the Commonwealth of Virginia was and is home to many other Indigenous people. We pay our respect to all of them, past and present. We also honor the enslaved African and African American people who built the University of Virginia, and we recognize their descendants. We commit to fostering voices from these communities through our publications and to deepening our collective understanding of their histories and contributions.

University of Virginia Press
© 2025 by the Rector and Visitors of the University of Virginia
All rights reserved
Printed in the United States of America on acid-free paper

First published 2025

9 8 7 6 5 4 3 2 1

LIBRARY OF CONGRESS CATALOGING-IN-PUBLICATION DATA

Names: O'Leary, Derek Kane, author.
Title: Archival communities : constructing the past in the early United States / Derek Kane O'Leary.
Description: Charlottesville : University of Virginia Press, 2025. | Series: From pamphlets to podcasts: an Institute for Thomas Paine Studies series | Includes bibliographical references and index.
Identifiers: LCCN 2024041091 (print) | LCCN 2024041092 (ebook) | ISBN 9780813953038 (hardcover) | ISBN 9780813953045 (paperback) | ISBN 9780813953052 (ebook)
Subjects: LCSH: Archives—United States—History. | Archivists—United States. | Archives—Social aspects—United States.
Classification: LCC CD3021 .O66 2025 (print) | LCC CD3021 (ebook) | DDC 352.3/870973—dc23/eng/20250225
LC record available at https://lccn.loc.gov/2024041091
LC ebook record available at https://lccn.loc.gov/2024041092

Cover art: iStockPhoto / Wylius
Cover design: Joel W. Coggins

To my mom and dad

CONTENTS

List of Illustrations	ix
Acknowledgments	xi
Introduction	1
1. Envisioning American Archival Exceptionalism	11
2. Contesting America's Global Archive	43
3. Washington's National Archive	82
4. State of the Archives	119
5. All History Is Local	151
Conclusion	181
Notes	185
Index	229

ILLUSTRATIONS

1. Silhouette of John Quincy Adams — 3
2. *Memoirs of the Historical Society of Pennsylvania* — 22
3. Silhouette of Sarah Josepha Hale — 26
4. Portrait of Carl Christian Rafn — 51
5. Diploma of RSNA membership for John Farmer — 55
6. Map of Norse discoveries from *Antiquitates Americanae* — 61
7. Portrait of Jared Spark — 95
8. Silhouette of Catharine Maria Sedgwick — 108
9. Engraving of George Washington — 111
10. Portrait of Edmund Bailey O'Callaghan — 146
11. James Savage bookplate — 156
12. Portrait of Frances Manwaring Caulkins — 157

➤ ACKNOWLEDGMENTS ◀

To my teachers: I thank my wonderful professors in the French Department at Amherst College, Leah Hewitt and Laure Katsaros, who supported my accent and stoked my curiosity to explore the world. To John Curtis Perry, friend, of the Fletcher School, who showed me how to love the life of the mind, though this book is likely less salty than he would have liked. To my advisor Mark Peterson, who guided this project and impressed upon me at a formative moment to "just make a good teapot," which I hope this is. And to paragons of teaching and scholarship at UC Berkeley, David Henkin, Jeroen Dewulf, Elisa Tamarkin, and Alan Karras.

To the institutions that supported me and this work: I thank UC Berkeley for being itself, as well as its Institute of European Studies, Social Science Matrix, Dutch Studies program, and History Department for their scholarly community, reassurance, and generous funding. In your own league for kindness and humor in student services, Erin Leigh Inama and Todd Kuebler, thank you. I send my gratitude to the staff of the libraries and historical societies, institutions that are actors in both this book and its creation: the American Philosophical Society, Harvard's Houghton Library, the George Washington Presidential Library, Massachusetts Historical Society, the Maine Historical Society, the New Hampshire Historical Society, the New London County Historical Society, and the American Antiquarian Society and its president, Scott Casper, who provided indispensable guidance. A special thanks to the wonderful editor Nadine Zimmerli of the University of Virginia Press, who from the early days of the pandemic advocated for this project.

My Berkeley friends and colleagues, Brandon Kirk Williams, Agnieszka Smelkowsa, Veronica Jacome, J. T. Jamieson, Russell Weber, and Franklin

Sammons, have my gratitude for their many years of interest and encouragement. To *JHI* bloggers emeriti, John Raimo, Sarah Dunstan, Spencer Weinreich, Cynthia Houng, and Nuala Caomhánach, thank you for reading so many scraps of this project as I pieced it together and for sharing your own compelling work along the way.

To Ayluonne, for building an archive with me.

And to my family, my first and dearest readers, who taught me that history is open to interpretation.

Two portions of chapter 1 were derived from earlier versions that appeared in "The Trouble with Antiquarianism in the Early U.S.," *Archival History News* (Spring 2019); and "Borrowed Books and Scholarly Interventions in Sarah Josepha Hale's *Genius of Oblivion* (1823)," *Libraries: Culture, History, and Society* 6, no. 2 (2022): 304–32. Thank you to the Society of American Archivists for their support and the thoughtful reviewers and editors for their guidance on these essays.

An earlier version of chapter 2 was published as "Scandinavian Archives, Transatlantic Historical Culture, and Carl Christian Rafn's Attempt to Rewrite American History in the Antebellum U.S," *Journal of Early American History* 12, no. 23 (2022): 169–210. I thank the journal's editors and reviewers for their support developing the article.

Two portions of chapter 3 were drawn from earlier versions that appeared as "Jared Sparks and Constructing the American Archive," in *The Representation of External Threats: From the Middle Ages to the Modern World*, ed. Eberhard Crailsheim and María Dolores Elizalde (Leiden: Brill, 2019), 294–318; and "Washington Writing in the Archival Space of Catherine Maria Sedgwick's *The Linwoods*," *Harvard Library Bulletin* (2020). Thank you to Houghton Library for their support in the revision of that article, in particular the excellent editing of Mitch Nakaue.

Several sections of chapter 4 emerged from earlier version of those episodes previously published in "Gender and the Archival Threshold in the Early U.S. Historical Society," *New Americanist* 4, no. 1 (2020): 29–58; "'The Historical Society Has Removed to Massachusetts': Edward Jarvis and the First Kentucky Historical Society," *Register of the Kentucky Historical Society* 121, no. 1 (2023): 5–50; "New Netherland, Archival Deficiency, and Contesting New York History in the Antebellum U.S.," *Dutch Crossing* 43, no. 3

(2019): 252–69; and "'For the Use of the State': Edmund Bailey O'Callaghan and the Work of New York's Archives," *Gotham: A Blog for Scholars of New York City History* (August 2021). Thank you to the editors of these essays for their support, in particular Daniel Burge and Stephanie Lang of the Kentucky Historical Society.

ARCHIVAL COMMUNITIES

Introduction

The United States of America had a problem, according to the New York Historical Society (NYHS). In 1845, a NYHS special committee "on a National Name" argued it was high time that Americans discard their inadequate moniker. The committee sent a pointed report on the issue to fellow historical societies and "eminent gentlemen" for their take. For an institution devoted to preserving America's past, the NYHS was frankly unsentimental about the name inscribed in the nation's founding documents and throughout its own archive. The committee's reasoning ranged from the grammatical to the existential. *United States of America* was an encumbrance—"being a phrase, from which it is impossible to derive an adjective," the committee griped, "we have no means of describing ourselves, but by a circumlocution." *American* would not do, "as it belongs to the whole hemisphere," and *United States*, if logical at the dawn of the Age of Revolutions, had become confusing in a hemisphere with multiple "United States"—four or five by the committee's count. For the NYHS, this absence of a suitable adjective for citizens of the United States of America reflected a more urgent problem than simply what to call themselves when traveling abroad: "If we are, what we boast, one people, and one nation, 'e pluribus unum,' with national traits, national impulses, a general history, and a common character, let us have a word significant of that unity. Let us have a sign in our language that such a nation exists."[1] The distinctive history and character of the nation, the name to encapsulate it, and its very existence were entwined.

The NYHS committee proposed a new national name grounded in the geography of their country. They summoned the words of Washington

Irving, a NYHS member whose fictional and historical writing—such as his widely read biography of Christopher Columbus—was renowned on both sides of the Atlantic, including in Spain, where he then served as US minister. Irving, they quoted, called for an "appellation" that made clear to all "that I belong to this very portion of America, geographical and political, to which it is my pride and happiness to belong: that I am of the Anglo-Saxon race, which founded this Anglo-Saxon empire in the wilderness; and that I have no part or parcel with any other race or empire, Spanish, French, or Portuguese, in either of the Americas. Such an appellation would have magic in it."[2] While the committee mused that the entire hemisphere should ideally be renamed *Columbia*, it agreed with Irving that the best word for the United States sprang from the land: *Alleghania*. The *U.S.A.* could be restyled the *United States of Alleghania*, or perhaps the *Republic of Alleghania*—its citizens, presumably, *Alleghanians*.

The committee saw the Allegheny Mountains as both a source and a symbol of the nation's interconnectedness, holding it together "as with a band of iron." The word for the mountain range, they believed, hailed from the "primordial race, more ancient than our nomadic tribes, beyond which no Indian tradition can go." Here they meant the Mound Builders, an Indigenous civilization that had emerged and thrived on the eastern half of the continent more than a half millennium prior, constructing large-scale earthen architecture before their decline and displacement by contemporary American Indians, or so a well-known theory shared by members of nineteenth-century historical societies went.[3] According to the committee, "that widespread people, whose mysterious history, dimly shadowed by their vast mounds in the wilderness, call up so many images of durability, of power, of wide embracing sway; images to which our progress of empire has given new vitality."[4] In the eyes of the committee, by appropriating the name *Alleghania*, the republic could claim both the imagined past of the Mound Builders and the expansive future that it envisioned for itself. Only a name commensurate with what they saw as their nation's triumphant progress through time and space would do.

The Massachusetts Historical Society (MHS) was among those urged by the NYHS committee to deliberate on a new national name, which the NYHS hoped might even lead to a formal petition by historical societies to the US Congress. Responding on behalf of the MHS, John Quincy Adams agreed that *America* was a historical mistake. He labeled it "a perpetual

FIGURE 1. Silhouette of John Quincy Adams, by Auguste Edouart, 1841. (National Portrait Gallery, Smithsonian Institution; gift of Robert L. McNeil Jr.)

memorial of human injustice, by conferring upon one man [Amerigo Vespucci] a crown of glory justly due to another," Columbus. As a younger man, Adams the diplomat had helped to negotiate the Treaty of Ghent with Britain (1814), orchestrated the Adams-Onís Treaty with Spain (1819) as James Monroe's secretary of state, and maneuvered US policy toward curtailing European imperialism in the hemisphere, which culminated in the Monroe Doctrine (1823). These and other diplomatic documents served to solidify the nation's southern and northern borders, enabling its westward expansion into Indigenous lands and territory claimed by competing European empires.[5]

Looking both backward and forward in time, Adams wrote in his draft letter to the NYHS that *Columbia* best suited the nation's "great and growing community"; he then crossed out "destined to cover the whole surface of this continent, and with the blessing of God to spread the rights of immortal man over the whole surface of the globe."⁶ Columbus represented the first stride of "civilization" across the hemisphere to Americans like Adams—the legacy inherited by the United States, as he saw it.⁷ *Columbia* had rung true to the nation's historical identity since the throes of the American Revolution and reverberated since, Adams observed. He shared with the NYHS committee an imperialist vision for the nation but was loath to rechristen it *Alleghania*, which, he carped, was "associated with no sentiment, but with the mere clod of earth, a mere chain of not even comparatively lofty mountains" when stacked alongside those of Europe, Asia, Africa, or South America.

The NYHS committee warned its influential correspondents that "nationality must express itself in words. If it finds none it will dissipate and disappear."⁸ Like Adams, historical societies from Vermont to Georgia and influential public figures from across the United States worried about this question but were ambivalent or outright dismissive toward the proposed name change. The Maryland Historical Society concluded that the "time has long since passed when the people of our Union would willingly consent to part with a title under which they have flourished and by which they are gloriously distinguished among the nations of the earth." Less diplomatic, a committee appointed by the New Jersey Historical Society to consider the matter queried, "Where upon earth is the country which has received its name from its mountains?" Most found the idea impractical or unnecessary. Henry Clay, the powerful Kentucky politician and Adams's former secretary of state, wished that the country's inhabitants "to the latest posterity, should be called Washingtonians," but thought it excessive to advocate for a formal name change. Less charmed by *Republic of Washington*, the esteemed historical novelist William Gilmore Simms admitted, "I conscientiously believe that if the nation was called 'Squash,' [our people] would not be conscious of any awkwardness" or receptive to a change imposed "by resolutions or enactments."⁹ In the end, even the NYHS decided against endorsing the committee's report.

Adams was not alone in airing his skepticism about the power of any name to unify a people far more attached to their separate states than to the union. "Our primitive motto was, 'out of many one,'" he remarked. "We adhere by the understanding and by good faith to the *many*. We cling, grappled to the soul with hooks of steel, to the *one*."¹⁰ The former president was not wrong. Rather than Alleghania, Columbia, the Republic of Washington, or any of the other names proposed to unite the nation in those years, Americans got the opposite less than two decades later: a Confederate States of America severed from the United States. A nation riven, its conception of history, past and future, divided.

Although a historical curiosity in the end, the NYHS committee on a national name hints at the stakes and challenges that these institutions' members perceived in their work to build archives that could authenticate narratives of the nation's origins, defining features, and historical trajectory. Although the NYHS and the MHS shared similar visions of the nation's destiny, they disagreed about where and when to locate its origins in the scope of global history, whether in a lost Indigenous civilization or the oceanic voyages that unleashed the colonization of the hemisphere. Both institutions worried about foreign perceptions and hoped to fashion a national historical consciousness that would distinguish Americans. But with no national entity equipped to preserve, interpret, and commemorate its history, historical societies in New York, Massachusetts, and nearly every other state promoted differing interpretations that foregrounded the singular history of their state. For the networks of influential Americans who supported these institutions and the broader public that consumed their narratives, these institutions' differing claims about the past could shape the historical significance of any local site within the nation: did a resident of the Alleghenies inhabit a "band of iron," as the NYHS viewed it, or a "mere clod of earth," as Adams sneered?

The year before Adams penned his response to the NYHS, he had been invited to address the audience of notables gathered in Manhattan for the society's fortieth anniversary. The lavish event doubled as a celebration of John Romeyn Brodhead's successful completion of an archival mission to Europe, where he had copied from collections in the Netherlands, Britain, and France some eighty volumes' worth of documents relating to New York's colonial period. The elite array of politicians, judges, merchants, clergy, and diplomats assembled before Adams likely nodded at his assertion that historical societies "must be regarded as the most useful Institutions upon earth." For these men and the many others engaged in the work of historical societies in the United States, these institutions were not just repositories for historical resources but shrines safeguarding the evidence for Americans' place within a transcendent history that connected past, present, and future. "When we go back to the discovery of this country, by Columbus," Adams sketched for his audience, "and then come down to the present day and review the history of that period, it will be found to be a mere progression of the condition of man upon earth."[11]

Since the turn of the nineteenth century, historical societies in Massachusetts, New York, and—by the time of his speech—throughout the expanding country had amassed archives of historical materials, text by text, object by object, in order to authenticate this historical vision. The many members of historical societies took it as their civic responsibility to preserve the record of what they deemed their nation's exceptional history and to use their burgeoning archives, growing networks of members, and public stature to shape how Americans perceived their past and envisioned their future. This, in turn, would enable Americans to document and emplot their own communities, families, and lives within the nation's history. History could thus unite, instruct, and guide Americans, they held. Much was at stake.

Yet these innumerable sources gathered by different institutions did not amount to one clear, unifying narrative for the nation. The historical record preserved in these archives remained incomplete, the contours of these emerging national narratives unstable. As Irving's musings about *Alleghania* and Adams's retort about *Columbia* suggest, historical societies struggled to distinguish their nation's historical identity from others in the Atlantic world. In addition, institutions in different states disagreed with each other over which materials should be archived and which narratives promoted. Advocates of historical societies also questioned their very capacity to salvage the full historical record and shape historical consciousness. In practice, the process of gathering materials and making sense of the past just as often obliterated historical materials and marginalized historical actors; after all, both *Alleghania* and *Columbia* disregarded Indigenous perspectives and validated the displacement of American Indians from the nation's history.[12] Establishing the archival threshold of these institutions, moving materials across it, and interpreting this historical record remained a challenging, complicated, and contested process.

One might hesitate to care much about the anxiety of the NYHS committee or hear Adams's claim at its anniversary gala as anything more than fanciful hyperbole—of interest only to these institutions.[13] Amid the teeming associational life of the early United States, historical societies and their networks can easily appear—if they appear at all—as just one of the many communities of busy Americans seeking some measure of belonging or diversion or reform. Historically minded Americans enjoyed many other vibrant means to engage with the past, as the rich scholarship about historical commemoration and writing in the early United States shows. Celebrations of anniversaries in the streets, pilgrimages to memorial sites, popular history books, lectures and historical paintings, and rituals of preservation and remembrance in homes: these and other forms enabled Americans to play their part in preserving the nation's past, constructing its historical narratives, and mediating the relationship between the living and the dead.[14] By contrast, historical societies might look like dusty, quiet, bloodless spaces, shielded behind stony facades. Within, they can appear as exclusionary redoubts for bookish white men, fanning their nostalgia with the page-by-page curation of the lives of greater ancestors. Their gleaning of historical materials can seem parochial, their production of historical narratives predictable.

However, *Archival Communities* shows that the work of historical societies was neither parochial nor predictable. The networks that these institutions activated and the wider publics that they engaged shaped the emergence of the historical discipline in the United States and the evidence and narratives that Americans used to make sense of their place in time. These archives and historical narratives emerged from a much larger international context, a wider array of people, and a more contingent process than we have imagined. Rather than siloed caches of historical materials, America's archives were collected and interpreted within a dynamic international context. Instead of cloistered groups of elite men, a wider array of hands on the margins of these institutions and much farther afield contributed to building and manipulating these collections. Far from inert, these materials and narratives were contested by individuals, institutions, states, and national governments between the nation's founding and the Civil War. Without this reframing, we cannot understand the emergence of archives and narratives that continue to influence how researchers and broader publics perceive American history today.

In its reframing, *Archival Communities* builds upon recent works on the gathering and writing of the nation's history by scholars such as Eileen Ka-May Cheng, François Weil, Lindsay DiCuirci, and Alea Henle, who have examined the construction of historical collections and narratives as part of the development of history as a discipline and the formation of national identity.[15] These excellent scholars reveal much about the world of archives and history writing, but they tend to limit their inquiry within the territorial boundaries of the United States. *Archival Communities* now shows that the building of the nation's archives and historical narratives was entangled in western European intellectual traditions, collections, geopolitics, and social networks. Often abetted by an expanding constellation of consular and diplomatic officials, collecting and deciphering American history took place in an international context from which America's archives and narratives derived their materials and meaning.

In examining the characters who built and interpreted the nation's early archives, this book acknowledges that archives were mainly the domain of privileged men, their work devised in patriarchal terms. The archival stories illustrated throughout this book show that their construction of archives actively built a threshold that included some and excluded other historical sources, people, and narratives. But a wider community of people influenced and engaged with these institutions by donating materials to archives, promoting the value of archives, and making sense of their meaning. This included women of letters whose gathering, preserving, and interpreting of historical materials actively shaped archives and Americans' relationship with their nation's past, which complements studies of women history writers by scholars such as Mary Kelley, Nina Baym, and Julie Des Jardins.[16] Examining women's archival work, even as they were regularly excluded from these institutions, expands our sense of "the gender of history" in the nineteenth-century United States, to use Bonnie Smith's now classic phrase.[17]

Within this broader geography and scholarly community, this book reveals the individuals, historical societies, states, federal forces, and foreign interlocutors who sought, examined, and contested a range of historical sources and narrative possibilities. Typically, scholarship has divided the work of building the nation's archives and crafting its prevailing narratives into separate studies that focus on a distinct historical period, such as Indigenous histories, the alleged medieval European colonization of North America, the colonial period, and the American Revolution.[18] However, this book brings together these various strands, recognizing that the same institutions, individuals, states, and federal actors were often engaged in the archiving and narrating of these different periods at the same time.

Whereas some materials and ideas came to be preserved and accentuated in archives, others were discarded or marginalized. What crossed the archival threshold, which individuals and institutions had the authority and responsibility to undertake this work, and how these materials and actors informed the nation's historical narratives, identity, and trajectory remained contested throughout the antebellum period in particular.

The Americans behind these archives envisioned, authenticated, and argued about their history within a series of overlapping frames, which provide the structure for *Archival Communities*: the global, the national, the state, and the local. As they undertook to authenticate America's past, construct a historical narrative for the nation, and mediate the public's relationship with it, the builders of America's archives sought to make sense of their historical record and past within these frames. After an opening chapter that describes the world of historical societies and the archives that they built, the following four examine the efforts to authenticate America's history within each of these frames, from the global to the local.

Each chapter illuminates an archival episode within that frame: in the global frame, chapter 2 untangles the response by America's archival gatekeepers to the evidence of Norse discovery of the hemisphere in the tenth century, a theory promoted by Denmark's Royal Society of Northern Antiquaries from the 1820s. Analyzing the national frame, chapter 3 follows Jared Sparks's effort to produce an archive of George Washington's writings in the 1830s that would encapsulate the nation's history and stir greater federal investment in archives and history writing. Within the frame of states, chapter 4 explores state-based efforts to distinguish their historical records, particularly New York's undertaking in the 1840s and 1850s to repatriate and republish its colonial archive. Finally, chapter 5 peers through the local frame at the work of the historian Frances Manwaring Caulkins as she developed a scholarly network, access to archival sources, and research practices that enabled her to craft local histories and cultivate the broader field of local history from the 1840s to 1860s. Although these chapters overlap chronologically, they chart a trajectory from efforts in the first decades of independence to gather America's full global and national history within one archive toward the undertakings by states and localities later in the antebellum period to comprehensively authenticate their distinctive place within those larger historical narratives.

From the title to the concluding sentence, the words "archive" and "archival" appear regularly throughout this book. Scholarly debates around archives in recent decades concern the types of historical materials and practices that form an archive, the role of power in the formation of archives, and the functions that an archive can serve. With reason, many object to the overly rigid and to the overly flexible uses of the term. This book defers to the understanding of an archive held by the historical actors who populate this story: an assemblage of historical materials by associations such as historical societies, entities like state and federal offices, and individual collectors that intentionally gathered and preserved these materials in order to authenticate, commemorate, or otherwise make use of the past.

The hopes and concerns that influenced the formation of these first American archives are only so distant from the roiling public debates over how we preserve, narrate, and relate to the American past today: When and where does the nation's history begin? Which materials belong within its archives, and who has the authority to decide? How do we interpret these materials? Which narratives and whose perspectives will we center? How do the answers to these questions impact our relationship with history and—more important—with each other, the nation, and the wider world? Such questions about the nation's archives and history were posed and contested from page one. We live but the most recent chapter of this longer story.

≽ ONE ≼

Envisioning American Archival Exceptionalism

In 1834, the aptly named librarian of the American Antiquarian Society (AAS), Christopher Columbus Baldwin, exhaled to his diary that he was "heartily glad [William Buell Sprague] has left New England." A Presbyterian minister normally based in Albany, New York, Sprague had recently swept through Connecticut snatching up coveted historical documents. These included "several bundles of manuscripts" left by Samuel Huntington, a signer of the Declaration of Independence who later governed Connecticut. Uneasy about his own prospects, Baldwin lamented, "I fear he has taken the meat and left me the shell, for he has so much fury about him in collecting autographs that he would carry off everything that had a name attached to it."[1] Such materials, Baldwin believed, belonged on the society's shelves and in Baldwin's neat catalogue, not in the grasping hands of an individual like Sprague.

Since its founding in 1812, officers, members, and other boosters of the AAS had hoped to preserve the historical materials that they deemed essential to authenticating American history, spanning from the earthen architectural ruins of Indigenous North America through the manuscripts of the American Revolution to the printed record of national progress since independence. Each individual piece of historical evidence could be placed within this arc. Like the Massachusetts Historical Society (founded in 1791) and New York Historical Society (1804), the AAS saw itself as a "National Depository" during a period when no such federal archives existed.[2]

Emulating European antiquarian societies, Baldwin's institution sought both private advocates and government patronage. But it was decidedly

American in casting this as a civic mission that its network of collectors, "residing in various sections of this vast continent," had a responsibility to perform.[3] The society foresaw that by "fathering around it the materials of History, aided by the good will of the public and the increased exertions of its members, it may, at no distant period, be made one of the noblest and most useful of the institutions of our Country."[4] Members were called on to "father"—an agricultural term for gathering a harvest—and deposit historical materials in a centralized archive in Worcester, described as "a handsome, commodious, and substantial building." Baldwin himself had lugged locust trees on his back from the local nursery to plant around the society's Antiquarian Hall.[5] Inside, the many vulnerable historical materials gathered from scattered households, offices, and other spaces could be secured in one place.

As this chapter shows, the nation's early historical societies believed not only that American history was exceptional but that the nation's archives and its citizens' relationship with these materials were too. Unlike the European countries to which these American institutions regularly compared themselves, America's full history was recent enough and so thoroughly documented, many held, that it could be comprehensively archived. This vision seemed within reach of historical societies, which reinforced their resolve to archive every last historical item that authenticated the nation's exceptional history, as they perceived it. Sprague's furious collecting for his own personal collection was at odds with this archival vision, which troubled Baldwin. This chapter introduces the archival culture that institutions such as the AAS and men such as Baldwin sought to build in their attempt to realize their vision of an exceptional archive. In the early United States, the belief that Americans should preserve certain papers within historical societies, that these papers bore national significance, and that archiving was a meaningful civic act all depended on the persistent exhortations that emanated from historical societies and their networks of boosters. Over the course of the antebellum period, this belief reverberated outward from these institutions into broader public consciousness, influencing federal and state government, representatives abroad, and local actors to engage in this work.

Archives as Tools for Nation-Building

During the American Revolution, the urgency to preserve the nation's historical record took hold of some Americans, a feeling that only intensified and spread during the first decades after independence. A similar urge to archive had followed destructive warfare in Europe, such as the political turmoil of seventeenth-century England and the conflagration of the French Revolution and subsequent Napoleonic Wars.[6] In the early United States, a determination to salvage papers deemed essential to telling national history gained momentum amid the daily, widespread loss and dispersal of historical materials: correspondence and diaries became insulation and kindling, public records were mislaid or destroyed by warfare or neglect, earthen architecture was plowed over, families migrated with papers in tow.

In the civil war of the American Revolution, the fledgling nation's texts seemed imperiled by both internal and external forces. This distressed New Hampshire's leading historian, Jeremy Belknap, who founded the MHS and whom John Quincy Adams later dubbed the founder "of all these historical societies, indirectly, throughout the country."[7] During the 1765 Stamp Act protests, the home of Massachusetts colonial governor Thomas Hutchinson was ransacked, his manuscript collection obliterated by "the vicious, the abandoned," Belknap recollected, including Hutchinson's intended *History of the Province of Massachusetts-Bay*.[8] The British occupying army, for its part, wrecked the major library and manuscript collection in Boston's Old South Church meetinghouse before it left the city in 1776.[9]

Materials like these, deemed integral to American history, seemed to disappear just as the conviction mounted among many Americans that their revolution was a providential event that had altered the course of history.[10] "Had we suffered [the irretrievable loss] by the hands of the Saracens," Belknap mourned in his *History of New Hampshire* (1784), "the grief had been less poignant."[11] In transposing the medieval Christian term for Arab Muslims and that existential religious war onto the British forces and Anglo-American imperial contest, Belknap suggested what some Americans already saw at stake in the preservation of historical documents: a practice that divided a civilized, divinely elected historical community from the uncivilized external forces threatening it.

Belknap believed that historical societies might withstand these destructive forces, but such institutions had no precedent in the British North American colonies or the newly independent country. As he vented to Vice President John Adams in 1789, "The want of public repositories for historical materials as well as the destruction of many valuable ones by fires, by war & by the lapse of time has long been a subject of regret in my mind."[12]

Only the former colonial records offices and a few scattered and relatively small libraries housed the nation's historical papers, paltry in comparison with the sizeable collections held by monarchs or learned societies in Europe. Although some important materials accumulated in federal offices like the US secretary of state's, no American federal institution prior to the Civil War was prepared to undertake the widespread collection and preservation of historical materials for the public's benefit.[13] Between public apathy and other legislative priorities, officials were not easily moved to action. Voluntary associations seemed the surest means to gather, preserve, and, as Belknap often advocated, republish the nation's historical materials.

For Belknap and his contemporaries, such as AAS founder Isaiah Thomas, the first historical societies in the United States drew inspiration from institutions in the empire with which the United States had just severed ties: the Society of Antiquaries of London (chartered in 1751), the Society of Antiquaries of Scotland (in 1780), and the Royal Irish Academy (1786).[14] Petitioning the Massachusetts legislature in 1812 to incorporate the AAS, Thomas insisted that "almost every nation indeed of the European world bears witness to the utility of similar institutions." Facing the members of the newly formed society, Thomas hoped to leverage their admiration for European learned societies while rousing their nationalism. He mused that the AAS "may in time vie with those of a similar kind in Europe, which are now so justly celebrated."[15] This situated historical societies as one of the many spaces in the early United States that remained "in the long shadow of the empire" left by British rule, in which Americans drew on European practices to refute perceptions of their own cultural inferiority.[16] Like those European antecedents, US historical societies built networks of voluntary members who wielded considerable social standing. As in Europe, the new archival communities that emerged in the United States sought materials connected with their nation's history, secured these in a permanent collection, paid dues, and subscribed to publications by the institution; they celebrated the whole undertaking among themselves, in conversation with learned societies in other states and countries, and before a broader public.

Although the first historical societies in the United States hoped to rival those in Europe, from the start Belknap's and Thomas's institutions had an ambitious civic aim that distinguished them from their transatlantic peers. Of course, European antiquaries did depict their work as serving a public or universal good that could redound to the prestige, glory, or welfare of their nation.[17] For instance, Thomas Pownall's *Treatise on the Study of Antiquities* praised the Society of Antiquaries in London as "one of the most useful literary Establishments ... as promoting and encouraging true and useful learning; as aiding and conducting the researches thereof to real and practical knowledge; the knowledge of our country; of our nation; of its actual history."[18] However, these claims about the relationship between the nation's past and present tended to be more measured than those made by Americans. While British men presumed the superiority of their nation, they did not assign to the archive the task of authenticating a triumphant historical argument about the nation into which they actively placed their own lives, as historical societies in the United States would.

Nor did Europeans advocate as earnestly for the civic worth of these archives. The Society of Antiquaries "was made up of private individuals who pursued antiquarianism out of personal professional interest, albeit often tempered by a sense of patriotism."[19] Many members of these societies came from a social echelon that did not exist in the United States. Unlike the admixture of elite, striving, and middling Americans who found ways to engage with archives on the margins of their generally busy professional lives, in Britain the antiquarians "were largely derived from a class where education was an unquestioned privilege and leisure an ample commodity."[20] One such man, Lord Buchan, founder of the Society of Antiquaries of Scotland and later one of the numerous foreign members of the AAS, confessed his modest hopes that their research into Scotland's past, from antiquity to the present, would be well received by the public. "And here I cannot but observe," he wrote, "that the name of Antiquary, from the frivolous researches of some of them, and the prejudices of the uninformed public, has, with other still more respectable appellations, become the butt of fashionable and humorous stricture." He continued, "I do not expect that we shall be able to introduce antiquities into the Morning Post at breakfast, or to make them light summer reading; but a great point would be gained, if they could be rendered interesting amusement for a long winter night."[21] By contrast, historical societies in the United States sought to provide the public with much more than amusement to fill breakfast or even a long winter night.

The earliest historical societies in the United States did not shy away from announcing their undertaking as a service to the national interest. "The cause of truth is interesting to all men," the NYHS addressed the public in 1809, "and those who possess the means, however small, of preventing error, or of elucidating obscure facts, will confer a benefit on mankind by communicating them to the world."[22] Upon the formation of its Historical and Literary Committee in 1814, the American Philosophical Society (APS) explained that its members were "sensible of the eminent usefulness of the exertions of the Societies established" in Massachusetts and New York and "anxious to concur in their patriotic pursuits," which led it to secure a site where historical materials "might be deposited for the public benefit and the advantage of posterity."[23] With this public purpose in mind, the MHS, AAS, NYHS, and the APS declared grand institutional designs to encompass not merely the history of their locality or state but *all* of American history. In the absence of serious national or state investment in preserving and publishing historical materials, these institutions argued continually through publication, petitions to state legislatures, and correspondence with their far-flung networks for their own public utility. Claims for the importance of archiving the nation's past would only rise with the swelling nationalism during the following decades and move others to undertake this work.

Throughout the antebellum period, historical societies, their members, and advocates insisted on the essential role of archives as an intermediary between past, present, and future American citizens. Although historical societies wrote constitutions, managed membership, and conducted meetings in the familiar fashion of all-male learned clubs in Europe, they asserted often their higher goal of building national identity. Archives, they contended, preserved history as a model for the living to both venerate and emulate, drawing American minds toward "the deeds and sufferings and opinions of the first settlers," for instance, as the Rhode Island Historical Society (RIHS) announced in 1837.[24] But the purpose was not to retreat into such poignant moments. Writing in 1826 to John Farmer, the nation's leading genealogist and a founding member of the New Hampshire Historical Society (NHHS), one advocate praised the society for "turning the attention of Gentlemen to the noble doings of their ancestors, strengthening the love of country by creating an interest in all that relates to home in its enlarged sense."[25] Understanding the past was widely believed to shape one's sense of belonging and conduct as a citizen, a pivotal concern for these first generations as an independent nation.[26]

As in the bevy of other historical societies founded around the fiftieth anniversary of the American Revolution, the leadership of the Historical Society of Pennsylvania (HSP) took for granted that it was a civic imperative to preserve the state's authentic historical record before it faded from view. In the preamble to its constitution in 1825, the HSP asserted that "to collect and preserve the evidence of its own history from the earliest date, is both the duty and interest of every political society, whether its progress has been prosperous or disastrous."[27] The Virginia Historical and Philosophical Society (VHPS) encapsulated the patriotic purpose of these institutions, "believing... as every American must do, that so exalted were the sentiments and so illustrious the achievements of our forefathers, that a correct and minute knowledge of them will be productive of great good."[28] Likewise, "is it not our imperative duty," listeners heard at the Maryland Historical Society (MDHS) in 1845, "to collect and to preserve every document, or record, or tradition, that, can transmit to posterity the legend of so honorable an ancestry and of so much virtue?"[29] The past was not a remote or lost place; historical societies did not want Americans to gaze nostalgically upon it. It was rather a mold for citizens and a guide for the nation's future.

In the absence of a national archive, these early institutions acted as archives of the nation, situating Americans in time as well as space.[30] They acted nationally—even internationally—by directing their members to gather materials in tandem with the territorial and maritime expansion of the United States. In doing so they both recorded the nation's history and charted its future trajectory. The MHS introduced itself in 1791 in a circular letter by calling to "every Gentleman of Science in the Continent and Islands of America" to contribute to its collections, which exhibited the society's aspiration to document a national community transcending Massachusetts.[31] They asked this broad audience "to collect, preserve, and communicate, materials for a complete history of this country, and accounts of all valuable efforts of human ingenuity and industry, from the beginning of its settlement."[32] In its early calls to the public for donations, the MHS announced its collecting aims, which ranged from "books, pamphlets, manuscripts and records, containing historical facts," to "a collection of observations and descriptions in natural history and Topography, together with specimens of natural and artificial curiosities."[33] The MHS and other early historical societies held a capacious notion of where this motley archive would be collected. "Belknap's quest had no geographical limits," his biographer, Louis Leonard Tucker, explains. "It extended from Boston to Europe and beyond."[34]

Although these encyclopedic collecting aims resembled the practices of eighteenth-century learned societies in parts of Europe, they intended to build a distinctively American archive that would authenticate the nation's progress while spurring it onward. An early circular from the Mineralogical Committee of the NYHS called on its members "to collect these scattered materials of our natural history, to display they riches of the mineral kingdom of each of our states; to inform the scientific traveller and citizen; to encourage the growing taste of this science in our country; to communicate discoveries and invite researches; are objects so useful, so important, that it would be impossible to doubt of the public favour being shown to this undertaking."[35] Emulating the MHS, the NYHS imagined the entire continent as the field from which materials could be collected. "Our inquiries are not limited to a single State, or district, but extend to the whole Continent," the prosperous New York merchant and NYHS founder John Pintard declared.[36] The AAS similarly hoped for a network of collectors spanning the country and regarded itself as a national repository. The society stated in no ambivalent terms after its first years of heady growth that "our Institution, in all its objects and concerns, is intended and considered as *national.*"[37] This growing archive would in turn inspire more collecting as the nation continued to expand. Not content to simply gather history, these institutions sought to propel America into the future.

These early efforts led to a deluge of donations that revealed the larger historical narratives that these new archives could support. The minutes from one 1793 meeting of the MHS record the seemingly dissimilar donations that had been recently archived:

For the Library:
    A new edition of the Captivity of Rev. John Williams, with additions by Rev. John [Taylor and others, 1793], from Mr. Thomas Dickman.
    Three Sermons preached before the Society for Propagating the Gospel, from Rev. Dr. Thacher.
    A printed copper-plate list of the First Purchasers and Settlers under William Penn, from Mrs. Russell, the wife of Mr. John Russell.

For the Cabinet:
    A Demarara Opossum, stuffed, from Captain Peter Chace.
    A Fish Hook, from Nootka Sound, from the President.
    An Indian Pestle, found at Newton, from Mr. William Googs.

Several Copper Coins and one Silver Coin, from Mr. James Thwing.
Shells taken out of the cliff at Rainsford's Island, from Mr. James Freeman.
A Portrait of Ankerstroom, from Captain Benjamin Homans.[38]

This could easily appear a jarring jumble placed at the archival threshold. But a closer look reveals accumulated proofs of a national narrative that spanned from seventeenth-century settlement through the new republic's global maritime expansion at the turn of the nineteenth century: encounters and contests with Indigenous societies, legal evidence of colonial claims to their land, and relics from the people who once held it; sermons to extend Christian civilization over these territories; specimens from New England's emerging transoceanic trade routes—Boston harbor, northeast Brazil, the Pacific Northwest. Such early accessions could all be woven into a historical narrative of progress. Meanwhile, practical knowledge accrued in archives about the spaces that the United States was expanding into and exploiting.

By the 1820s, historical societies shifted from an attempt to archive the entire nation toward a focus on authenticating the distinctive history of their individual state within the nation's history. Newer historical societies modeled their efforts on the better-established institutions in the Northeast. Upon its founding in 1839, for instance, the founding officers of the Georgia Historical Society (GHS) recognized that their undertaking "comes in as auxiliary to the many similar associations already existing." Yet they also stressed the distinctive origin and the challenges that its state had overcome, "whether as a colony planted by the benefactions of the philanthropist; as a frontier settlement, exposed to the horrors of Spanish and Indian invasion; as the youngest of the old confederacy, and yet among the first to proclaim her rights, and demand redress; or as burdened, harassed, and almost eradicated by the war of the Revolution." Its founding officers claimed their society "is laboring in a distinct field for our common country, and aims to enrich American literature, by treasuring up, and publishing the memorials of this important member of the Union."[39] By emphasizing the significance of its state within America's larger history, the GHS and other new historical societies could claim a meaningful role for their institution in the wider, unceasing work of archive building.

A regular feature of their pitch to the public was that historical societies were impartial collectors of these facts, conduits for the nation's texts from past to future, and repositories from which future historians could compose history. According to Gouverneur Morris, a framer of the US Constitution and an early president of the NYHS, these "authenticated facts" made up the "Skeleton of History." In his visceral metaphor, Morris explained at an annual meeting of the NYHS that historians pieced together the disconnected bones and added muscles, "which give symmetry, strength, and grace." "At last the goodly form," Morris went on, "complete in all its fair proportion, when language spreads a finish over the promoethian frame, how must its appearance be affected by the colouring it receives? The same event, treated by different historians, comes white from one hand, tinged with a rosy blush from another, and from another black."[40] In portraying the nation's historical archive as a sort of catacomb from which the historian drew and reanimated skeletal remains, Morris used an uncommon metaphor to make a common claim. Historical societies were impartial repositories, furnishing historians with authentic facts that could be fashioned into a range of narratives.

To construct collections, these institutions used an important text of their own: the circular letter. Published and distributed widely, the circular specified materials that members and the broader public should locate and donate. These circulars were regularly issued and amended, sent to members by mail, inserted in newspapers, and reissued in published collections. Circulating, these evidentiary wish lists nudged Americans to empty out their household libraries and garrets, survey their local communities and lands, and document oral traditions, all of which they could send from the corners of their state or sometimes across states lines to a historical society.

Whatever their claims to neutrality, the historical narrative envisioned by the society preceded the archive that it built. Historical societies tended to trace the script for the narratives that would be constructed from these archival sources, often reiterating the collecting mission detailed in a historical society's own founding documents. The NHHS, for instance, called on citizens in its 1823 act of incorporation to contribute all materials "as may illustrate the early history of the State; and of acquiring and communicating a knowledge of the natural history, the botanical and mineralogical productions of the State."[41] The society was mainly interested in texts tied to symbolic sites and events within its historical trajectory from colonization to the present. These included accounts of early settlements and "contests with the aboriginals"; information on the establishment of churches, seminaries, schools, and newspapers; details of "the character, customs, and general history" of local American Indian tribes; all manuscripts about the early settlers; climatic data as it related to epidemiology, mortality, and longevity; information on "Indian fortifications"; and topographical, mineralogical, and geological descriptions of towns.[42] The first circular of the RIHS in 1827 similarly called for topographical surveys of towns, accounts of their settlement, commerce, industry, and arts; biographies of "original settlers, revolutionary patriots, and other distinguished men" in the state; any original manuscripts documenting this history; printed works such as sermons and orations; and finally, "accounts of Indian tribes which formerly inhabited any part of this State, their numbers and condition when first visited by the whites, their general character and peculiar customs and manners, their wars and treaties and their original grants to our ancestors," as well as the place names they left behind.[43]

The argument that these new archives were just records for the historian to interpret belied the influence that preexisting notions about history had on what was collected in the first place. Collecting priorities such as the accomplishments of a colony's early settlers, the wars and treaties that dislodged Indigenous societies from their lands, and the natural endowments and distinctive accomplishments that drove progress all sustained certain narratives and snuffed out others. Once gathered, such materials served collectively not just to authenticate but to justify the colonization of Indigenous lands and development of colonies and states.

Archival Expansions

Propelled by this sense of purpose and equipped with these tools, historical societies multiplied into the dozens, and membership expanded into the thousands over the course of the antebellum period. Both Maine's and Pennsylvania's membership, for instance, went from a ceiling of fifty members upon their founding in the 1820s to almost two hundred a quarter century later. "The members of an historical society ought to be numerous, perhaps unlimited," the HSP president announced during his inaugural address.[44] A large and powerful membership of leading men of politics, law, commerce, religion, and letters within a given state—a historical establishment—signaled the prestige of a historical society, promoted the public value of its work, and applauded their own belonging within the historical narrative authenticated by its archive. Societies intentionally extended membership

FIGURE 2. Cover page of the first *Memoirs of the Historical Society of Pennsylvania* (1826). (Image from HathiTrust)

to individuals dispersed throughout their state, to specific families with known access to important manuscripts, and to prominent men in other states and abroad with materials and prestige to lend the society. In part, this reflected a distinctly American conviction that the work of archives was an essential civic task in which everyone should engage. It was also a practical concern for institutions that depended on the donations, access to historical materials, wealth, and power provided by members. Although many smaller societies had formed to collect historical materials by the Civil War, one major historical society in each state tended to consolidate the authority and capacity to gather a comprehensive archive of the state's history, as its leading members conceived it.

For many members, belonging to a historical society became both a relationship and a ritual. Corresponding secretaries courted prospective members, whose responses were often noted at meetings and recorded. New members were nominated, invited, confirmed, and bestowed with a diploma of membership. Donations from members were announced at meetings, inscribed in accessions logs, and regularly appeared in historical society publications. Parties and lectures brought members together for anniversaries of pivotal historical events, frequently recounted in the press. Members became subscribers and readers of historical society publications.[45] Some historical societies conducted affairs and stored archives in prominent buildings. From its formation into the 1830s, the MHS was granted the space above the central arch in the architect Charles Bulfinch's Tontine Crescent in Boston, an innovative curved rowhouse that had been constructed with the MHS in mind.[46] In Connecticut, the Wadsworth Athenaeum, the premier cultural institution in Hartford, hosted the Connecticut Historical Society (CHS) collections and meetings. One's very belonging endorsed the member's own virtuous affiliation with the patriotic undertaking to preserve their place within the history of their locality, state, nation, and even the world.

Although the large majority of most historical society members resided in or at least hailed from the society's home state, these archival communities were entwined with each other across state lines. Leading collectors, historians, and other advocates of archives from one state were nominated to institutions in other states. Sometimes, a historical society called on geographically distant individuals to reaffirm their identification with their home, such as the Exeter, New Hampshire, native Lewis Cass. While serving as Michigan's governor, where he also founded the Historical Society of Michigan in 1828, he accepted his appointment to the NHHS in 1831. "This honour is the more grateful," he responded, "as it comes from the land of my nativity."[47] These fraternal exchanges papered over the competing collecting aims and notions of the nation's narrative that often divided historical societies in different states. But this practice did create a community of men—almost without exception men—that crossed state lines in the larger project of collecting the nation's historical record.

In the official invitation and acceptance letters dispatched and received by corresponding secretaries, both historical society and individual member could affirm their patriotism and virtue. Historian William Willis, a leading member of the Maine Historical Society (MEHS) in the antebellum era, carefully preserved his collection of diplomas received from historical societies in Massachusetts, Vermont, New Hampshire, New York, Pennsylvania, Maryland, Georgia, Wisconsin, and Florida.[48] Societies seized on symbolic anniversaries to host large celebrations, typically inviting representatives from other societies. In 1843, John Quincy Adams delivered the oration celebrating the two-hundredth anniversary of the New England Confederation, held by the MHS, which invited historical society delegations ranging from Georgia to Quebec. These practices knit together a national fraternity of collectors who shared an organizational structure, a commitment to historical preservation, a method for acting on it, and an ideology about how citizens should relate to the past.

On their membership rolls, historical societies hoped to count prestigious individuals from Europe and, less often, the newly independent Spanish American republics. The AAS was especially ambitious in expanding the network of corresponding members who supported its work. True to its name, the first volume of their *Archaeologia Americana* (a title borrowed from the Society of Antiquaries' serial *Archaeologia*) claimed as its object all of American antiquity, by which they meant Indigenous civilizations prior to contact with European colonists. AAS leaders hoped that European readers would come to appreciate the erudition of the *Archaeologia Americana*. To the Franch emigrant scholar Pierre-Etienne Du Ponceau (or Peter Stephen Duponceau to some American peers), an AAS member and leader at the APS in Philadelphia, the AAS corresponding secretary promised in 1816, "the time I am persuaded *will come,* when . . . Europe in general, will voluntarily accord to us the merit, which may be due to our exertions as a constituent member of the republic of letters."[49] This reflected the society's aim to shine as an equal in an international constellation of European learned societies.

Collecting a cosmopolitan membership might also distinguish their institution's work, the AAS hoped. It was certainly quick in its first decade to induct illustrious foreign members who had taken an interest in American history and supported the new republic from abroad: the Prussian scientist who had written extensively on the natural history of America, Alexander von Humboldt; the Italian historian Carlo Botta, whose *Storia della guerra dell' Independenza d'America* (1809) continued to be read in translation and taught in American universities by professors like Jared Sparks for decades; the German bibliographer Christoph Ebeling, who had assembled the largest collection of Americana in Europe; the famed French fan of the American Revolution, the Marquis de Lafayette in Paris; and Simón Bolívar, whose new Colombian republic seemed to carry the torch of the American Revolution.

Other American collectors, historians, and members of historical societies continually sought to prove the quality of their institutions to foreign audiences by conscripting elite Europeans as corresponding members and then disseminating historical publications to European institutions. In 1817, for instance, the MHS sent its full published *Collections* to the Royal Library in Paris. In Paris, these were received by David Bailie Warden, an American consular officer and notable book collector and scholar.[50] Warden conveyed these volumes to the head of the king's personal library, who in 1818 returned the thanks of Louis XVIII with a box of books for the MHS.[51] Their eagerness for royal endorsement of the US republic's new archives represented Americans' hope to prove their nation's cultural parity with Europe while distinguishing its archival record and historical identity. In practical terms, honorary members in Europe might also help Americans gain access to private collections and public archives that could be used to authenticate America's own history. Vindications from abroad clearly flattered American historical society members, but these international exchanges also accentuated their authority as stewards of the nation's historical record in the absence of substantial investment by their own federal government.

Men dominated these expanding institutions, but women found numerous ways to engage in the work of building and interpreting the nation's archives. For instance, in her first major publication, *The Genius of Oblivion* (1823), the prolific author and editor Sarah Josepha Hale crafted an eponymous historical poem about the original settlement of North America that both drew on and responded to the work of historical societies.[52] The poem depicted a young man wandering westward across the Alleghenies to examine the Indigenous earthen architecture that many contemporaries attributed to an extinct mound-building civilization, which intrigued historical societies and a broader public eager for evidence about this seemingly lost civilization.[53]

As Hale prepared the poem in early 1823, she established contact with Jacob Bailey Moore, a Masonic brother of her recently deceased husband. Moore was a leading printer of historical materials in New Hampshire and soon-to-be librarian of the NHHS, founded that spring. She maintained

FIGURE 3. Silhouette of Sarah Josepha Hale, by Auguste Edouart, 1842. (National Portrait Gallery, Smithsonian Institution; gift of Robert L. McNeil Jr.)

that whatever the poem's faults, "you will find the *subject* and *plan original*—the scenery and *sentiment American,* which I flatter myself will be some recommendation to gentlemen of your taste and patriotism."[54] Partnering with Moore through the winter and spring of 1823, Hale called on him to provide access to resources that would bolster the poem with credible scholarship, making it more than just a work of fancy. She shared with Moore her plan to "considerably enlarge the notes and add some fugitive pieces which have appeared in your paper with others which were never published."[55] To do so, she sought materials about Indigenous architecture that were beyond her reach as a widowed woman with limited wealth. Writing to Moore in early spring, she explained her predicament: "You, sir, have access to many records and documents which are not in my power to obtain and if you have leisure and inclination to make a transcript of such further particulars respecting those antiquities as, you judge, would be useful and entertaining to insert in the notes I should esteem it a great favor."[56] To make it fit for publication, Hale believed that the poem itself and its endnotes should reflect the best contemporary knowledge about the origin and significance of the Indian mounds—or "antiquities," as she and many contemporaries labeled them.

Hale's endnotes to the poem showed her engagement with the scholarly materials Moore shared about the history and architecture of Indigenous American civilizations. This included Caleb Atwater's survey of Indian mounds in the Mississippi valley, which formed the keystone of *Archaeologia Americanae* (1820), the inaugural publication of the AAS, which Hale quoted to justify her depiction of this civilization's origins in the poem.[57] Atwater concluded that the mounds he surveyed "were erected by a race of men widely different from any tribe of North American Indians, known in modern times."[58] This study was sold by the AAS to influential readers, learned societies, and libraries around the country, as well as through its network abroad. It validated the fiction that contemporary American Indians, deemed incapable of advanced sedentary society, had violently displaced this former mound-building civilization.

In her notes, Hale shored up her poem with scholarly scaffolding for readers interested in the historical inquiry within the poem.[59] The dynamic between poem and endnote, however, revealed Hale's perspective that early scholarship had not produced convincing answers to crucial questions about America's past. In the poem, Hale suggested that no rational inquiry could uncover the history of the mounds:

> How earnest, yet how impotent—
> To know from whence, and who these were?
> How came—how perished they? And where
> The archives of their history,
> Their tomes of kings, forgotten lie?
> But vain these wishes throng his mind,
> Vain as yon Circle's end to find!
> Ages untold have drawn their shroud—
> Nor human powers may pierce the cloud.[60]

Such skepticism pervaded the work, implying that the myriad men who had already examined innumerable mounds and poured over accounts of them were incapable of reliably archiving and narrating the history of the Mound Builders. Hale combined this skepticism with credible evidence in the endnotes to support her own theory: the mounds were built by exiles from the ancient Phoenician city of Tyre during the Babylonian siege of the city in the early sixth century BCE—"and hence Columbia's *first* inhabitants, / The authors of these monuments of old."[61] In her endnotes, Hale reasoned that one could deduce from the "great antiquity" of the mounds and the "knowledge and skill" used to build them that "the settlers emigrated from a country, where the arts that embellish and defend communities were for that age of the world well understood." Echoing the argument of scholars like Atwater, she concluded from this that "they could not be savages, according to our idea of the term."[62]

These imagined founders resembled the English settlers extolled in her 1823 ode, published in the same volume, to New Hampshire's founding two hundred years previous, when

> The white man breathed his ardent vow,
> And rais'd his altar here;
> From Albion's haughty, sea-girt land,
> "Laconia's" Ancients come;
> A patient, firm and dauntless band,
> To seek a peaceful home.[63]

Hale in this way fashioned an antique American origin story that could simultaneously displace contemporary American Indians from that first founding and provide a historical analogy for the later founding, progress, and westward imperial expansion of her American civilization. Like nearly all historical societies, New Hampshire's barred women from membership during this period, but Hale expressed a vision of the American past and future that aligned with the beliefs of that institution while questioning its leaders' capacity to decipher the past.

The emergence throughout the expanding United States of historical societies like New Hampshire's created an archival landscape in sharp contrast to the centralized national archives developing in those very years across the Atlantic. Europe was hardly devoid of voluntary associations devoted to the collection of historical materials. Throughout the British Isles, local antiquarian and archaeological societies formed in the late eighteenth and early nineteenth centuries. In France, the local nineteenth-century historical society was especially active.[64] But such local archival practices were adjuncts to the centralized state archives in imperial capitals such as London and Paris: the Plantation Office and, later, State Papers Office, and across the English Channel, the Archives de la Marine et des Colonies and the Archives des Affaires Etrangères. In this comparative perspective, the archives of early US historical societies were not secondary to a government project to collect and publish the nation's historical records. Rather, they formed the main institutions for the work of collecting and publicizing the historical record, built by influential citizens laboring alongside each other.

In addition to a broader public who engaged with their work, such as authors like Hale, historical societies could count on some help from their state government and occasionally the federal government, though the degree of patronage varied among these institutions and took sundry forms. Often, claims for state support for US historical societies emphasized the advantages enjoyed by European institutions, supported by the wealth of nobles and monarchs. "Donations, legacies, contributions, and royal patronage, are the support of those in Europe, and have raised them to a state of eminence," the AAS observed.[65] In the United States, however, petitions for states to demonstrate their "liberality" found different degrees of purchase on state legislatures. With the exception of Georgia and Louisiana, historical societies in the antebellum South were far less active and well-supported than those in many northern and some western states. Even the oldest and most firmly established historical societies struggled to gain the state resources on which their aspirations often depended. The NYHS, for instance, was deeply indebted and then peripatetic among different buildings before major infusions of state funding in 1827, thanks to a five-thousand-dollar bailout ushered through the state's senate by its corresponding secretary.[66] Yet many smaller forms of state support helped to grow historical societies. Secretaries of state, for instance, responded to historical society requests for donations of their published legislative record and other public documents.[67]

The most visible endorsement that a state could make, and often an important factor in a society's success, was the use of public buildings. In New Hampshire, historical society meetings were held at the Court House in Concord.[68] Though haphazardly organized for years after its 1831 founding, the VHPS held its annual meetings in Richmond when all three branches of its state government were in session, assembling "many enlightened and influential persons from the country."[69] In addition to receiving five hundred dollars in annual support, the RIHS held meetings in the state's senate chambers and lodged its collections in an adjoining room.[70] The Wisconsin Historical Society (WHS) enjoyed a five-hundred-dollar fund each year from the state, its addresses were delivered in the state assembly hall, and its meetings held in the room of the governor, who doubled as the society's president. Use of state buildings afforded both the symbolic support of the state and the physical protection of the archive.

State support for building and republishing archival materials would mount during the antebellum period, but that these archives could be called *public* had less to do with state sponsorship. Rather, they were built by prominent public figures, preserved what they defined as the public's historical record, and served what they deemed a public need, even as they denied access and representation to the large majority of the public. The amount of direct support from each state fluctuated over the decades. Throughout, however, historical societies were run by cohorts of influential men who reflected structures of power within their state. Each of these historical establishments took upon itself the task to preserve and promote its state's history as these individuals conceived it. Upon incorporation in 1822, the MEHS counted Governor Albion Parris as its president; the brigadier general, Bowdoin College overseer, and future secretary of state Edward Russell as its corresponding secretary; chief justice of Maine's highest court, Prentiss Mellen, as treasurer; and Portland's leading Congregationalist pastor, Edward Payson, as its librarian.[71] For these officers, preserving history and then crafting a narrative for the state was bound up with their own work leading its political, commercial, legal, and spiritual life.

These leading men dominated historical societies in most ways. They convened as officers, dictated the collecting aims, petitioned state legislatures and the federal government for support, and motivated the domestic and foreign corresponding members who helped fill their libraries. They made the popular annual addresses, often recounting the labors of their ancestors. Typically, only members could nominate new members, request access to a society's library, or vouch for another's privilege to borrow material. When they generated enough subscribers or revenue for a publication, they selected and arranged manuscripts for publication. When they died, their passing was often announced at a society meeting, their eulogy read and published, their belonging in the society celebrated, their personal records donated—archival accessions all.[72]

Summoning Oblivion, Salvaging History

Historical societies across the United States sought to choreograph how Americans would perceive and engage with the nation's historical record.

To galvanize members and build these archives, historical societies and their advocates portrayed the nation's historical record as perennially on the cusp of destruction. Archives, they argued, were crucial to salvaging it. For these advocates of preservation, this fear of loss surged amid the material wreckage of the Revolution and intensified alongside the unprecedented changes to the rhythm, scale, and complexity of life in the industrializing, sprawling, and increasingly fragmented nation. Through these decades, historical societies in nearly every state called on citizens to perceive their homes, cities, and landscapes as sites where the nation's historical record could be saved. Family papers abandoned under floorboards and in garrets, Indigenous artifacts and architecture threatened by natural elements and human recklessness, data about agricultural productivity and commercial growth, wartime recollections of aging veterans, innumerable printed documents: these materials had to move from the precarity of private hands to the common archival storehouse of a historical society.

By the antebellum period, the MHS, NYHS, AAS, and APS had imposed a set of tropes onto the matter of historical collecting, which they pressed their members and the broader society to adopt. The act of salvaging precious papers from the ravages of time became the aesthetic framework in which historical societies depicted the civic imperative of preserving historical materials. These institutions evoked images of historical materials subjected to disorder, darkness, decay, and waste, against which they juxtaposed the archive as a site of order, clarity, permanence, and utility. Historical societies positioned themselves as bulwarks against destructive forces and storehouses where precious historical materials could accrue value for the future benefit of American society. The MHS deployed these metaphors from its founding. Recording a 1791 meeting, Thomas Wallcut wrote that the preservation of American historical materials "must always have a usefull tendency to rescue the true history of this country from the ravages of time and the effects of ignorance and neglect."[73] By the nineteenth century, these images had become commonplace. Addressing the public in 1809, the NYHS announced its purpose "to rescue from the dust and obscurity of private repositories such important documents, as are liable to be lost or destroyed by the indifference or neglect of those into whose hands they may have fallen, will be a primary object of our attention."[74] At its annual meeting in 1814, AAS president Isaiah Thomas likewise portrayed the landscape of imperiled historical materials that Americans must save: "At this day, there are numberless old books, newspapers and magazines, and many relicks of antiquity, crowded together in garrets and store houses, of no use to any one, and hastening to destruction by means of the weather and vermin."[75] Myriad papers seemed scattered among many individual hands and private homes across the country, where human neglect, natural phenomena, and the ravaging force of time worked upon them. Although historical societies regularly struggled to find affordable, reliable, and secure space for their meetings and collections, they repeated this claim.

Year after year, historical societies argued that although much had already been lost, time remained to rescue the historical record. From the insecurity of households and landscapes to the orderly permanence of the archive, these institutions envisioned a mass movement of authentic historical data moving across their threshold. "A depository like this," the AAS claimed, "may not only retard the ravages of time, but preserve from other causes of destruction, many precious relics of antiquity . . . which once lost could never be restored."[76] As a generation of veterans from the Revolutionary War passed away, historical societies were especially anxious to gather records and testimony from them.[77] For the RIHS, the revolutionary history "rested solely in the fast fading memory of those that participated," and the state's early history "was only to be gathered from mere fleeting tradition and documentary evidence, scattered over every part of the State."[78]

Yet time was running out. "We have scarcely begun the great work which has been assigned us," the RIHS Board of Trustees announced at their first annual meeting.[79] "Time, the great devourer of all things," Nathaniel Adams mused in the NHHS's voluminous first *Collections* in 1824, "preys upon the evidence designed to perpetuate virtuous actions with unabated appetite."[80] As he tried to establish the Dorchester Antiquarian and Historical Society in the 1840s, Ebenezer Clapp argued to one correspondent that their generation had nearly miscarried their duty to remember their ancestors: "Many of the early settlers of this Town, were persons whose lives and characters would have done honor to any age, who nerves were nerves of iron, and who were inflexibly firm in every post of duty:—many of them have passed away, leaving no line to tell their story, no stone to mark their last resting place, no descendants to cherish their memory."[81] To another, he insisted that "the Time for learning the history of our progenitors is fast passing away, and very soon will be added to the vast amount irretrievably lost."[82]

This archival jeremiad lamented the failure to preserve history but promised redemption if Americans acted before it was too late.[83]

The imperative to collect seemed even more urgent to the major historical societies founded later in the antebellum period, such as in Kentucky, New Jersey, Georgia, and Maryland. Prompting the aged politician John Rowan to commit his own biography to paper for the Kentucky Historical Society (KHS), one hopeful donor to their fledgling archive let the society know in 1841 that "by some exertion I have obtained and committed to writing some very interesting facts and incidents, which inacted in this county, or by those who had become its citizens—facts well worthy of a place in the history of our country, and which by the death of a few old men, would have been consigned to oblivion."[84] In its 1845 constitution and by-laws, the New Jersey Historical Society (NJHS) implored Americans to transfer manuscripts "from the dust and darkness of private repositories."[85] Rev. Dr. John Proudfit, professor at Rutgers, wrote to the NJHS that, "the Past, right as it is in instruction, in delight, and in all elevating influences, is swiftly receding from us—and we surely do well in securing such of its precious fragments as are still floating within our reach on the stream of time, beneath the surface of which they will soon sink and disappear forever."[86]

In Georgia, Judge William Law lectured the historical society in 1840, "As we recede from the period of our origin and infancy the means of correct information must constantly diminish, while time and accident will obscure and obliterate much that is valuable and worthy of preservation."[87] Speaking to the MDHS, novelist-politician John Pendleton Kennedy announced that same year, "This society has come into existence just in time to rescue some of the fragments of our youthful annals from irrecoverable oblivion." He continued, "Would that some earlier generation had conceived the happy thought of addressing itself to the same task, when full stores of the treasures of our young Antiquity might have been garnered into a magazine safe enough to deliver them unmutilated into our hands!"[88] Americans still had time, historical societies insisted during this period, to secure the nation's historical record, but not much.

On this imagined landscape strewn with historical materials, advocates of preservation conjured the metaphors of ruination and illumination. Uncollected historical papers were portrayed to Americans as textual ruins in a country with fewer architectural ruins than in Europe.[89] Whereas the collector, traveler, or artist in contemporary Europe could derive pleasure from their encounter with a ruin or relic, historical societies in the United States applied that traditional antiquarian practice to the recovery of far more recent documents.[90] The Board of Trustees at the newly founded RIHS announced in 1824 that "an ample and, in some respects, unexplored field is open before [American collectors]. By their efforts the fading memorials and records of oldentime scattered throughout this state are to be rescued from destruction and preserved for the benefit of future generations."[91] Here, the lone collector could experience the thrill of encountering the ruined historical object, salvaging it, and contributing it to the sacred civic space of the archive. Speaking in Hartford, Connecticut, in 1843 not far from the state's fabled Charter Oak, in which its colony's charter was once hidden, Reverend Thomas Day waxed that the tree itself "has escaped the ravages of fire; and has withstood the assaults of hail, and snow, and vapour, and stormy wind. Still Decay has exercised dominion over even the charter-oak. Some of its boughs have withered . . . the heart of its trunk has mouldered into dust; and the remnant of that trunk has ceased to chronicle on its wood the years of its life."[92] The seeker cast light, figuratively and often literally, upon the document. Documents in turn illuminated the past for the living and posterity.

By claiming to perform a vital civic role, enlisting the privilege of influential men and state resources, and wielding these metaphors, US historical societies positioned themselves as institutions poised not only to accomplish their local labor of building archives but to take on a work of global significance by authenticating the exceptional history of the nation that they envisioned.

Archival Exceptionalism

According to archival advocates in the United States, the materials held in these institutions, the history that they revealed, and the relation that Americans had with them were all exceptional. In contrast with the archives of Europe, they argued, America's archives contained the materials to authenticate the nation's entire history. In even starker contrast with the history of Europe, moreover, the history revealed by these materials reflected the democratic array of actors who had participated in the exceptional history of the nation. Consequently, they reasoned, the relationship between Americans and their historical record was exceptional, too, because each historical trace produced by an American could figure into the archive authenticating this democratic history. As the Massachusetts politician, diplomat, and man of letters Edward Everett stated in his wildly popular 1850s "Oration on the Character of Washington," "in little more than a century and a half, the English Colonies passed between the feeblest provincial infancy, and powerful, vigorously acting, earnestly projecting, self-reliant national manhood."[93] The entirety of this national trajectory could be authenticated, historical societies argued, an exceptional archival opportunity that distinguished the nation.

By placing this fraction of the American population and their historical record at the center of the archive, historical establishments inscribed their blinkered vision of America's past onto the records they sought and the narratives they elevated. By enumerating desired materials through circular letters and other publications, historical societies implicitly enumerated what should fall beyond their archival threshold, such as the histories of people enslaved throughout the colonies, American Indians' ongoing struggle for sovereignty, and the increasing population of new immigrants. But the notion that the nation's archives had the distinctive potential to encompass its full history proved appealing to those who built and made use of these collections. Over the decades, this claim reverberated from historical societies outward toward a larger public, which the leaders of these historical societies in turn hoped could be induced to donate materials and further their mission.

From the start, emerging historical societies in the United States and their boosters contrasted the nation's archives with what they imagined of Europe's. John Pintard stated in the first NYHS circular letter, published in 1805, that "without the aid of original records and authentic documents, history will be nothing more than a well-combined series of ingenious conjectures and amusing fables."[94] Implicitly, Pintard stereotyped the history of other nations as unsubstantiated. The builders of American archives maintained that this was a distinctive trait of many foreign archives. European history, the first *Collections* of the MEHS implied in 1831, was lost in the fogginess of a mythic past to which Europeans traced their origins.[95] GHS founding officer William Law similarly opined that the lack of authentic materials had misled other nations to fabricate their history: "Prompted by pride and vanity all nations have desired to increase the lustre of their origin, and the fame of their ancestry, by filling the 'immense vacuity,' which lies beyond the limits of well authenticated memorials, with the splendid inventions of fable." By contrast, Law continued, "there is a land, in relation to whose origin, all fiction vanishes and truth is realized . . . a land whose origin depends upon no legendary tales drawn from an obscure and remote antiquity, but is revealed with unerring accuracy, and recorded in the simplicity of uncolored truth.—That land is our Country."[96] In 1844, when John Quincy Adams rose in Manhattan to extol the importance of historical societies, the presiding officer reminded everyone that "our national origin differs from that of all the people of antiquity, in that we do not look for the founders of our Empire in the fables of gods and goddesses."[97] America's archives, in their eyes, were different.

Advocates of American archives juxtaposed the seemingly fuzzy origins of other nations with the vivid history of the United States, which they believed could be fully authenticated. From Jeremy Belknap's initial call in 1791 to "collect, preserve, and communicate, materials for a complete history of this country" onward, many posited that the entirety of American history existed in texts that could be gathered. Speaking to the NYHS in 1828, Chancellor Kent explained about New York that "our origin is within the limits of well-attested history. This at once dissipates the enchantments of fiction. . . . It is sufficient honour to be able to appeal to the simple and severe records of truth."[98] As the nation's origin "was nearly contemporary with the invention of Printing," John Romeyn Brodhead explained to the NYHS, American collectors and historians could document the nation's entire history from settlement through independence and into its expansion as a nation.[99] This seemed to place American history on a solid archival foundation that was unavailable to Europeans. The CHS laid out this argument in its inaugural address in 1839: "There is not a nation on earth that has existed two hundred years, the sources of whose history are more abundant and authentic than those of our own. Its origin was not in a barbarous age; its first settlers were not savage and ignorant men; the monuments of their liberties were not merely traditions and customs. The very foundations of our civil polity and the framework of the superstructure rest on enduring records."[100] In this comparative historical vision, the exceptional abundance and authenticity of the nation's archives enabled not just the writing of history but held up the very structures of government and society that made the United States exceptional.

This insistence on distinguishing America's archives from those of Europe also demeaned the capacity of American Indians to preserve and narrate their histories.¹⁰¹ The Maine historian William Willis made this argument in a speech at the Maine statehouse, claiming that "the origin of the old nations of the earth, is like that of our aborigines, hidden in obscurity or lost in myth and fable; while upon this continent, it is our privilege to be able to explore the foundations on which our empire is erected."¹⁰² Here Willis appealed to the anti-Indian prejudice of his audience to argue that Europe's history stood on a shaky foundation that could not be authenticated. America's relative newness, he suggested, stabilized its historical identity rather than undermined it. This reflected an assumption endemic to history writing in this period, according to which "the nation is distinguished from unnamed ignorant and semibarbaric others by a precise documentary record that symbolizes civilization."¹⁰³

Within this context, the trouble that the AAS librarian Christopher Columbus Baldwin saw in William Buell Sprague's omnivorous documentary collecting habits comes into focus. Sprague was a hoarder of autographs, amassing some forty thousand "specimens" over the course of four decades.¹⁰⁴ In addition to his own travels throughout New England and to Mount Vernon, where he took a variety of autographed papers bequeathed by George Washington in 1815, he built a network of fellow collectors in the United States and Europe to expand his personal collection.¹⁰⁵ As a young pastor in the 1820s, he struck up a transatlantic exchange with the Reverend Thomas Raffles, the most notable English autograph collector of the time. By the late 1820s, Sprague admitted to having become "quite an enthusiast in the business of collecting autographs."¹⁰⁶ From Raffles, Sprague requested autographs of European poets, statesmen, bishops and clergymen, historians—truly, any distinguished person enticed him. In turn, the Englishman sought America's colonial clergy, its revolutionary leaders, the presidents of its colleges. The two men corresponded through the 1830s and 1840s, Sprague often hectoring the Englishman when he delayed shipments.

As Sprague emerged as a nationally respected preacher, he situated himself at the center of an epistolary network of historical collectors who constantly traded autographs with one another. Writing in the summer of 1845 to Eliza Allen, for instance, he offered one of Joseph Hewes, a signer of the Declaration of Independence from North Carolina. "If you have already a specimen of this I will ask you to retain it," he explained, "as I have two or three other friends who are very desirous of obtaining it, but I much prefer you should have it, unless you are already supplied."¹⁰⁷ He exchanged such lists of "desiderata" with his avid correspondents, who shared their own must-have lists with him.

For Sprague, it was the comprehensive ownership of autographs within a given category—the signers of America's founding documents or German professors in Göttingen—that moved him rather than close observation of any one piece of paper.[108] He simply wanted them all. An autograph collection, the *Southern Literary Messenger* observed in 1856, was "a mass of manuscripts from the pens of great personages characteristic of them, and illustrative, to a greater or less extent, of their modes of thought and graces of style."[109] By this definition, a writer's "autograph" was a synecdoche for the full manuscript it was traced upon, which reflected the mind and character of the individual who produced it. The trouble with Sprague's autograph collection was that this mass of individuals did not coalesce into a larger, meaningful story. While historical societies sought to document the exceptional history of their locality, state, or the nation as a whole, Sprague's collection sprawled, encompassing far more than America and Americans. Now held by the HSP, each one of Sprague's hefty indexes of foreign autographs reflects this cosmopolitan compendium. They arrange thousands of autographs from British, French, German, and other Europeans, Latin Americans, a smattering of "Asiatics," and a few Africans. Many are compiled by alphabetical "class": authors followed by British admirals, judges preceding ladies of the nobility, sculptors and secretaries to the nobility arranged one on top of the other.[110]

This acquisitive, autographic gaze around the Atlantic world irked historical society leaders like Baldwin and leading collectors such as Jared Sparks. Throughout the antebellum era, Sparks labored to gather a comprehensive record of George Washington's writings, the war for independence he led, and the Atlantic diplomatic context in which the Revolution triumphed. He saw this as a national record that should be published for a broad audience and ultimately preserved in Washington, DC. By contrast, Sparks found Sprague's collecting habits weird, albeit valuable. Sprague helped Sparks obtain original letters that made their way into the latter's own publications; in return, Sparks offered autographs of French nobles, "scraps of Franklin," "Lafayette a plenty."[111] The two men played the collecting game for different stakes: Sparks was constructing a collection that would enable US historians to tell a unifying story of revolution and independence, secured in print for public benefit; Sprague was amassing distinguished Atlantic individuals without a clear chronology, narrative bounds, or civic purpose.

This could strain Sparks's patience and his vision of what the nation's archives should be. In 1832, he exclaimed to Sprague, "You autograph maniacs are the most ravenous animals, that I have ever heard of, not excepting sharks and alligators . . . you are all-devouring. Old papers, the scorn of moths and mice, seem to be your most precious morsel."[112] Here Sparks inverted the trope of the citizen salvaging papers from oblivion, making Sprague not the preserver but the predator of manuscripts. Although Sparks endorsed Sprague's collection of autographs of revolutionary leaders, he worried that by detaching these papers from their rightful place in a historical society and instead adding them to his own private collection, Sprague *consumed* rather than *preserved* them. Years later, as Sparks completed his mammoth project to edit and publish the writings of George Washington, Sprague again managed to pick through those papers for more autographs of Washington before they were transmitted to the State Department to be archived.[113] Through an array of other correspondents, Sprague built an unprecedented personal collection of autographs, but in neither donating them nor crafting them into a narrative account, he went off script, as far as men like Baldwin and Sparks had written it.

Sprague embodied a relationship between American citizen and the archive that ran against the claim by historical societies that Americans had not only an exceptional archive and history but an exceptional relationship with the nation's documentary record. In numerous statements throughout this period, historical societies and their advocates argued that not just the doings of elite Americans but an American's every act was historical, eligible to enter these growing archives. "The least favour will be acceptable," the MHS circulated in 1813, "the smallest document, illustrative of our history, will be gratefully acknowledged, and carefully preserved."[114] If European archives appeared crowded by the documentary traces of nobles and monarchs, historical societies claimed, America's were populated by a wider array of figures.

The accession catalogues of historical societies frequently show the many small gestures by individuals to write the mundane facts of their community or family into the archive, such as Reverend and Portland journalist Asa Cummings, who in 1824 submitted his own sermon delivered upon his election as deacon to the First Church in North Yarmouth to the Maine

Historical Society.¹¹⁵ To Americans in the early republic, the historical record did not constitute a remote history from which the living were detached. Rather, it was understood as a cumulative record, one in which Americans could situate their own lives. This dynamic between individual and archive was facilitated by the innumerable calls by historical societies to gather the comprehensive record of the nation within their archives. Societies such as the RIHS sought "all those works of the early settlers."¹¹⁶ Responding to the call by the Dorchester Antiquarian and Historical Society for records of early settlers, the novelist and avid student of history Sylvester Judd eagerly responded with a long list of the first inhabitants of Dorchester. The generation of such lists, whether of first settlers or anniversary sermons, reflected the common vision of the American historical record as comprehensible— as something to be comprehended if only enough citizens preserved it.¹¹⁷ However exclusionary these institutions were in fact, for the builders of archives in the early United States, generating these seemingly comprehensive collections made the writing of national history possible.

The donation of papers or artifacts inscribed the living into archives in a way that was unavailable to other nations, these institutions contended. Donating and receiving material to this end became a rite, indicating the significance of each item submitted to the archive and celebrating the citizen's belonging within it. The donor's contribution was announced at society meetings and often attributed in the subsequent publications of the society. Often, that person would receive a certificate or letter of recognition, which they too could archive. It was a way of performing publicly the act of gathering and transmitting to the archive. This made the preservation of historical traces a visible, legible, civic gesture, rather than marking the self-interested penchant of an individual. "Despise not the day of small things," the NJHS implored American citizens in its first circular. "The suggestion of a single useful thought; the transmission of the smallest valuable pamphlet, manuscript or specimen; the ascertaining of a single fact, however apparently trivial, pertaining to our early history, may be of great value to us, and will certainly be received with gratitude by the Society."¹¹⁸ In this light, any trace produced in the course of America's history—including by one's own life—could sustain an archive that claimed to distinguish the American nation from any other.

German bibliographer Hermann Ernst Ludewig captured this aspect of America's archival exceptionalism in his 1846 survey of America's local historical literature. Ludewig compared American archives, libraries, and emerging historiography to Europe's, which as a wide-ranging member of both sundry US historical societies and European learned societies, he knew better than perhaps anyone:[119] "No people in the world can have so great an interest in the history of their country . . . for there are none who enjoy an equally great share in their country's historical acts."[120] Ludewig perceived an organic archive that grew with every act of free men on American soil. In this sense, US archives were founded as progressive institutions that looked toward the future—one which, without exception for these institutions, was perceived as the upward trajectory of a national history that could be comprehensively authenticated through records.

In frontier cities, this became especially important. The newer historical societies in states outside the narrative arc of colonial settlement and the events of the Revolution became more likely to build their collections around more recent events, proudly centering the settler-colonial conquest of the continent. In Wisconsin, the historical society repeated the familiar aim to "never falter in its noble mission of gathering from the mouldering records of the past, the scattered fragments that yet remain." This mainly meant "securing complete memorials of the present," and the works of those who labor "to advance the honor and prosperity of our State, or to enlighten, improve, or ameliorate the condition of man!"[121] To this end, Lyman Draper left his Puritan-descended New York family, of which various relatives had fought in the formative battles of the nation in the American Revolution and War of 1812, and traversed thousands of miles during the 1830s to build an archive of "trans-Alleghany pioneering," hagiographic portraits of men who had forged westward.[122] As earlier societies on the East Coast had formed around the passing of the revolutionary generation, Wisconsin's, like others in the US West, formed to "collect from the pioneers then alive, such facts in regard to the early history of Wisconsin as they might possess, as well as to treasure up those concerning the future."[123]

Historical societies were often among the first settler institutions established on lands violently appropriated from American Indians and built up before white citizens' eyes—"the settlement and improvement of this State by its present possessors," their president, Senator Benjamin Tappan of the Ohio Historical and Philosophical Society, called it. Of more interest than the "relics of antiquity" of Indigenous earthen architecture in the state, he argued that "the commencement of each village, of each farm indeed, may be ascertained and preserved; and their progressive advance marked, from the first rude hut or log cabin to their present improved condition."[124] In one breadth, this conception of the historical record expanded the archival threshold to include the lives of otherwise unknown settlers while excluding those whom they displaced. Whether new or old, these historical institutions believed that in collecting the past they could trace the nation's exceptionalism into the present and future.

The significance ascribed to historical societies, their expansive membership, and the urgency that filled their archives were all driven by a widely shared sense that the nation's exceptional history could be authenticated in its exceptional archives. Pronouncements by historical societies might suggest that the contours of this historical record were clearly defined, the nation's historical narrative established. However, as the following four chapters illuminate, the threshold for the nation's archives, interpretations of the materials that might cross it, and the narratives that these could sustain were in flux throughout the antebellum period.

⇥ TWO ⇤
Contesting America's Global Archive

Intrigued, many Americans in the 1830s weighed the claim by the Danish scholar Carl Christian Rafn to have uncovered "testimony, the most authentic and irrefragable, to the fact, that North America was actually discovered by the Northmen towards the close of the tenth century."[1] From the helm of the Royal Society of Northern Antiquaries in Copenhagen, Rafn had set his sights on the record of Norse exploration in the North Atlantic world since the institution's founding in 1826. A decade later, Rafn put before European and Americans readers what he deemed indisputable documentary and archaeological evidence that these medieval mariners were the first Europeans to have discovered North America—the first to practice Christianity there, to settle and extract economic value, to procreate, and to record their experience. These would have been the earliest events within American history that archival evidence could authenticate. If authentic, such proof would vastly expand the threshold of the archives that Americans were building in the antebellum period and revise the global history of early America.

Rafn's transatlantic intellectual maneuver was unprecedented. Deploying his own prodigious energy and the resources of the state-funded Royal Society, he aimed to convince the leading archival gatekeepers and influencers of historical consciousness in the United States of this Norse theory. Alongside a profusion of correspondence and publications, the main vessel for his argument was the great collaborative work he constructed and saw published by the Royal Society in 1837: *Antiquitates Americanae, sive scriptores septentrionales rerum ante Columbianarum in America (American*

Antiquities; or, Northern Writers on Pre-Columbian America). Evidence culled from Old Icelandic sagas stored in Danish archives and archaeological sites in Iceland, Greenland, and New England filled the elaborate tome, which included Latin and Danish translations of the Old Icelandic manuscripts as well as commentary in French and English. Though beyond the means of most Americans to access and decipher, its argument filtered through US historical societies and bookish publications before trickling outward into popular culture in the 1830s and 1840s.

How to situate America within global history is perhaps the oldest and most enduring intellectual question generated by the encounter between European colonists and the Indigenous peoples and lands of the Western Hemisphere.[2] Within this broader inquiry, the evidence arrayed for the Norse theory challenged American readers to reconsider the place of their past—as a nation, in particular states, and at a local level—within the global history of European exploration and colonization. Rafn's theory carried the potential to add dramatic interest to the narratives that US historical societies supported and that the public eagerly consumed. At the same time, by expanding the contours of the archival record that could authenticate that history, *Antiquitates Americanae* revealed the global dimensions of American history and provoked Americans to ponder seriously where the threshold of America's archives should lie.

American historians, historical societies, and a broader public were immersed in an international context in which they sought, received, and analyzed foreign historical sources and claims like Rafn's. Yet despite the best efforts of the Danish Royal Society to promote its materials and the genuine interest of sympathetic American readers, most Americans in the antebellum United States ultimately felt ambivalent about the evidence and the implications of the theory. Rather than revise the dominant narrative of America's place within global history and expand the archive for it, most Americans pushed this theory and its evidence to the margins of both.

Although Americans were drawn into such transatlantic intellectual currents as the theory of Norse discovery, they also navigated and redirected these currents according to their own notions of what belonged within the archival record and what the nation's narrative should be. To explore in detail the transatlantic context in which Americans reexamined the archival record for their place within global history and to map the international networks in which these American archival advocates operated, this chapter charts the intellectual history of the Norse theory, from Rafn's attempt to breach the established archive and narrative of America's discovery to the Americans who resolved—for the moment, at least—to leave these materials on the shoreline.

Columbus vs. Northmen

In the early United States, the archival materials that could attest to a Norse discovery of America were neither widely known nor especially interesting to most Americans.[3] Not Northmen bound for New England but a southern European alighting in the Caribbean was emblazoned on the first page of the nation's history books—the name Columbus immortalized, from poetry to place-names. However, as the country's commercial and diplomatic influence expanded after the Napoleonic Wars, knowledge about a possible Norse discovery became available to more American readers. The expanding cohort of American men appointed to diplomatic and consular posts in western Europe became conduits for an assortment of archival materials and intellectual notions, including the Norse theory. During the 1820s and 1830s, their interest in Scandinavia infused books and journals published in the United States at the same time that Rafn launched his campaign to convince influential Americans of the Royal Society's revisionist account of what many perceived as the most significant event in global history.

Some well-read and well-traveled Americans in the early United States had studied the theory of Norse discovery, but they tended to demote the importance of these transatlantic voyages and the reliability of the evidence. As late as 1828, the literary phenomenon Washington Irving shared such thoughts in his *History of the Life and Voyages of Christopher Columbus*, published in the United States, Britain, and France. Irving had relocated to Madrid at the insistence of US Minister Alexander Hill Everett, who hoped to entice Irving with the newly available materials about Columbus's voyages. These had been published by Don Martin Fernandez de Navarrete, the secretary of the Royal Academy of History, an institution supported by the Spanish Crown since 1738. Hosted by Obadiah Rich, US consul and assiduous collector of American historical materials, Irving enjoyed full access to Rich's expansive personal library and materials at the Royal Library, the Jesuit College of San Isidroo, and a number of other noble family collections, including the descendants of Columbus. "As far as authenticated history extends," Irving stated in the introduction to *Christopher Columbus*, "nothing was known of terra-firma, and the islands of the western hemisphere, until their discovery towards the close of the fifteenth century."[4] The authenticated history of European colonization of the Americas—the first pages in its archives—began with Columbus.

Irving belittled claims that the Norse had made landfall in North America, disputing that the records of these alleged voyages influenced Columbus five centuries later. If "the legends of the Scandinavian voyages be correct," Irving assured readers, the Norse "had but transient glimpses of the new world, leading to no certain or permanent knowledge, and in a little time lost again to mankind."[5] For Irving, the dearth of archival evidence left by those North Atlantic crossings reflected their historical insignificance. This contrasted with the archival plenty produced by the southern voyages of Columbus, which led to the uninterrupted colonization of the hemisphere. Irving situated Columbus's exploits at the threshold between America's history and the authenticated past, leaving the Norse vessels in the historical mists beyond it. Irving's popular biography won him membership in Spain's Royal Academy of History and a major award from Britain's Royal Society of Literature, in addition to his membership in US historical societies.

By the 1830s, however, new diplomatic and intellectual links between the United States and Denmark drew Americans to Scandinavian history, including the oceanic voyages linking Scandinavia with the lands that had become the United States. Henry Wheaton, a Rhode Island native and a leading scholar of international law, departed for his diplomatic post in Copenhagen as the United States avidly expanded its commercial empire. The US chargé d'affaires to Denmark between 1827 and 1835, Wheaton hoped to relieve the "*ennui* of banishment" that he felt abroad by mingling literary pursuits and extended European vacations with his diplomatic work—a work-life balance that was becoming common for US representatives abroad.[6] Rubbing shoulders with the Danish royal family and the learned elite in Copenhagen, Wheaton immersed himself in the study of Scandinavian languages, literature, and history. This enabled him to act as an intermediary between Denmark and men of science and letters in the United States, such as Pierre-Etienne Du Ponceau of the APS and David Hosack of the NYHS. In his research, he was aided by the leading European scholars on the region. These included the foremost Danish linguist, Rasmusson Rask; Icelandic literary scholar and archaeologist Finnur Magnússon; and Rafn himself.

His place within the expanding US diplomatic infrastructure enabled Wheaton to access foreign library and archival collections and to convey this knowledge from Europe to the United States. Wheaton had the chance to visit Denmark's national libraries, the royal family's vast natural historical collections, and "northern antiquities" held at the Rundetårn, or Round Tower, a seventeenth-century astronomical observatory repurposed as an archive.[7] Like Everett and Irving in Madrid, Wheaton entered national archival institutions that far surpassed those in the United States. Based on his extensive research, Wheaton's *History of the Northmen* appeared in London and Philadelphia in 1831 as the first serious study of Scandinavian history by an American, earning him honorary membership in several historical and archaeological societies in the United States and Europe.[8]

Influenced by his new network and research in Copenhagen, Wheaton came to admire Scandinavia and perceive a meaningful transatlantic connection with the United States. In Denmark, Wheaton found the fountainhead, as he wrote in the prominent Boston journal *North American Review*, of "our languages, our laws, and whatever it is that peculiarly distinguishes us from other races of men."[9] Wheaton observed a legal, linguistic, and deep cultural kinship between Scandinavians and Americans. Yet he was not swayed by the evidence that medieval Norsemen had first colonized the lands that had become the nineteenth-century United States or that such an event should supplant the historical significance of Columbus. His study of Norse history only briefly addressed the voyage captained by Leif Erikson to North America at the end of the first millennium. Judging the dates and daylight recorded about the southernmost point of that voyage, Wheaton added in a footnote, "Supposing this computation to be correct, it must have been in the latitude of Boston, the present capital of New England."[10] Although more inclined than Irving to connect the Norse voyages with contemporary US territory, Wheaton shared Irving's ambivalence toward the evidentiary record of Norse settlement in the hemisphere and its significance for American history.

For the moment, a Norse landing in Massachusetts Bay could be deduced from the medieval Norse historical record but was not worth emphasizing within the history of local American sites, any state, or the nation. In an appendix to his final volume of *Christopher Columbus*, Irving admitted more than in the book's introduction, recognizing "no great improbability" that "such enterprising and roving voyagers as the Scandinavians may have wandered to the northern shores of America." But he noted no evidence that the Norse ventured farther south than Newfoundland, in contemporary Canada. Irving did not read the original Old Icelandic accounts of these voyages, assessing instead interpretations by recent European scholars. "Learned men," he insinuated, "are too prone to give substance to mere shadows, when they assist some preconceived theory." Even if the Old Icelandic manuscripts were "genuine, free from modern interpolation, and correctly quoted," Irving concluded, that knowledge never circulated beyond Scandinavia to Columbus.[11]

Wheaton argued similarly that even if Norse discovery could be authenticated, "there is not the slightest reason to believe that the illustrious Genoese was acquainted with the discovery of North America by the Normans centuries before his time."[12] This dismissed the possibility that Columbus could have learned about the Norse accounts when he visited Iceland in the winter of 1477 to 1478, prior to his transatlantic crossings. For Irving, Wheaton, and their readers, this apparent archival rupture—between the documentation of medieval Norse voyages to North America and the records that Columbus could access centuries later—proved the originality and significance of what Columbus had accomplished. This burnished him as a national symbol in their eyes. Reviewing Wheaton's book, one American periodical reassured readers that although "the spirit of the north was noble, original, and bold in all things . . . the honour of being the first Europeans who penetrated to the shores of the New World" remained with Columbus.[13]

Such praise of Columbus was rampant in this period, blunting the appeal of the alternative narrative of Norse discovery briefly pondered by Irving and Wheaton. During the American Revolution, Columbus emerged as a potent symbol for the United States, "one that not only transcended British imperialism but also placed the establishment of the nation within a larger historical process that understood the progress of mankind as inexorably moving westward, thereby also affirming Americans' notions of the importance of the new republic to the world."[14] Columbus represented the first stride of what white Americans deemed "civilization" across the continent. His voyages had produced the first documents in the archive of the Americas. For many Americans, he had written himself onto the first page of their history.

This conviction suffused American culture, whether in such popular children's texts as *Peter Parley's Book of the United States* (1837), massive artworks such as John Vanderlyn's Landing of Columbus in the Capitol Rotunda (commissioned in 1836 and installed in 1847), or volumes such as George Bancroft's canonical History of the Colonization of the United States (1834–40), in which Bancroft deemed Columbus's Atlantic crossing "the most memorable maritime enterprise in the history of the world."[15] Affiliation with Columbus was strongest in the Northeast, although located far from the disembarkation of those Spanish voyages and colonial projects. Reviewing Irving's work in the North American Review, Alexander Hill Everett contended that Columbus's voyages were "the very best subject afforded by the annals of the world."[16] Although these transatlantic voyages did not cross into other regions of the globe, antebellum Americans saw them as a pivotal event within the broader frame of global history that centered the exceptional history of the United States.

In such interpretations, Columbus became detached from what many saw as the repellent imperial legacy of monarchical Spain and recast in a republican mold as a "simple mariner," "who, by his hardy genius, his inflexible constancy, and his heroic courage, brought the ends of the earth into communication with each other," as Irving put it. Irving captured the tone of contemporary praise for Columbus as an agent of progress who embodied qualities important to Americans.[17] He and other Americans often distanced Columbus from the depredations of Spanish conquest of Indigenous lands.[18] In Vanderlyn's depiction of Columbus in the US Capitol, he gazes toward the heavens after landing in the Caribbean, his sword facing downward; meanwhile, his entourage menaces the Indigenous inhabitants and digs hungrily for gold behind him. This preserved Columbus as a noble innovator and agent of historical progress who symbolized the ongoing civilization of America—a historical vision of America's past and future within global history that the inconsequential Norse settlements in North America could not satisfy.

The evidence for the Norse theory could not yet authenticate an earlier discovery that might displace Columbus, but Americans by the 1830s were becoming more interested in Scandinavian history and impressed by its archives and scholarship. Influenced by Rafn and others in Copenhagen, Wheaton praised the contemporary Danish archives and the research over the preceding decades that had made Norse history and literature knowable. Based on his experience in Danish archives and libraries, Wheaton wrote in his History that "these sources embrace the most authentic and valuable historical monuments of early transactions possessed by any European nation, which have been illustrated with a diligence and critical skill that may fairly be said to be unrivalled by the antiquarian labours of any other country."[19] In touting Scandinavian sources and scholarship, Wheaton surely sought to endorse his own research, but he also shared a perspective that was becoming increasingly popular among American intellectuals. In contrast to those of other European nations, Scandinavian archives seemed distinctively well-suited to authenticate medieval history.

In an 1829 *North American Review* article, Wheaton insisted that the labor of Scandinavian scholars merited special praise for salvaging this archive. Among the scholars across Europe whose research had "recently turned with renewed and fresh interest to the cultivation of their own native literature, language, and history ... none have labored with more zeal in this patriotic work than the Danes and Swedes." According to Wheaton, the quality of these archives and this archival labor distinguished Scandinavia, such that "there are no nations of modern Europe who can trace back the authentic history of their ancestors so far in written records."[20] The historical connections between Scandinavia and the United States seemed to extend to their archives: more than those of other European nations, Scandinavia's archives looked like the collections that historical societies in the United States strived to construct, an authentic—though perhaps not comprehensive—record of the nation's past, diligently preserved for scholars to examine. Across the Atlantic, Americans like Wheaton admired this archival community and its practices at a moment when they sought to foster their own. Moved by these global currents, Americans became more receptive to the narrative of the Northmen.

An Atlantic Network for *Antiquitates Americanae*

From his vantage in Copenhagen, Rafn recognized both the stature of Columbus in American historical consciousness and these shifting perceptions about Scandinavian archives and scholars. Beginning with the very conception of *Antiquitates Americanae* in the 1820s, he asked Americans to integrate the archive and narrative of Norse settlement into their perception of history. Undertaking this project, Rafn contended that the manuscript and archaeological record documented in the compilation authenticated a vast arc of Norse exploration across the North Atlantic: from Scandinavia through Iceland, Greenland, and into North America, landing somewhere in New England in the eleventh-century colony of Vinland, and perhaps venturing even as far south as contemporary Brazil. In the United States, this argument entered a cultural and intellectual context within which it had only recently become possible for Americans to appreciate that these foreign archives and scholarship could reveal something about America's own history, even if it meant challenging strongly held beliefs.

In the decade preceding the publication of *Antiquitates Americanae* in 1837, Rafn used the Royal Society as a hub for assembling the historical materials and building the network of European and American institutions and readers that he hoped to reach. Inspired by the extraordinary assortment of manuscript materials at the University of Copenhagen, where he had worked closely with the Arni Magnusson collection, Rafn formed the Society in 1826, which soon received royal sponsorship from King Frederick VI. Rafn developed relationships with an international array of scholars who helped to gather, interpret, and publicize the historical traces of

FIGURE 4. Portrait of Carl Christian Rafn, by Julius Magnus Petersen. (Royal Danish Library)

the Norse Atlantic world. He managed this international network from his office, which became known as the "real Foreign Ministry of Denmark," serving as "a veritable clearing house for the exchange of manuscripts."[21] In collaboratively undertaking this major scholarly work and then presenting it to an elite Atlantic audience, the Royal Society hoped to inspire a broader transnational community to appreciate Denmark's place within the global history of America's discovery and colonization.

In staking Denmark's historical identity and scholarly reputation on the Norse theory, Rafn and the Royal Society used his international intellectual network toward nationalistic history writing. Upon the completion of the book, the Royal Society boasted, "In order to perpetuate the glorious memory of our ancestors, it reclaims for them their rightful honor in the history of the universe, of science, of trade, and navigation."[22] A humbled post-Napoleonic Denmark, detached from the kingdom of Norway, had declined in stature. The historical record reconstructed in *Antiquitates Americanae* connected the now middling nation-state with a much grander historical identity. The investment of the Danish government in this historical narrative underscored the significance of the Norse past for Denmark's present. The Royal Society enjoyed the regular support of the Danish monarchs Frederick VI and Christian VIII, whose interior ministers opened the annual meeting of the Royal Society. Addressing the Royal Society, its president, Johan Mosting, head of the king's library, spoke on behalf of the Danish monarchy when he insisted on the link between the study of history and nation-building: "It is the study of antiquity to which we devote ourselves that conserves the root of the venerable source from which the young stalk emerges under which the crown must one day protect our nation."[23] According to the Royal Society, the significance of its archives and the sophistication of Danish scholarship enabled them to comprehend their nation's distinctive past in a way that served its present.

To substantiate this historical vision, the early Royal Society invested the bulk of its resources and aspirations in its Committee on the Ante-Columbian History of America. This research group worked to collect evidence that would authenticate the arc of Norse exploration and settlement.[24] Rafn supported their work by looking to a transnational community of collectors who would help substantiate this history of exploration, including historically minded Americans and historical societies in the United States.

As the Royal Society began to translate and annotate the volumes of medieval Icelandic sagas into the more accessible Latin and Danish, Rafn initiated contact with correspondents at historical societies throughout the northern United States. Denmark's minister to the United States, Chevalier Peter Pederson—Wheaton's counterpart during these years, and like him an archival intermediary—and other Danish representatives helped to mediate these exchanges. As soon as the Royal Society was founded, Rafn announced the scope of his project to his American contacts. Writing to the NYHS in German in 1826, he envisioned "a collection of descriptions of the old Scandinavians voyages of discovery to Vinland, which I God willing hope to eventually send the Society."[25] He established similar lines of communication and self-promotion with historical societies in New England. In so doing, he hoped to recruit boosters for his project who would procure evidence that could support Rafn's argument for Norse settlement and then endorse the book, find subscribers, and distribute copies in the United States when the volume appeared.

Historical societies in the United States were eager to welcome this unprecedented level of engagement with a learned society in Europe, even though its historical inquiry was tethered to the aspirations of another nation-state, at odds with prevailing depictions of American history, and based on unfamiliar archival materials. John Farmer, New England's preeminent genealogist, captured the early enthusiasm toward Rafn's project. Responding to Rafn in 1828, he anticipated that the inquiry into Norse history "will be to some of the members of [the New Hampshire Historical Society] the means of directing their attention to inquiries beyond the sphere of our region, and to ages with which our acquaintance has been much circumscribed."[26] Farmer, like many of Rafn's American correspondents, was thrilled at the prospect of documenting what he and others called the "ancient" history of the Americas.

As much as the historical interest of this archival evidence or the Norse theory itself, the opportunity to engage with a leading European learned society attracted Americans and influenced how they perceived this revisionist history. In the next few years, Rafn was elected an honorary member of various historical societies that were receptive to his inquiry into their own continent's past and eager to expand their Atlantic network to include the Royal Society: the New Hampshire Historical Society in 1828;

the American Philosophical Society, Massachusetts Historical Society, and Historical Society of Pennsylvania in 1829; Rhode Island's in 1833; the American Antiquarian Society in 1836; and, after the publication of *Antiquitates Americanae* in 1837, historical societies in New York, Georgia, Maryland, and Wisconsin, as well as the New England Historic Genealogical Society in Boston.[27] Rafn could reasonably expect that the Norse theory might well sate the appetite of those Americans who were, as one leading scholar on this subject has put it, "hungry for a romantic history they could call their own."[28] This drew Americans into the widespread fascination with the Middle Ages in Europe, where many historians and their state sponsors sifted through their medieval archives in hopes of constructing distinctive narratives for their own nation-states.[29] For Americans who had perennially worried about both their lack of compelling precolonial historical associations and the modest stature of the nation's new and often poorly funded archives, the theory of Norse discovery offered to cast light on a medieval period in America while the Royal Society offered to integrate US historical societies as peers in a transatlantic fraternity of scholars.

As Rafn fanned enthusiasm about the Royal Society's research, the Dane became a privileged foreign correspondent of American scholars and historical societies. His letters were read aloud at historical society meetings, and notable American scholars and historical society leaders paid membership dues to the Royal Society.[30] Americans soon formed a small but important cohort among the Royal Society's expansive network, which would comprise two thousand members and numerous learned societies across several countries by midcentury. In New England, soon-to-be US minister to Britain Edward Everett, Harvard librarian William Thaddeus Harris, Harvard president Josiah Quincy, and Massachusetts Historical Society officer John Winthrop became members. They were joined by the influential historian and editor Jared Sparks and scholar of the Spanish empire, William Hickling Prescott, as well as the Harvard poet-professor Henry Wadsworth Longfellow, who along with Vermonter George Perkins Marsh was the most avid American student of Scandinavia. New Hampshire politicians and leaders of historical preservation William Plumer and Levi Woodbury also paid dues, as did a number of notable advocates of historical preservation in Rhode Island: Thomas Webb, Judge William Staples, Mayor Samuel Brigham, and Brown University professor Romeo Elton. Beyond New England—the alleged site of Norse discovery—members subscribed from New

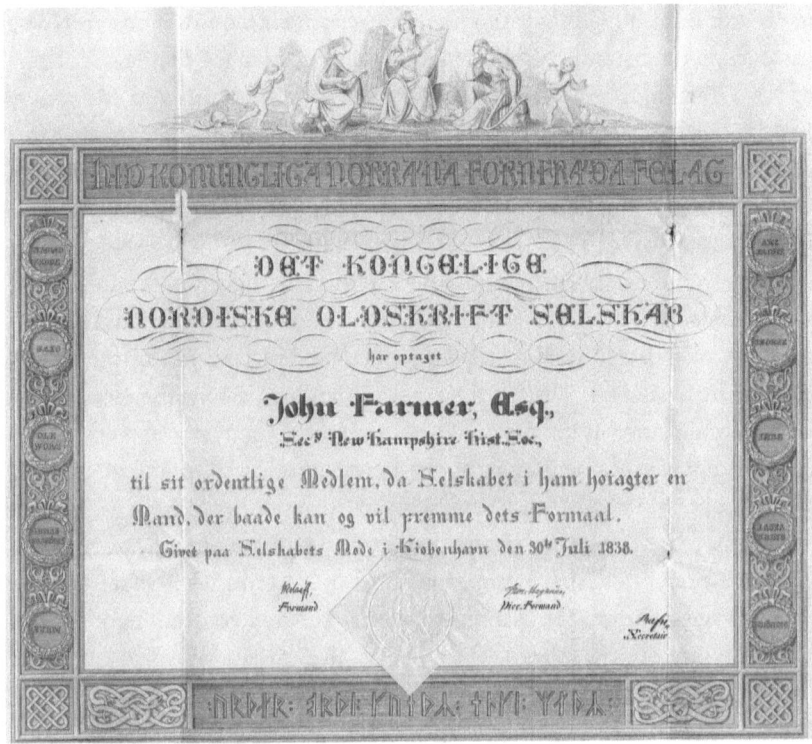

FIGURE 5. A diploma of membership in the Royal Society of Northern Antiquaries depicting the recording of the Norse sagas, preserved by John Farmer, New Hampshire genealogist. (Courtesy of the New Hampshire Historical Society)

York and Pennsylvania. From Copenhagen, the diploma signifying membership was sent to each new member.

As excitement around *Antiquitates Americanae* mounted, the *American Quarterly* published a detailed description of the diploma that members could look forward to receiving, endorsed by the king of Denmark and the Royal Society's officers. The icon of the Royal Society depicted a sagaman, the medieval recorder of history, on an Icelandic landscape in the act of inscribing Gothic runes on parchment—the transmission of oral tradition to the very texts on which the theory of Norse discovery was based and which American readers were asked to trust.[31]

During the years of correspondence that preceded the publication of *Antiquitates Americanae*, Rafn pushed Americans to see New England within the arc of Norse history and to imagine themselves on a landscape bearing its traces. Rafn hoped that *Antiquitates Americanae* would impose a Norse cartography, substantiated by medieval sources, onto the familiar coastline of New England: "Furdustrandir" for Nauset, Chatham, and Monomoy Beach; "Krossanes" for Gurnet Point or Point Alderton; "Straumsey" for Martha's Vineyard or Egg Island; "Straumsfiordr" for Buzzards Bay, and "Hop" Mount Hope Bay.[32] Rafn promised the MHS, for instance, to have identified "the precise spots where the [sic] antient Northmen held their intercourse," and even urged its members to inscribe eleventh-century Norse place-names on future maps and geography books of New England.[33]

Rafn collaborated with members of the Rhode Island Historical Society (RIHS) in particular, seeking their help in authenticating the evidence of Norse architecture in the region. RIHS secretary Thomas Webb enthusiastically supported Rafn's inquiry about architectural, archaeological, and linguistic traces of the Norse in New England. Responding to Rafn in 1830, he exaggerated that it had "long been the received opinion of many of our most learned Antiquaries" that Europeans knew of America well before Columbus's voyages. The proof was in the mysterious characters seemingly chiseled with iron implements into rocks across North America, of which American Indians had no knowledge, he argued. Webb lamented to Rafn that the tide of development swept more swiftly over the continent than the man of science could study it: "Scarcely a year passes, but what, in the progress of civilization, and the consequent settlement of the lands in the West, some of these are not swept away; being employed for building, or for making walls; and after the lapse of a short period, hardly a vestige of them will remain. The clearer of wild lands is not a virtuoso; he sees in those rocks nothing but unmeaning scrawls of, as he supposes, the idle [sic] indian, who had spent his time in this lazy manner."[34] Webb's commonplace complaint about the destruction of historical materials also distanced American Indians from the evidentiary record of, he imagined, possible traces of Norse settlement. This implied that more evidence of Norse settlement might only further marginalize American Indians from the nation's archives and historical narratives.

As the Royal Society prepared the work, the RIHS Committee on the Antiquities and Aboriginal History of America visited sites of possible Norse activity, where they recorded data that the Royal Society could corroborate with medieval manuscripts in Copenhagen in order to determine the location of Norse settlements. They copied inscriptions on rocks from sites such as Dighton Rock in Massachusetts, which Rafn and others suspected as evidence of European settlement prior to Columbus, described nearby topography and animal and plant life, and recorded proximate natural features such as tides and weather that might correspond with Norse accounts of the region. By using this data and then reprinting his letters with Webb as part of *Antiquitates Americanae*, Rafn drew on this transatlantic exchange as evidence to substantiate the Royal Society's theory and endorse the Danish attempt to rewrite the dominant narrative of American history.

For years, Rafn used such exchanges to generate American interest in *Antiquitates Americanae*—Denmark's "national relics," as the *North American Review* labeled it.[35] As one circulating advertisement for the book quoted, "It may be confidently asserted that no historical work has been looked for with more anxious expectation by those who knew of its being in progress."[36] This helped Rafn stoke curiosity among potential readers. Corresponding with Rafn during his own travels through Scandinavia in the 1830s, Longfellow promised to "do all in my power to make the Literature of the North better known to my countrymen, on the other side of the Atlantic."[37] In his correspondence with George Perkins Marsh, Rafn asked Marsh to gauge popular interest in the forthcoming work in the United States and do what he could to promote it.[38] Though he would later cast doubt on the Norse discovery theory, George Bancroft flattered Rafn's undertaking as the work went to press as "a subject of very high moment . . . still more as vindicating for a glorious race of hardy adventurers the honor of having made a real and pregnant discovery of the New World."[39]

As the Royal Society prepared *Antiquitates Americanae* for publication, Rafn activated his American historical society contacts as literary boosters and agents, hoping they could excite popular interest and commit subscribers to his unprecedented, though admittedly uncommon, work. Rafn distributed to them a sensational advertisement, which soon appeared widely in the popular press. His insistence that this work contained definitive proof of Norse discovery—"testimony, the most authentic and irrefragable"—echoed again and again in newspapers across the nation.[40] Intrigued Americans subscribed through the historical societies of Massachusetts, Rhode Island, and New York, as well as the APS in Philadelphia. After this long-anticipated work was printed, stitched, and dispatched from Denmark in the autumn of 1837, Americans could finally examine this evidence for themselves. This would soon foment a scholarly debate in the United States about the import of these historical materials and narrative.[41]

In form, however, the book was an unlikely stimulus to the scholarly—and, increasingly, popular—debate that ensued. As advertised by Rafn to American consumers, *Antiquitates Americanae* was "a critical apparatus of variorum readings." Like the collections irregularly issued by US historical societies and the many learned societies throughout Europe, the volume was a historical compilation, drawing together multiple primary sources paired with scholarly commentary produced by the publishing institution. But compared with publications by other learned societies, *Antiquitates Americanae* was a much larger, more collaborative, and intellectually ambitious production that aimed to make a major intervention in Europeans' and Americans' understanding of history.

It was an amalgam of medieval geographies, historical narratives, commentaries on the voyages and geography of Norse settlement, epistolary exchanges between men like Rafn and Webb, appendices including timetables and genealogy—all serving as scaffolding to the republished original Old Icelandic manuscripts and their dual translation into Danish and Latin.[42] Aside from a few letters between Webb and Rafn, none of the text was in English. The Old Icelandic materials consisted mainly of two major thirteenth-century accounts of the late tenth- and early eleventh-century voyages of Eric the Red to Greenland and Thorfinn Karlsefni to Vinland, alongside fifteen other reprinted manuscripts; these were published in the original with translations in Latin and Danish, along with infusions of French commentary. In addition to the language barriers this posed, relatively few Americans would purchase the twelve-dollar book. Still, upon publication in 1837, several hundred copies were circulated by traveling agents to universities, libraries, and learned societies.[43]

Like Wheaton in his *History of the Northmen*, Americans praised the extensiveness and integrity of the Danish archives, where some two thousand manuscript sagas had been amassed and kept in "a high state of preservation," the *Knickerbocker* reported.[44] To encourage American readers to examine the source texts, George Perkins Marsh published an Old Icelandic grammar the following year, which he hoped would "awaken the attention of American scholars to the remarkable language in which the ancient and curious memorials contained in that volume are embodied."[45] In practice, however, very few Americans would have accessed the theory of Norse discovery through the source material republished by the Royal Society.

Recognizing this, Rafn sought to increase access to the text itself, enabling the evidence and theory of Norse settlement to emanate outward from a handful of American literary gatekeepers to a broader public. Urged by Marsh, Rafn released an abridged English-language version in New York in 1839, the title of which distilled his major claim: *America Discovered in the Tenth Century*.[46] In a few dozen pages, compared with several hundred in the original, Rafn surveyed the major voyages catalogued in the Norse sagas. By downplaying the folkloric elements of the sagas, he made this archive appear as "reliable evidentiary documents," one scholar has explained.[47] In the preface to the abridged American volume, he underscored the distinctiveness of the archives and of the scholarship that authenticated this history: "After having perused the authentic documents themselves, which are now accessible to all, every one will acknowledge the truth of the historical fact, that during the tenth and eleventh centuries, the ancient Northmen discovered and visited a great extent of the eastern coasts of North America."[48] Salvaged from obscurity and examined, the medieval Icelandic accounts served "to shed an unexpected light on this remote period, formerly supposed to be wrapped in Cimmerian darkness." In employing the figurative language of light and darkness to describe primary sources, Rafn evoked metaphors familiar to historical societies, which habitually urged the public to illuminate the past. For its American audience, the Royal Society's history of America's first European colonization claimed to cast light upon a material record, a space, and a period that had lain in "the obscure recesses of antiquity" and to inscribe this global origin within the arc of American history.

Moreover, Rafn had made the publication of *Antiquitates Americanae* a bookish transatlantic event that predisposed American readers to perceive the archival evidence as authentic and the scholarship as credible. Affiliation with the Royal Society bestowed prestige. "This society," the *Providence Journal* embellished to readers, "is one of the oldest and most eminent in existence; it enrolls among its members many of the best known and most distinguished savans in Europe."[49] Press accounts celebrated the transatlantic archival, fraternal community that linked the United States with northern Europe, "whose scholars share with us in the sentiment, that such literary undertakings ought not to be confined within political boundaries, but, on account of their extensive tendency, have also a claim to active participation from other countries."⁵⁰ This cosmopolitan scholarly exchange was especially appealing to Americans in states where Norse colonists allegedly landed, sites of vanished settlements that might enrich the significance of their state's past within the nation's history. The RIHS in particular garnered kudos for engaging as a peer organization in the production of this international publication.⁵¹

Rafn worked letter by letter, year after year to build these transatlantic links and promote the Norse discovery theory, which arrived in 1837 in an American context that had become more inclined to lend it credence. His efforts reveal that archival gatekeepers in the United States operated in an international context and could be enticed to broaden the threshold for the archival materials that informed their understanding of America's past. At the same time, the significance of these materials remained contested. These gatekeepers and a broader range of American readers would critically examine the volume as they appraised its impact on their understanding of the nation's history and the materials that should fall within its archives.

America Appraises the Norse Archives

In *Fantastic Archaeology*, the archaeologist Stephen Williams writes that scholarship by Rafn "started the frantic and almost unending search for Viking remains."⁵² Americans analyzing *Antiquitates Americanae* did indeed lend credence to these historical sources, motivating some to seek material traces of Norse settlement lingering within the borders of the United States. At the same time, they critically assessed the sources that the Royal Society and fellow Americans had arrayed to substantiate the theory of Norse discovery. In doing so, influential Americans—less frantic than measured—participated in the transatlantic intellectual exchange initiated by Rafn while continuing to patrol the threshold for America's archives.

Antiquitates Americanae presented a collection of thirteenth-century Old Icelandic sagas translated into Latin and Danish from the originals archived in Copenhagen—sources both intellectually and physically inaccessible to nearly all American readers. In fact, these published sources were compilations of formerly oral traditions fashioned by many mouths and hands over the course of many years, which the Royal Society used to center its nation's place in global history.⁵³ In contrast, US archives tended to prize legible, discrete texts produced by identifiable historical actors that could

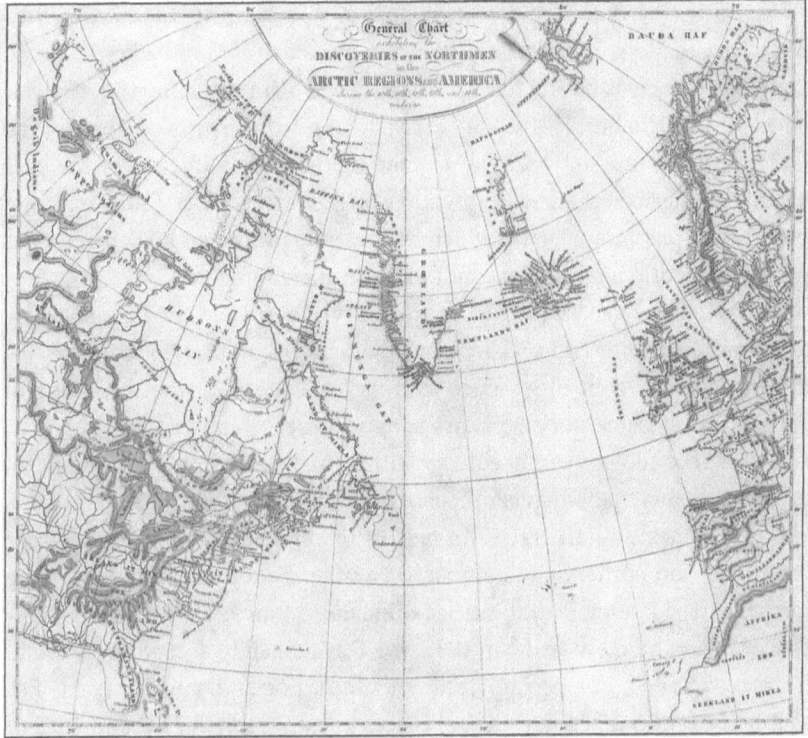

FIGURE 6. *General Chart Exhibiting the Discoveries of the Northmen in the Arctic Regions and America*, published in *Antiquitates Americanae* (1837). (Image from Archive.org)

authenticate the exceptional upward arc of the nation's settlement and progress.[54] Whereas American historical societies and their networks took it upon themselves to conduct the research and craft the narrative of the nation's past, the evidence for Norse discovery and settlement was assessed and curated by scholars in Europe. In sum, although the evidence about Norse settlers was scarce by American archival standards, of questionable authenticity and validity, and primarily construed by foreigners for their own ends, many Americans took it seriously as a potential addition to their nation's historical record and an intervention in the prevailing narrative of America's discovery and colonization.

Given the focus of American historical societies on amassing texts that could authenticate their history as colonies and a nation, the widespread receptiveness toward the medieval sources behind the Norse theory could seem surprising. Just a few years before *Antiquitates Americanae* reached American readers, reviewers of Wheaton's *History of the Northmen* judged the Icelandic sagas as "mixed up more or less with mythological and poetical embellishments."[55] By the release of the work in 1837, however, the materials presented in the work seemed increasingly authentic in the eyes of Rafn's American readers. In this they largely agreed with Rafn's insistent public relations campaign, in which he tirelessly promoted his "endeavor to give to the world a faithful account of these ancient records."[56]

In part, this reflected the successful effort by Rafn and the Royal Society to convince an international scholarly audience that its medieval archives distinguished it from other European nation-states. During the first half of the nineteenth century, scholars across Europe employed new research methods in philology, archaeology, and history to examine the medieval past as a means to distinguish their respective nation's identity in the present.[57] As Wheaton had argued in his *History of the Northmen*, the relative intactness and authenticity compared to other European archives for the medieval period endowed these Scandinavian archives with special significance. In an annual meeting in 1838, the Royal Society argued that the full history of Russia, northern Germany, France, England, and America "has as much need to delve into the resources of our archives as the history of Rome depended on Greece and Asia in order to know its origin."[58] Reviewing a book on the medieval history of Greenland, where the Royal Society had examined evidence of Norse colonies for *Antiquitates Americanae*, the society's 1836 *Mémoires* contrasted the significance of these materials with those available for medieval histories of other European countries: "any morsel of history, recording facts of that remote corner of the globe, from a period in which the annals of the most civilized countries in Europe are so meager and the history so dark, must be as welcome to the student of history as a fertile oasis in a dreary waste to the traveller."[59] The Danish institution anticipated that its archive of wide-ranging Norse trade and conquest in Europe and North America would attract a number of European countries to examine their own national histories in this early period.

Editions of Rafn's abridged account of the Norse theory were published in German, French, as well as Polish, Spanish, Portuguese, and Italian. Eulogizing Rafn in 1864, the Royal Society found that he was largely successful in convincing fellow Europeans, winning nomination to more than one hundred learned societies across Europe and the Americas along the way. "Mr. Rafn has also the great merit of having, by this work," one eulogist wrote, "brought these events, formerly doubted by so many celebrated scholars of Europe, to such an incontestable clearness, that no one can, for the future, deny the truth and exactness of these historical facts."[60]

Influential Americans, for their part, came to perceive the medieval authors of these texts as reliable historical recorders. An essay on the distinctiveness of Scandinavian literature by Peter Erasmus Mueller, translated into English by George Perkins Marsh in 1841, observed that no other literature more clearly showed the transition from oral tradition to written history.[61] Some American readers similarly touted the distinctive oral role of Icelandic skalds and the scribal role of the sagamen who had preserved memory of the Norse voyages and produced the Old Icelandic texts. In so doing, Americans constructed an image of these medieval figures as trustworthy historical observers and compilers. As Marsh explained in the *North American Review* a year before *Antiquitates Americanae* appeared, the skalds "united in themselves the functions of the historiographer and of the poet. . . . They were the interpreters of the gods, the ambassadors of kings. . . . Skaldic poetry was a regular art and science."[62] Accompanying kings, skalds closely observed the course of history in real time, which they converted to oral poetry that would later be transcribed.

In contrast to the "monkish legends" produced by medieval clergymen in Europe, Edward Everett elaborated in the same journal the following year, "The Skalds were men of the world;—warriors, rovers, chieftains, they mingled in the stir of life; they were trained, not within the cloister, but in the open air of the mountains and the vales, and amidst the wild creations of Arctic nature."[63] For Everett, the narratives that these skalds preserved reflected their engagement with the "stir of life," as compared with chroniclers of history who worked in monasteries. These qualities infused the historical accounts that the sagamen (literally "story men") crafted into prose from the poetry of the skalds.

In fact, the oral traditions of the skalds could have an extraordinary documentary power. Reviewing several recent translations of the *Saga of Frithiof*, the *North American Review* waxed that "the modern Scald has written his name in immortal runes; not on the bark of trees alone, in the 'unspeakable rural solitudes' of pastoral song, but on the mountains of his fatherland, and the cliffs that overhand the seas, and on the tombs of ancient heroes, whose histories are epic poems."[64] Unlike the typical treatment that white Americans accorded Indigenous histories, American readers were impressed by "the power of oral traditions," as one periodical labeled it, when appraising this Norse archive.[65] The materials then accumulating in archives at US historical societies were valued in part because they embodied firsthand experience of what was commonly seen by white Americans as the exceptional narrative of colonization, settlement, and progress of the nation. Based on descriptions from such influential intellectuals writing in esteemed publications, American readers could recognize in the authorship of those foreign manuscripts a similar proximity to historical events and reliable method for recording them.

Rather than consign Norse history to the mists of unauthenticated time, many American readers concluded that records attesting to Norse settlements in North America fell within the scope of verifiable history. "What are these manuscripts, where are they preserved, what is their age, and what their claims to authenticity, what is their exact purport, and why are they not published?" Edward Everett asked of the Old Icelandic sources in the *North American Review*. He assured his readers that Rafn had faithfully answered all of these fundamental questions. The "obviously fabulous" did persist in these sources, the influential southern periodical the *Democratic Review* admitted, but that "only further proves that the accounts were indeed produced in a half-civilized age, and thus confirms, instead of shaking, the authenticity of the narrative."[66] Americans were receptive to the liminal archival space—betwixt oral tradition and written text, pre-Christian and Christian Europe—that these sources emerged from, where the obscurity of the remote past transitioned into the realm of verifiable history. "The light of authentic history is here shed upon what otherwise must have remained, to a great extent, the 'fabulous age' of our country," recorded Henry Rowe Schoolcraft, a leading ethnologist well-known for his accounts of Indigenous oral traditions, in 1839.[67] Scandinavian sources and scholars, in other words, could cast light on a period of American history that Americans and their archives could not.

American experts on Scandinavian literature also encouraged readers to appreciate its aesthetic qualities. Over the course of a half century, George Perkins Marsh assembled the largest nineteenth-century library of Scandinavian history and literature in the United States. He maintained this collection at his home in Burlington, Vermont, where in the 1820s his study of the law first stirred his interest in northern European legal antecedents, which led to his realization that literature on Scandinavia was mostly unavailable in the United States. Writing Rafn in 1833, Marsh shared his aspiration to enliven interest "in a land where Scandinavian literature is wholly unknown."[68] Rafn provided encouragement to Marsh as he built his book collection and studied Scandinavian languages. In particular, he directed Marsh to the work of Rasmus Rask, the leading scholar of Old Icelandic and an advocate for the preservation of its language and literary heritage.[69] Through the Danish consul in Boston, Rafn ferried Rask's works to Marsh, as well as guidance from himself and other scholars at the Royal Society.[70] Marsh sped up the publication of his long-planned *Compendious Grammar of the Old-Northern or Icelandic Language*, a unique edited translation of grammars previously assembled by Rask. Just as Rafn's *Antiquitates Americanae* reached American reviewers in 1838, Marsh hoped his *Grammar* would encourage American scholarly interest in Old Icelandic and "facilitate access to the literary treasures of which the Old-Northern tongue is the vehicle," as he put it.[71]

Marsh and other influential readers believed that the Norse saga offered a special literary experience that attested to its authenticity. Some found in it a consummate example of the sublime, "a grandeur in its rudeness, a sublimity in its wildness, while in the midst of its homely figures, and strange and startling descriptions, glimpses of deep and mysterious meaning, flashes of strange and bewildering light, as though from another and more ancient world, gleam awfully upon us."[72] One reviewer of Wheaton's *Northmen*, for instance, praised him for leading readers on a journey "through the dark and illimitable regions of the North; amid all its gloomy mythology—its savage wildness—its desperate adventure—its untameable freedom."[73] Historian George Folsom commended the "simple and unvarnished style of the Icelandic writers" in an address to the New York Historical Society, using the very language often employed to praise authentic narratives.[74] "In the opinion of those most competent to judge," Marsh explained, "it has never been surpassed, if equaled, in all that gives value to that portion of history which consists in spirited delineations of character, and faithful and lively pictures of events, among nations in a rude state of society."[75] In his popular lectures about the Norse discovery theory, Asahel Davis—plagiarizing the Danish scholar Rasmus Rask and Wheaton—claimed that the "copiousness, energy, and flexibility" of Old Icelandic "rivals every modern language . . . and enables it to enter into successful competition with the Greek and Latin."[76]

Readers saw the sophistication of Old Icelandic literature as a reflection of Icelandic society and government, as they construed it, during an otherwise barbarous age across Europe. According to this historical account, the government of medieval Iceland was a bastion of liberty, its people purified by Christianity, and its culture devoted to learning when these oral traditions were committed to writing. Reviewing a new history of Iceland in 1832, the *North American Review* praised the "beautiful form of civilization which started into life among these cold and barren rocks, like the magical vegetation of a polar spring, at a period when thick darkness covered the nations."[77] The political enlightenment seemed to exist in inverse proportion to Iceland's dark northern climate. "Their arctic isle was not warmed by a Grecian sun," one journal reflected when reviewing the Royal Society's work in 1838, "but their hearts glowed with the fire of freedom."[78] According to Asahel Davis, Iceland was "the Athens of the North, during the Dark Ages."[79] As one scholar has noted, "many nineteenth-century Americans grossly exaggerated both democratic and republic features of this system"—namely, the functioning of its deliberative body, the Althing, and its alleged kinship with Americans' own democratic institutions.[80] Nonetheless, this interpretation of Icelandic history colored many Americans' perception of the archival evidence for the Norse theory.

In part, these readings of Scandinavian literature and history reflected the self-perception of American readers as they approached *Antiquitates Americanae* and the Norse discovery theory. By the middle of the nineteenth century, emerging notions of race and historical identity increasingly racialized the significance of the Norse for white Americans. Undergirding this shift was a narrative of northern European history in which the Norse, untainted by Roman influence, made the "fresh irruptions" in Anglo-Saxon England, as the author Lydia Maria Child wrote in 1846, that reaffirmed the exceptional character and institutions that would be conveyed by European colonists to North America.[81] Figures such as the preeminent transcendentalist philosopher Ralph Waldo Emerson agreed that the Norse transmitted important qualities into Anglo-Saxon civilization when invading medieval England. This enabled some Americans to knit the Norse into the larger trajectory of liberty from its origin among the Teutonic people of Europe to its standard-bearers in America, part of a triumphal story about the progressive arc of civilization from a benighted Europe to North America.[82]

Yet New Englanders were also hesitant to fully integrate the Norse into the racialized historical narrative that assigned a special historical role to the Anglo-Saxon race.[83] In an attempt to interweave Norse and American genealogy, an appendix to *Antiquitates Americanae* presented a genealogical tree that traced children born in the Norse North American settlements back into Scandinavian history, documenting the descendants of the first American-born Norse from the eleventh century to the present. Americans, however, were more likely to perceive a cultural analogy between themselves and the Norse rather than a direct genealogical or explicitly racial link. In 1849, a *Massachusetts Quarterly Review* article on *Antiquitates Americanae* and its translations and abridgments observed that "the restless activity, the impatience of control, and the practical faculty which distinguish the Yankee" are "strikingly characteristic of the old Norsemen."[84] Commentators such Alexander Hill Everett depicted the Norse "as proto-Americans and precursors of the hardy Yankee seamen of his own day."[85] These terms for the Norse were becoming racially coded, but it would be misleading to conflate the plainly white-supremacist appropriations of the Norse that occurred later in the century with the reception of the Norse discovery theory in the antebellum United States.[86]

In extending credence to medieval Icelandic sources and ascribing proto-American qualities to the Norse, Americans deferred to a foreign archive and scholarly society to an unprecedented degree—a remarkable move for a country that was striving to build archives and historical narratives that could distinguish the United States from the rest of the world. Foreign scholars in a state-sponsored archive working with an uncommon textual source base sought to inform America's early global history; leading American men of letters, in turn, endorsed this for a wider national audience. However, rather than fully offshore the archival collecting, analysis, and historical writing for this revisionist account of America's global origin, many influential American readers came to respond critically to the argument made by Rafn and the Royal Society, marginalizing the Norse rather than placing them in the foreground.

Northmen on the Shore of American History

Rafn projected confidence that *Antiquitates Americanae* would sway American readers, but whether Americans would fully trust these materials and firmly inscribe this Norse chapter narrative within America's global history was a less certain matter. As there were considerable impediments to directly accessing *Antiquitates Americanae,* content was parsed, filtered, and mediated to a broader public by influential reviewers such as Edward Everett, whose interpretations were subsequently commented on by others, resonating outward from the source material. These accumulating summaries and commentaries about the sagas soon eclipsed the original text itself, becoming the main way that many Americans engaged with the theory of Norse colonization in New England.

US historical societies remained ambivalent about whether the evidence presented in *Antiquitates Americanae* proved Norse activity in the lands that would become colonial New England and later the United States. Between 1838 and 1839, moved by *Antiquitates Americanae,* RIHS leader Thomas Webb continued to closely research and document the cylindrical stone structure in Newport, Rhode Island, thought by Rafn to be a baptistry constructed by Norse settlers eight centuries previous. In theory, the tower would have placed Europeans, advanced technology, and Christianity on the American landscape far sooner than commonly believed. Webb's ongoing exchanges with Rafn were discussed at Royal Society meetings and included in its 1839 *Mémoires*. In Webb's 1839 account of the stone structure, reproduced by Rafn in an English-language *Supplement to Antiquitates Americanae* in 1841, the Rhode Islander demonstrated how the evidence for Norse settlement had led him to revise his narration of his state's colonial history. In one laborious passage, he insisted that "the State of Rhode-Island was first settled by the whites in Post-Columbian times, (using that expression, by way of distinction from the Ante-Columbian times, as, since the satisfactory evidence that has been adduced of the early visits of the Northmen, it would be manifestly incorrect to speak of the period we are now referring to, as that in which the first white settlers located themselves here,) we repeat, the State of Rhode-Island was first settled by the whites or Europeans, in Post-Columbian times in the year 1636."[87] While validating in parentheses the Royal Society's evidence for Norse landings in Rhode Island, Webb doubted that Newport's stone structure predated the "Post-Columbian" white settlement of Rhode Island given the lack of early colonial documentation about a preexisting structure. To substantiate his interpretation of the tower, Webb sent Rafn detailed drawings of the tower by Frederick Catherwood, who became famous for his sketches of ancient Mediterranean and Mesoamerican architecture. In several reprinted letters Webb admitted that despite his long-running endorsement of Rafn's argument, his own "mind is not conclusively made up." Webb was similarly unconvinced that the well-known Fall River skeleton, unearthed in that Massachusetts village in 1831 and famously animated a decade later in Henry Wadsworth Longfellow's "The Skeleton in Armor," was the entombed Norse settler that Rafn wished to make it. "We are far, however," Webb wrote to Rafn, in an exchange republished in the Royal Society's next *Mémoires* in 1844, "from being willing to decide that this was or was not one of the Aborigines," by which he meant the Indigenous people of the region displaced by seventeenth-century European colonists.[88]

Rafn pushed back against the ambivalence of Webb and other Americans. After a detailed comparison between the tower and the architecture and art of medieval Scandinavian architecture printed in its 1838–39 *Mémoires,* Rafn emphatically concluded, "I am persuaded that all who are familiar with Old-Northern architecture will concur, that this building was erected at a period decidedly not later than the 12th century."[89] Webb sent metal articles disinterred with the Fall River skeleton to Denmark, where Royal Society fellow Baron Jacob Berzelius performed a metallurgical study of their qualities alongside an old Danish artifact, a Japanese coin, and a piece of modern brass. Presenting this inconclusive report in 1840, Rafn nonetheless assured readers that even if the Fall River skeleton's particular artifacts were not made by the Norse, "on many occasions such antiquities may reasonably be assumed to originate from the descendants of the ancient Scandinavian colonists, who, on the cessation of all communication with the mother country, would naturally get intermingled with the wild natives," such that subsequent articles might just be "fabricated after Scandinavian prototypes."[90] At the Royal Society's 1842 annual meeting that examined local samples of wood sent by Webb, Rafn linked each sample with the name assigned to it in the Norse accounts of North America.[91] The Royal Society also continued to seek artifacts as proof of Norse settlement throughout the Western Hemisphere. In 1840, the Royal Society sent a scientific committee to Bahia aboard the Danish king's ship to authenticate this possible site of Norse settlement.[92] Other accounts of stone settlements in the Americas allegedly built by ancient European populations, ranging from Wisconsin to Mexico to Brazil, trickled into the Royal Society.[93]

For all this ongoing effort by the Royal Society, Webb's response suggests that while the Old Icelandic manuscripts were deemed reliable sources, Americans hesitated to accept Rafn's assertion that medieval stone structures, skeletal remains, and other archaeological traces were. How, Webb and others asked, could they have gone unremarked during the settlement of New England in the seventeenth century? Edward Everett, in both his *North American Review* dissection of *Antiquitates Americanae* and in his popular lectures, dismissed Rafn's claims about Norse runes on such sites as Dighton Rock in Massachusetts. Speaking in Boston in 1838, Everett cited the notable ethnographer and artist of American Indians, George Catlin, who claimed to have seen hundreds of such inscriptions elsewhere, "which would have filled a volume of more than a thousand pages."[94] George Bancroft agreed. In the third volume of his mammoth *History*, the first since *Antiquitates Americanae* appeared in the United States, he complained, "By unwarranted interpolations and bold distortions, in defiance of countless improbabilities, the plastic power of fancy transformed the rude etching into a Runic monument."[95] According to such appraisals, the Danish scholars had deviated from the sober analysis of authentic sources that historians were supposed to practice.

While Webb and others were intrigued by the Royal Society's arguments about the Norse archaeological record in New England, they did not simply defer to Scandinavian expertise. They recognized the significance of the historical questions raised, considered the evidence in different ways, and reached varying conclusions about whether and where the Norse fit into the historical narrative of America. Speaking before the NYHS a decade after the publication of *Antiquitates Americanae*, Schoolcraft again applied this critical lens. While he concurred that the medieval sagas and ballads furnished "historical proof" for Norse settlement as far south as Massachusetts, he cast doubt on hypothetical claims about the specific locations and artifacts that "the bold spirit of northern research" had led the Royal Society to assert. He cautioned that the question of Norse settlement "invites a careful and candid scrutiny, with a sole eye to historical truth," rather than a lapse into speculation and fabrication.[96]

This same doubt seeped into other publications, such as history textbooks, where the Norsemen began to appear as a brief prelude to Columbus. In the opening paragraphs of the 1840 edition of his popular *History of the United States*, Salma Hale explained that the Royal Society had recently published materials documenting the Norse voyages. "They are not universally credited," he continued ambivalently, "but the reasons for believing them are more cogent than those by which many undoubted historical facts are supported."[97] The very application of this scrutiny in public forums and publications gave Americans the opportunity to vaunt their critical engagement with a major work from a leading European institution.

Beyond historical societies and prominent publications, a wider array of Americans appraised the Norse theory as well, including through the genre of poetry. In Lydia Sigourney's 1845 collection of poems, *Scenes in My Native Land*, she explored symbolic historical places such as the First Church at Jamestown, the Charter Oak in Hartford, and the Washington Elm near the general's wartime headquarters in Cambridge. Such sites could sketch a rough chronology of American history from settlement to colonization to national independence.[98] Notes followed each poem, placing the location in context. However, "The Newport Tower" was conspicuous among the historical associations marking the poetic landscape of the collection, standing out like the thing itself, a "Dark, lonely Tower, amid yon Eden-isle," set atop a hill in Rhode Island, overlooking Narragansett Bay.[99]

In the poem, Sigourney echoed some of the theories about its shadowy origins:

> Say, reared the plundering hand
> Of the fierce buccaneer thy massy walls,
> A treasure-fortress for his blood-stained gold?
> Or wrought the beings of an earlier race
> To form thy circle, while in the wonder gazed
> The painted Indian?

While few had in fact reckoned it a pirate fortress, some had attributed Newport Tower to the architectural feats of a mound-building people distinct from "the painted Indian," which by the 1840s was well-trodden scholarly ground. Sigourney disagreed, however. Nor was she convinced of the tower's supposed colonial origins in the seventeenth century, a notion that she mocked:

> Some there are, who say
> Thou wert an *ancient wind-mill.*
> Be it so!
> Our pilgrim-sires must have been much in love

> With extra labor, thus to gather stones,
> And patient rear the Scandinavian arch.
> And build thine ample chamber, and uplift
> Thy shapely column, for the gadding winds
> To play vagaries with.
> In those hard times
> I trow king Philip gave them other work.

The ornate arch would have been an unlikely aesthetic flourish by English settlers viciously warring with King Philip—or Metacom—whom her readers knew as the tragically famous Wampanoag sachem killed in the blaze of violence in 1670s New England known as King Philip's War. As elsewhere in the collection, she invited readers to see from the perspective of an inanimate historical object in order to comment on how her contemporaries viewed their history. Speaking to the tower, she bantered,

> Had'st thou the power,
> I think thou'dst laugh right heartily to see
> The worthy farmers, with their sacks of corn,
> Mistaking thy profession, as of old
> Don Quixote did mistake thine ancestor;
> If haply such progenitor thou hadst.

In other words, nineteenth-century observers, including writers from historical societies and leading journals, were tilting at windmills in their characterizations of the tower.

Throughout this collection, Sigourney revealed historical traces and hidden histories in the landscape that she treads. Reflecting on past European and Indigenous warfare in the "Vale of Wyoming," she wrote,

> Yet still, deceitful Vale,
> So lulled, and saturate in deep content
> With thine exceeding beauty, though dost hide
> A blotted history, of tears and blood,
> A dire, Vesuvian, lava-written scroll.[100]

Such poems and their accompanying notes illuminated historical sites, recovering them almost as one would salvage a manuscript for the archive. Sigourney portrayed these sites as documents of a sort, as "a blotted history" or "lava-written scroll," difficult to decipher but legible. By contrast, Newport Tower appeared illegible in the poem, beyond popular understanding, "A mystery and paradox, to mock / The curious throng." It was less the tower itself than "the curious throng"—such as inquisitive RIHS members, perhaps—that had obscured its origins. Popular perception of the tower rested more within the realm of "Fancy" than "Antiquity," which Sigourney depicted with feminine and masculine imagery.

> Fancy spreads her wing
> Around they time-scathed brow, and deeply tints
> Her fairy-scroll, while hoar Antiquity
> In silence frowns upon the aimless flight.

Unlike the Vale of Wyoming, this metaphorical scroll of the tower was tinted, the reading of it aimless, flighty.

Speaking again to the tower, Sigourney herself frowned at the flawed efforts of her contemporaries to sound its origins. Her own commitment to historical inquiry notwithstanding, she questioned the very instinct of her fellow New Englanders to seek historical knowledge:

> Thou wilt not show the secret of thy birth!
> Nor do I know why we need question thee
> So strictly on that point; save that the creed
> Of Yankee people is, that through the toil
> Of questioning, there cometh light, and gain
> Of Knowledge to the mind. (240)

Despite this censure, she too had been drawn to the tower, "And 'neath thy shadow weave my noteless song," she wrote. Sigourney claimed instead to offer her poem as a tribute to the antiquity of the site, reasoning that "whatsoever bears / The stamp of hoary time, and hath not been / The minister of evil, claims from us / Some tribute of respect." For all her insistence on the tower's inscrutability, true to Yankee form she tried to decipher it. In her note at the end of the poem, she sketched a spectrum of theories about the tower's origins: on one extreme, the "matter-of-fact man" who saw it as a colonial windmill; on the other, "the child of imagination" who imagined the "Skeleton in Armor" (1841), Longfellow's fanciful poem inspired by the tower, to be a "text-book." Between the two, she placed "the erudite scholar, who discovered in it the architectural marks of the ancient Norse-men."

Sigourney in the end agreed that Newport Tower could only be of Norse construction, yet unlike other sites throughout *Scenes in My Native Land*, she did not emplot it within the arc of American history and onto its historical landscape. The Norse presence in North American in the late tenth and early eleventh centuries "is matter of grave history," she noted, adding that Irving's *Life of Columbus* (1828) identified Norse settlement as far west as Canada.[101] And their landing farther south "seems to rest on stronger foundation than conjecture," which she derived from "Professor Rafn." Quoting from *Antiquitates Americanae*, she added that, "'of the ancient structure at Newport, from such characteristics as remain, we can scarcely form any other inference than one.'" In a country "almost destitute of the vestiges of antiquity," Norse architecture was an alluring historical association for her, but she also *dis*associated it from national history. The historical monument at the center of the poem appeared documentable, but on the margins of the nation's historical record. It did not exercise the same emotional or psychological sway on the living as the other monuments described in the volume. In another poem about Connecticut's Charter Oak, the legendary tree in which the colony's charter was hidden from royal interference in the 1680s, she noted that "some of its pressed leaves, or small articles made from a supernumerary branch . . . are found to be acceptable gifts, both to the antiquarian and the patriot."[102] Newport Tower attracted curious gazes but offered no such relics.

Rafn's words seemed to settle for Sigourney the historical question of the tower's origin, but they were not the last in her notes on the poem. She instead quoted seventeenth-century English poet Sir Thomas Brown as consolation for those "who adhere tenaciously to the 'old wind-mill' creed." "'Oblivion,' quoth he, 'reclineth semi-somnous, making puzzles of Titanian erections, and turning old glories into dreams, while History sinketh down beside her. The traveller asketh of her, amazedly, who builded these? And she mumbleth something, but what it is, he heareth not.'" Neither lost in the depths of time nor chronicled in the colonial record, the tower seemed on the threshold of Oblivion and History. Sigourney, great advocate of historical inquiry into the nation's past, wavered on whether the monument could be demystified and placed within that history. Whether in scholarly reviews or poetry informed by scholarship, the Royal Society encountered critical readers of its evidence in the American press.

Rafn's attempt to convince American readers of the significance of the Norse within American history also collided with the primacy of Columbus within American historical narratives and the broader culture. Whether advocates or critics of Rafn's work, American readers were loath to let the Norse diminish Columbus within a national narrative that typically took his fifteenth-century discovery as a point of departure. In Britain, readers of the abridged British version of *Antiquitates Americanae* might accept that as the Norse discoveries were "made at a much earlier period, and in a much more complete manner, by the inhabitants of a distinct and remote nation, the honour which has surrounded [Columbus's] name should be transferred to them," as the major British abridgment of the theory argued.[103] But Americans commenting on the hemisphere's past routinely apotheosized Columbus and were far less likely to dislodge him. Edward Everett wrote in his 1838 review of Rafn's work that "no single event in the history of civilization is of equal importance with the discovery of America."[104] The historiographical and symbolic stakes for Americans remained high.

Sensitive to this intellectual context, the Royal Society argued that Columbus had gleaned his initial knowledge of the Americas during his 1477 visit to Iceland, where he would have learned of the thirteenth-century Icelandic accounts of the Norse voyages. Irving had argued against this in his biography of Columbus a decade earlier, reasoning, "though, from time to time, some document has floated to the shores of the old world, giving to its wondering inhabitants evidences of land far beyond their watery horizon; yet no one ventured to spread a sail, and seek that land enveloped in mystery and peril."[105] By contrast, the Royal Society suggested that Columbus's Caribbean landing should be viewed in the light of these earlier Norse discovery voyages, but that his knowledge of them did "not at all diminish the glory that he acquired through the high intelligence and untiring zeal with which he braced all the obstacles and perils."[106] Through the media of Royal Society proceedings, correspondence, publicity, and *Antiquitates Americanae*, Rafn narrated that knowledge of the Western Hemisphere was first acquired by the Norse, transmitted to Columbus during his travels to Iceland, and only then put into practice in his voyages to the Caribbean.

Excitedly, some American newspapers reiterated the claim. "What serves in no small degree to enhance the value of these documents," the

National Gazette and *National Intelligencer* published in 1836, "is the great apparent probability, amounting indeed almost to certainty, that it was a knowledge of these facts that prompted the ever-memorable expedition of Columbus himself!"[107] Some American readers, in fact, saw the Danish argument that the voyages of Columbus had depended on Icelandic sources as further evidence of the navigator's greatness. As *Antiquitates Americanae* neared publication, the *Boston Courier* anticipated that this proof of Columbus's knowledge of prior Norse discoveries "will increase the common admiration of the character of the illustrious Columbus for perseverance and intrepidity."[108] Another reviewer assessed that in light of this new information, Columbus appeared more than a "bold adventurer," voyaging westward by intuition alone; rather, he was elevated to "a sagacious discoverer," a "master-mind," who skillfully employed the insights of the Norse.[109]

Most American readers objected, however, claiming that Columbus could not so easily be displaced along the timeline of American history. As Irving's *Christopher Columbus* made clear, his voyages derived their dramatic force from their originality, an oceanic expression of an individual's genius that had transformed the history of the world. Despite the far earlier Norse discoveries, Columbus remained "an original discoverer" in the eyes of many.[110] As the popular lecturer Asahel Davis reassured his many audiences in the 1840s, "the laurels given to Columbus will not wither on his brow."[111] Even readers inclined to believe Rafn's theory of Norse settlement in New England tended to balk at any imputation against Columbus and his unassisted discovery of the Americas. Some refused outright to acknowledge that Columbus had learned of the medieval Norse voyages during his brief visit to Iceland in 1477.

American skeptics diminished Rafn's revision of Atlantic history by doubting that Columbus could have even accessed information buried in Old Icelandic manuscripts, which in the late fifteenth century were already several hundred years old, in an inaccessible language, and unknown to continental European scholars. "At all events," one reviewer argued before *Antiquitates Americanae* was even published, "there is not the slightest reason to believe that the illustrious Genoese was acquainted with the discovery of North American by the Normans five centuries before his time, however well authenticated that fact now appears to be by the Icelandic records."[112] Columbus's landing was "of such an astounding character," Henry Rowe

Schoolcraft later insinuated, "that it is no wonder other countries of maritime borders, should rake up the arcana of their old traditions to share in the glory."[113] The Danish, in other words, were putting national pride before rigorous research.

Those Americans who did accept the Danish argument about an earlier discovery still managed to diminish the significance of the Norse discovery relative to the preexisting hagiography of Columbus. When the historian George Folsom spoke to a large audience at the NYHS in 1838, he insisted that it was "one of the most powerful causes that inspired the mind of that great man, (whose glory cannot in any degree be impaired by the prior achievement)." He went on to emphasize that what truly mattered was Columbus's "discovery of the New World under circumstances that necessarily led to its immediate, uninterrupted, and constantly increasing colonization and occupation by the energetic and intelligent races of Europe."[114] Opening a history of the Americas in 1851, Charles Goodrich, congregationalist minister and brother to Samuel, the popular children's history writer, was similarly ambivalent about Norse settlement. Even though Goodrich accepted the Scandinavian argument and integrated the Norse into American history books, the impact was more chronological than meaningful. "On the supposition that the records are true, which in general may be admitted, the colony could not have had a long continuance, and it is certain that no remains of it have ever appeared. . . . It was not until the era of Columbus that the world was awakened to the enterprise, or even to the thought of discovering land beyond the Western ocean."[115] For Folsom and Goodrich, Columbus maintained his status within American history due to the historical process that he set into motion, which could be traced, uninterrupted, to their present in the nineteenth century.

In this global narrative of discovery, conquest, and progress, the Norse did not displace Columbus's significance but were rather engulfed by it. In the late eighteenth and early nineteenth centuries, an American conception of its empire was central to the formation of national identity, and Columbus was an important symbol in this.[116] The extraordinary symbolic power of Columbus and his centrality in American historical consciousness helps to explain the mixed response to the Danish attempt to revise America's prevailing historical narrative. For Americans concerned with the ongoing course of empire across their continent, the fifteenth-century Italian agent of the Spanish Crown in the Caribbean was a far more useful historical metonym than the brief beachheads claimed by medieval Norsemen in the North Atlantic, which were not points of departure for territorial conquest in the Americas.

Reviewing Joshua Toulmin Smith's slim and accessible English distillation of *Antiquitates Americanae* in 1839, the *Christian Examiner* assessed that the Norse settlement in North America "possesses not so much an historical, as an antiquarian interest and importance." Echoing Irving's earlier distinction between Norse settlement and Columbus's voyages, the critic wrote that the former were not "the first of an uninterrupted series, by which this continent was so rapidly put into the possession of its new inhabitants, and brought so completely within the range of European civilization."[117] Columbus was, in contrast, an "inherently imperial" figure who could be appropriated to advance the interests of different imperial actors over time, including Rafn's readers in the antebellum United States.[118]

Of the European nations that had colonized (however briefly) North America, the Scandinavians—both the medieval Norse and early modern Swedish and Danes—were the only one lacking a major work of romantic history authored by an American. William Hickling Prescott published his accounts of the Spanish conquest of Mexico in 1843 and Peru in 1847, Francis Parkman released the first of his many accounts of France's North American empire in 1851, John Lothrop Motley published his histories of the Dutch Republic from 1856, and from the 1830s into the 1870s George Bancroft delivered his vastly influential histories of British settlement and Anglo-American conquest of the continent. The remoteness of the Norse settlement, its brevity, the inaccessibility of its material traces, and the disjuncture between it and the historical landscape of the colonial contest for North America explain why leading American historians did not take it up as a subject. Even the first professor of Scandinavian languages and literature at New York University, the Dane Paul Sinding, argued in his *History of Scandinavia* (1860) that the authenticity of the Norse's earlier discovery had not "eclipsed that splendor which never will cease to invest the name of this unexampled discoverer [Columbus]."[119] What mattered was the transformative imperial process that Columbus initiated, to which Norse discovery could only tenuously be prefaced, left on the shore of America's grand historical narrative.

For most, the grand attempt by Rafn and the Royal Society of Northern Antiquaries to revise the nation's history remained inconclusive. In the 1840s and 1850s, Henry David Thoreau took four walking tours of Cape Cod, and his vignettes of these appeared in his 1865 travel account *Cape Cod*. Musing about the local fishermen along one stretch of the coastline, Thoreau wrote, "I was frequently reminded of the Northmen here." At the same time, when Thoreau gazed at the Cape Cod coastline in the 1850s, he was unimpressed by Rafn's argument about Norse discovery and settlement—which he borrowed from the Harvard library and, judging by the footnotes, closely read following his first tour of Cape Cod.[120] In that scene, Thoreau recounted a mirage appearing on the Cape Cod sand dunes, which according to Rafn was also observed during the voyage of the Icelandic explorer Thorfinn Karlsefni from Greenland to North America in the year 1007. Thoreau pondered: "But whether Thor-finn saw the mirage here or not, Thor-eau, one of the same family, did; and perchance it was because Lief the Lucky had, in a previous voyage, taken Thor-er and his people off the rock in the middle of the sea, that Thor-eau was born to see it."[121]

Punny, surely. Comical too, given that few figures in American letters could seem further from the bookish, land-hugging Thoreau than the sea-roving Leif Erikson, likely the first European to step foot on North America since the continent's much earlier peoplings. Thoreau in this aside displayed his ambivalence about the authenticity of the evidence behind the theory of Norse discovery and settlement of New England. He allowed that, *perchance*, Norse migration to North America had something to do with the later European colonization of New England and with his own existence in the nineteenth-century United States—an expanding terrestrial empire that was swiftly conquering the rest of the continent. In his final word on the Norse in *Cape Cod*, Thoreau concluded that, as the medieval Norse historical records "have not mentioned the latitude and longitude distinctly enough, though we have great respect for them as skilful and adventurous navigators, we must for the present remain in doubt as to what capes they did see. We think that they were considerably further north."[122]

By the time Thoreau looked out on the littoral of Cape Cod, such was the scholarly consensus about the evidence and the import of the Norse theory: after rigorous analysis, the evidence for Norse migration, somewhere at least, to North America was convincing, despite its remote provenance. But the claim that Americans should reinvent their narrative of the hemisphere's colonization was less so. Like Lydia Sigourney in her note appended to "The Newport Tower" (1845), Thoreau found the theory intriguing and worth musing upon, but ultimately the stuff of a footnote.

Despite the wide interest generated around the publication of *Antiquitates Americanae*, the Norse settlements appeared as historical islands for many American readers prior to the Civil War. Whatever the Norse discoveries, and despite Rafn's insistence that Columbus had learned of them, most agreed with Edward Everett that, "it had no effect upon the mind of Europe at large."[123] Few were inclined to see the wellspring of Columbus's insight about the Western Hemisphere in Iceland. The Norse may have been the first Christians to land, worship, trade, and procreate in North America, but the architectural and human legacy of that was so scarce, questionable, or nonexistent that it was hard to draw a link between the medieval period and later European settlement. For many, the Norse were inserted within American history as a peculiar prelude that—for the moment, at least—did not mean all that much.

Reflecting on the American landscape in 1836, a year before *Antiquitates Americanae* reached American readers, the famous artist Thomas Cole enthusiastically observed, "you see no ruined tower to tell of outrage—no gorgeous temple to speak of ostentation; but freedom's offspring—peace, security, and happiness, dwell there, the spirits of the scene."[124] In Cole's eyes, the very vacancy of the landscape prior to European colonization differentiated America from Europe; the absence of such historical traces as towers and temples signified America's separation from a global history connecting the hemispheres. At the same time, he revealed that his awareness of national history and identity was immersed in a global context, similar to the American readers of the oceanic archive and historical narrative offered by the Royal Society. For Americans with the power to build the nation's archives and craft its narratives, engaging with the institutions, scholars, collections, and claims that emerged from places like Scandinavia provided an opportunity to demarcate their own archival threshold.

Cole's claim, echoed by many authors and artists throughout this period, offered solace to Americans who sought a more ancient and impressive historical record. This apparent vacancy helped set the stage for the unfurling of their seemingly exceptional national history, authenticated by material traces that were distinct Europe's. As suggested by the American reception of the Norse theory, Columbus appealed to many because of the uninterrupted process of colonization that they could trace from his voyages to their own history, documented page by page, whether as an entire nation, in the distinctive history of individual states, or in local communities.

THREE

Washington's National Archive

Alexis de Tocqueville's *De la démocratie en Amérique*, published in France in 1835 and 1840 in the United States, offered a mixed appraisal of Americans' relationship with their history. Whatever his esteem for the historical significance of the United States, he shook his head at the nation's capacity to preserve its past. If he admired the widespread associational spirit that moved, for instance, historical societies to coalesce and build archives, he questioned the ability of the federal government to safeguard the nation's historical record. In his chapter titled "Instability of the Administration in the United States," Tocqueville observed that men flitted in and out of the tumult of American politics. "The public administration is, so to speak," he wrote, "oral and traditionary. But little is committed to writing, and that little is wafted away for ever, like the leaves of the sibyl, by the smallest breeze."[1] Compared with the modern archival practices of France, he implied that Americans managed their historical record in an uncivilized fashion. "In fifty years," he predicted, "it will be more difficult to collect authentic documents concerning the social condition of the Americans at the present day, than it is to find remains of the administration of France during the middle ages; and if the United States were ever invaded by barbarians, it would be necessary to have recourse to the history of other nations."[2] The Frenchman's critique turned on its head the notion espoused by historical societies and their advocates that the nation's comprehensive record could be gathered and used to authenticate Americans' exceptional history.

At a time when Americans pondered their place within global history, assessed the wide-ranging archival materials that should inform it, and engaged with scholars and archival institutions across the Atlantic, Tocqueville's reproach of America's archival practices was discouraging. The American editor of *Democracy in America*, John Canfield Spencer, pushed back against Tocqueville's critique of American archival practices. The New York politician, and later secretary of state and of treasury, insisted in a rare footnote that Tocqueville was "certainly mistaken" about the condition of American public records. "The journals of congress, the journals of state legislatures, the public documents transmitted to and originating in those bodies," he pointed out, "are carefully preserved and disseminated through the nation; and they furnish in themselves the materials of a full and accurate history."[3] These published materials were regularly distributed to library collections and historical societies, where they contributed to the archiving of national history in real time.

Beyond such political records, however, Tocqueville was right to observe that the US federal government had invested less in the preservation of its historical record than nations across the Atlantic. Preserving select American governmental records did not come close to Europeans' use of national resources and leadership to build historical archives and publish compendia of significant national documents, as seen in Britain, Spain, Belgium, Denmark, Germany, or his own France, where the state had built national historical archives and published major volumes of critical historical documents. The historian François Guizot, from his perch as French minister of public education, formed the state-funded Society of the History of France in 1833, which produced volume upon volume of original historical documents.[4] Other state-sponsored projects, such as the tomes published by the Royal Society of Northern Antiquaries in Denmark (discussed in the previous chapter), proliferated by the 1830s.

Jared Sparks, a member of multiple historical societies and editor of several major documentary projects, would have understood Tocqueville's dim impression of American recordkeeping compared with that of European nation-states. The two had met during the Frenchman's 1831 tour of the United States, Sparks helping him to understand the history of local government in Massachusetts. Tocqueville later returned the favor as Sparks plumbed French state archives for American materials the following decade. Sparks became a booster of Tocqueville's work, seeking a translator and publisher for the American edition.[5] Yet their visions for America's archive diverged. Rather than sharing Tocqueville's dismal outlook that recent US history could become as inscrutable as France's during the Middle Ages, Sparks envisioned a brighter future for the nation's archives. More than any other American prior to the Civil War, Sparks argued for the importance of preserving and examining the nation's documentary past, especially the record of its revolutionary struggle and founding. For Sparks, the writings of George Washington embodied this history more than any other documents. For a decade, his hope to collect, edit, and publish Washington's writings led Sparks throughout the original states and to European archives as he prepared his twelve-volume *Writings of George Washington*, which reached readers between 1834 and 1837.

Sparks assembled, edited, and promoted what he saw as the cornerstone of the nation's archives. He did so in an era when the federal government remained remote from the work of building archives and writing history, and historical establishments in most states narrowed their focus to their own state's past. Amid the broader national debate about how to preserve Washington's legacy, the federal government had not asserted responsibility for Washington's former home at Mount Vernon, physical remains, or extensive archival materials. For their part, historical societies did not hesitate to praise Washington and seek stray documents that linked the man to their state, but no state attempted to gather a comprehensive record of his papers. Sparks stepped into this void. Drawing on the methods, networks, and materials of historical societies and the resources of the federal government, he produced a national archive that institutions and Americans across the country could access.

Initially, this national archive was not an institution but a collection of Washington's writings curated by Sparks in order to preserve the record of the nation's early history, connect dispersed Americans with their past, and serve future writers of national history. Although criticized by some contemporaries for infusing his New England bias into this project, he imagined in Washington a figure whose writings drew the nation together—a connection between citizens and the documentary record quite unlike the evidence of Norse landings in spare corners of coastal New England. By casting light on Washington's written legacy, Sparks contributed to the most significant archival accession by the federal government prior to the Civil

War. To tell this story, this chapter situates Sparks in the tumult of the revolutionary Atlantic world in which he developed his approach to building a national archive for the United States, what he initially perceived as a global frame for the revolutionary independence movements in the Americas. It then shows how Sparks narrowed his view to a national frame centering Washington and his writings, which he saw bringing together the nation's disconnected states, leaders, and peoples as no other figure could.

Archivist of Atlantic Revolutions

Around the fiftieth anniversary of US independence, Sparks leapt into his lifelong work to collect, edit, and disseminate crucial portions of the nation's historical record.[6] As new republics emerged from the ruins of Spain's American empire, the revolutionary upheaval in the hemisphere formed part of the landscape in which Sparks approached the archive of his own nation's revolutionary origins. Daily, these new American republics seemed to produce archival materials for a larger hemispheric story of liberty and progress that could trace its origins to the American Revolution. Although Sparks's initial interest in the Spanish American republics faded with their apparent political fortunes, in seeking to archive and make sense of their unfolding national histories he developed an archival practice that would propel his work to build an archive for his own nation.

Hailing from a relatively humble upbringing in New Hampshire, Sparks joined a cast of elite, bookish, Unitarian ministers who left a lasting imprint on America's archives and the writing of American history. Like them, he graduated from Harvard as it established itself at the epicenter of American Unitarianism. He set up his ministry in Baltimore's First Independent Church while serving as the chaplain to the US House of Representatives. Sparks soon returned to Cambridge, however, and in 1823 published his first substantial work, the two-volume *Collection of Essays and Tracts in Theology*, which presented American readers with a range of otherwise unavailable European theological texts.[7] This was his last theological work and, by all evidence, engagement in American religious life. He left the pulpit, sold much of his theological library, used the proceeds to purchase his stake in the *North American Review*, and as its editor began to gather and examine the record of American history, including the new American republics to the south.

Like fellow Unitarians such as Edward Everett and George Bancroft, Sparks brought his authorial power and scholarly practices from the spiritual community of the church to a virtual reading community. As did other leading Unitarians, Sparks called on the individual to exercise freely their rational judgment of textual evidence in their religious practice.[8] As one leading scholar put it, "For the rational, orthodox Unitarian, who had been repelled by trinitarian dogma, theology itself was a historical science, to be based on verifiable evidence."[9] In this sense, Sparks's shift from preaching to publishing, from rigorous reading of theological texts to new publications in the *North American Review*, was not such a leap.[10]

Sparks and other Unitarian historians also found in both faith and history a means of guiding believers to understand their lives within a universal story. Historians like George Bancroft thought that "history was the unfolding of a vast Providential plan, and the laws of the moral world were the links between the ages.... The historian had a didactic as well an artistic duty to arrange apparently disconnected events in their proper order."[11] Sparks shared the belief that through the close analysis of historical source material the individual could comprehend how providence acted upon human affairs. Importantly, as theology's influence waned in New England, literature succeeded it as "an important means of social control as well as an invaluable aid to personality development."[12] History, and in particular the prolific genre of biography, was deemed essential for modeling virtue to citizens in a republic.[13] Both theology and this conception of history writing enabled Sparks and others to emplot an individual or a community within a historical arc according with divine design.

As he began to steward the *North American Review* in 1824, Sparks dined with some of the men in the United States most informed about Spain's American empire and excited for the future of the new American republics that had dismantled it. At the Boston home of George Ticknor, Sparks joined Daniel Webster and William Hickling Prescott to fete the Marquis de Lafayette, the beloved French hero of the American Revolution.[14] Lafayette was on his sensational tour through the United States, where the famous foreigner inspired hundreds of thousands of Americans across the country to greet him.[15] To hail Lafayette was a Janus-faced reflection for these Americans: they looked backward at the triumph of the nation's independence and forward at the legacy of that world-altering event beyond the United States, including Spanish America. Lafayette had remained a vocal champion of liberalism in the Western Hemisphere and Europe, from the American Revolution through the Spanish American wars of independence and, in subsequent years, to the 1830 Polish uprising against Russia, which was quashed before his death in 1834.[16]

Seated with Lafayette was Congressman Webster, one of the nation's most ardent advocates of liberal independence movements abroad. Just days before, he had implored Congress to send aid to the Greek patriots rebelling against Ottoman rule—the "struggle of an interesting and gallant people, in the cause of liberty and Christianity," he described it in one fiery speech. America bore a historical debt to Greek civilization, as Webster saw it, and their descendants now appealed to the United States in the very spirit of America's own war for independence.[17] In the following months, Webster urged the United States to support the newly independent republics of Spanish America in the name of defending these same principles.

Also at the table, Prescott and Ticknor were among the leading American students of Spain's Atlantic history. As Harvard's professor of Spanish and French, Ticknor was the foremost scholar of Spanish language and literature and owner of the largest library of Spanish works in the United States.[18] Encouraged by Ticknor, Prescott began orienting his scholarly interest toward the rise and fall of the Spanish empire, which would lead to a number of major publications, beginning with *Ferdinand and Isabella* in 1837.[19] As Prescott's vision deteriorated, Ticknor, Sparks, and others sent him books and documents relating to Spanish history gathered during their European travels. Next to these scholars of the Spanish empire and champions of its downfall, Sparks was becoming an expert on the new Spanish American republics; just that week, he had met with the Colombian minister to the United States, who brought Sparks original documents.[20] By the fiftieth anniversary of the Declaration of Independence, he would refashion the *North American Review* into the nation's main source of political and historical analysis about the new republics to the south.

These American men shared in the popular exuberance about the Spanish American independence movements, which one could hear expressed in July Fourth toasts and children named after the independence leader Simón Bolívar, the "Washington of the South." Institutions such as the American Antiquarian Society even unanimously elected Simón Bolívar and the Peruvian jurist and independence leader Manuel Vidaurre as honorary members.[21] Through news reports and firsthand accounts of these events, many American observers saw in Spanish America the ongoing historical contest between the forces of liberalism and tyranny. The foreign policy of the Monroe administration toward the region reflected the widespread enthusiasm and anxiety about the course that history would take in the hemisphere. In 1822, the United States officially recognized the republics and sought a congressional appropriation of one hundred thousand dollars for new diplomatic missions to their governments. For a US political system still hostile toward "diplomatists," this unprecedented infusion of federal funding to build relations with the new republics reflected the administration's vision for an integrated hemisphere.[22] In his annual address the next year, Monroe underscored his commitment to their independence from European meddling, in what later became known as the Monroe Doctrine.

This was a canny diplomatic move orchestrated by Secretary of State John Quincy Adams and a signal of the administration's ambitions in a hemisphere mostly purged of European sovereignty. At the same time, it reflected American anxiety (however improbable it would later seem) that resurgent monarchism in Europe, incarnate in Russian Tsar Nicholas's Holy Alliance, would seek a new foothold in the Americas and halt the historical course of liberty across the region.

Popular interest and federal policy echoed Sparks's sense that these new republics embodied the spirit of the American Revolution and that the hemisphere would become increasingly united within one historical trajectory. As the Monroe and then John Quincy Adams administrations imagined a more integrated commercial and political future for the Americas, Sparks compiled an archive of these American revolutions and new republics. He perceived these events within a global frame that included his nation's own history—the documents emerging from the new republics within a vast archival record of revolution and independence. By 1825, his *North American Review* regularly featured news and analysis of events unfolding in Spanish America for its growing readership, including policy-makers in Washington, DC.

To gather evidence and analyze these transformative events, Sparks knit together a network of US expatriates and Spanish American correspondents with access to developments and documents in the new republics. Over the following two years, he routinely exhorted these correspondents to collect and dispatch historical papers and analysis to Massachusetts, where he worked them into the *North American Review*. To better communicate with his Spanish-speaking correspondents and understand the materials he gathered, he began studying Spanish at Harvard.[23] In April 1824, in the first of many such letters, he sent a documentary wish list to Juan García del Río, Peru's minister plenipotentiary in Europe. Sparks included requests for original copies of "the proceedings of Spain in regard to the colonies from the year 1808 till the restoration of Ferdinand in 1814; and also the transactions in the colonies during the same period; particularly accounts of the juntas in Old Spain, and the juntas of the different colonies," as well as "History of the Revolutionary proceedings in the colonies from the beginning, both in regard to the civil governments and military operations."[24] Sparks hoped to compile every relevant public document and the most recent periodicals and political publications.

To bolster this inchoate archive of Spanish American revolution and independence, he called on Secretary of State John Quincy Adams to activate US consuls and diplomats throughout the region.[25] Sparks pressed US Minister Caesar Rodney in Buenos Aires to send all documents concerning Argentina's revolution and independence. He prompted William Tudor in Peru and Robert Lowry in Colombia for the records in those countries. And he corresponded with Joel Poinsett in Mexico, a leading commentator on the region in his own right.[26] When a correspondent disappointed him, Sparks guilted him to act more like those who "supplied me very abundantly" from other diplomatic and consular posts.[27] Endorsed first by Adams's State Department and then by the incoming Adams administration in 1825, he implied to these US representatives that they had an official obligation to assist his private undertaking.

To foreign correspondents, he argued in loftier terms for the importance of sharing documents about their national histories. Writing in 1825 to Mexico's first secretary of state, Lucas Alamán, a historian and founder of Mexico's national archives, Sparks emphasized that sharing these materials would fortify mutual understanding, shared interests, and cooperation within the Americas.[28] Acting as a proto–public diplomat, Sparks fused his study of the Spanish American republics with a diplomatic vision of an integrated hemisphere. This resulted in a reciprocal traffic in paper: Spanish American official documents and newspapers sailing north and copies of the *North American Review* heading south. To Colombian governor Jose Manuel Restrepo, who was emerging as the new nation's leading historian,

Sparks promised that the *North American Review* would be "the vehicle of intelligence respecting the revolutionary history" of Spanish America.[29]

Briefly, it became just that. Sparks coordinated with Heman Allen, US minister to Chile, to transmit documents from the Chilean independence fighter and politician Manuel de Salas, Colombia's chargé d'affaires in Chile. In exchange, Sparks proposed that Salas contribute to the *North American Review*, "to strengthen an attachment between the U.S. and Chile." Sparks reasoned, "The more we can diffuse the light of knowledge, the faster prejudice will disappear, and the stronger the empire of liberty and truth will become established."[30] In recognition of the Chilean's account of their revolution, he furnished a copy of the *North American Review*. "I hope you will be gratified with perusing it," he wrote, "and find that it inculcates liberal and just principles, and cherishes a good spirit towards the new Republics in South America."[31] Salas would indeed have found enthusiastic commentary on Spanish American affairs in those pages.

As one historian has documented, Spanish American agents were avid publicists for their cause in the American press, as they "spent their lives scribbling—writing articles, contacting printers, and translating foreign news clips into English for publication."[32] Alongside analysis by leading American commentators such as Joel Poinsett, the revolutionary voices of Restrepo, Luis López Méndez, and Bernardo Monteagudo spoke through the pages of the *North American Review* to American readers and the growing transatlantic distribution network that Sparks fostered with Europe. In educating Americans on these developments, Sparks explained to Restrepo, the Colombian statesman offered a "service to the cause of liberty, in diffusing widely, the light of truth and knowledge," which he hoped would "enable the friends of liberty throughout this western hemisphere to be animated by the same spirit."[33]

On the same ships that John Quincy Adams hoped would entwine American commerce, Sparks saw a tightening epistolary network that could document the historical alignment within the hemisphere. As US foreign policy leaders anticipated the geopolitical and commercial consolidation of American independence from Europe, Sparks devoted considerable time to an archival and intellectual counterpart based on his perception of the distinctive trajectory of the American republics within global history.

Sparks sought to gather the textual traces of these new national histories as the prospect of an international congress in Panama approached, where

Bolívar planned to coordinate the region's internal and external relations. In his first annual address in late 1825, President Adams insisted on extending commercial reciprocity and most-qualified-nation status to the rest of the newly liberated republics, which he called "indispensable to the effectual emancipation of the American hemisphere from the thralldom of colonizing monopolies and exclusions, an event rapidly realizing in the progress of human affairs."[34] To this end, he accepted the invitation from Colombia, Mexico, and the Central American Republics to send a delegation to Panama. Yet in early 1826, he fumed about congressional opposition to US participation in Panama.[35] Adams assured a leery US Congress that these delegates would not undermine US neutrality with Europe, but his intent was clearly to promote national interests in the hemisphere against the perceived illiberal threat and commercial challenge posed by Europe.

These geopolitical stakes mapped onto the historical significance that Sparks identified in Panama. Sparks placed the national histories of these new American republics within an arc that spanned from his nation's own revolutionary origins, creating a vast though scattered American historical record documenting these exceptional developments. In the spring of 1826, he promoted this argument in his correspondence and through the *North American Review* while the stormy debate over whether to send a diplomatic mission to Panama roiled the US Congress. To Alamán, he announced, "Let this large portion of the globe be a sanctuary sacred to liberty and the rights of man, never to be subdued by any alliance of despotic powers."[36] He assured Alexander Hill Everett, in Madrid as US minister to Spain, "I have the fullest faith that no event in history has been the first spring of more wide and lasting effects on the condition and progress of the human race, than this assemblage at the Isthmus." Sparks mused, "I had rather be a representative from Columbia or Mexico at the first congress of Panama, than to have sat on the throne of kings, or commanded the armies of empires."[37] The developments in Panama appeared part of an extraordinary historical process.

Everett readily agreed, linking the Panama Congress with another in Philadelphia a half century prior. In the work he was then composing, *America: A General Survey of the Western Continent* (1827), Everett placed the new American republics within the longer history of the American Revolution, as if part of a shared genealogical tree. "This consummation," he wrote, "of which our own revolution was the first great act, which is now proceeding in Spanish America, and will ultimately be completed by the emancipation of the remaining British colonies, exhibits the final development, in one of its great branches, of the revolution in the old European political system, or rather of the formation of a new one."[38] Sparks went further, arguing that the ongoing revolutions in the Western Hemisphere would in turn bear on Europe. Writing to US Minister Poinsett in Mexico City, Sparks argued that "the time will come when the renovation of the old world will date its origin in the revolutions of the new."[39] In gathering manuscript and printed materials about these unfolding events, he imagined that he was building an archive to a political phenomenon that "has no prototype in the annals either of ancient or modern story."[40]

Over the course of 1826, however, the public and political enthusiasm for hemispheric unity eroded. Sparks's commentaries on Spanish American affairs were the main source of facts for many Americans readers at this time, including in the US Congress. Ironically, the *North American Review* did not influence congressional debates in the ways Sparks had intended. To his chagrin, he learned so that spring when visiting Secretary of State Henry Clay to seek access to diplomatic records from the American Revolution.[41] Drawing on coverage of Spanish America in the *North American Review*, many southern representatives painted Panama as a supranational entity committed to abolitionism, a severe threat to national sovereignty. Southern politicians came to condemn what they saw as a presidential plan to abet an antislavery congress that might extend this platform to Cuba and the United States.[42] The heated exchanges filled many hours and hundreds of pages in the congressional records. Although the US Congress finally appropriated funds for a two-person mission to Panama, one diplomat died en route, and the other never attended the inaugural but anticlimactic meetings that September.[43]

As the geopolitical vision for the hemisphere fractured, Sparks's sense of historical kinship between American independence and the newly liberated republics frayed. His enthusiasm for the historic opportunity in Panama dimmed as the new republics' constitutions and historical trajectory seemed to deviate from those of the United States.[44] Contrary to his grand expectations months before, Sparks increasingly diminished the historical significance of Panama as he reviewed the newest intelligence channeled through his network. From the opening remarks of the Panama Congress, Sparks hoped for "a paper like those which issued from the first congress assembled at Philadelphia," he wrote to Alexander Hill Everett.[45] Instead of a founding document kindred to his own nation's, Sparks found Peruvian delegate Manuel Vidaurre's opening address lackluster—one more paper in an archive that increasingly seemed to document a lesser historical arc diverging from the exceptional history of the United States.

By the following spring, Sparks had excised Spanish America from his own sense of America's history. Reflecting in his diary on his ongoing correspondence with the Colombian statesman Restrepo on the relationship between the United States and the new American republics, he sighed, "no conclusion can be drawn from the example of the United States, respecting the descendants of the Spaniards in South America . . . the people of the two countries are as different as day from night."[46] His shift in perception was soon evident in the pages of the *North American Review*, where articles emphasized the discrepancies between the United States and Spanish America.[47]

Sparks's interest in the larger history of Spain's Atlantic empire had always been limited. He cared about these revolutions and the prospects of the new republics to the extent that they might fall within the exceptional historical trajectory of the United States. Compared with the other leading American students of Spanish history gathered around Lafayette that evening in 1825, his attention span toward the region was short. Sparks did not share with Ticknor and Prescott a broader interest in the historical archives, literature, and culture of the Spanish Atlantic world. He soon stopped studying Spanish and suspended communication with his Spanish American network.

The hemispheric geopolitical scope in which Sparks forged his interest in American history, broadly conceived, faded from view. In turn, a more narrowly defined chronological and geographical framing of his nation's archival record and history took form in Sparks's mind. Though short-lived, Sparks's first foray into the collection and interpretation of historical documents allowed him to develop his approach to gathering, editing, and publishing a national archive. Sparks had learned to foster a network of correspondents dispersed across political borders who endorsed his research into pivotal historical events. He gained confidence navigating institutions and calling on government support to pursue this work in the name of the public interest. And he insisted on the link between gathering documents and forming a shared historical identity for a broader imagined community.

Shifting the global frame through which he had viewed the historical record of his own nation and the Spanish American republics, Sparks reframed his historical inquiry around his own sprawling nation, for which he planned to be build a national archive with one unifying figure at its center.

Assembling a National Archive

Over the following decade, Sparks narrowed his archival gaze to the record of his own nation's revolution and founding, which he examined synchronically within the history of the United States rather than diachronically within the longer history of republican revolutions in the hemisphere. Like other historically minded Americans, Sparks held that the history of the American Revolution had yet to be properly written. Just weeks before the former president's death in July 1826, Sparks shared his disapproval with Thomas Jefferson: "In perusing the histories of the revolution hitherto written, I have been forcibly impressed with the belief, that the best of them exhibit only the shadow of the great events of that period. Some of the prominent deeds of the actors in the scene are set forth, and no doubt faithfully represented; but the original impulses, the moving springs, and efficient principles of the revolution, it appears to me, have never been developed with any adequate degree of accuracy or justice."[48] To begin gathering the materials for such a history, Sparks departed on a "Southern Tour" of the United States in the summer of 1826 as his optimism waned for the approaching Panama Congress. As some Americans still looked hopefully to Simón Bolívar as a Washingtonian figure, Sparks trained his eye on George Washington himself, seeking his papers. Although Sparks would never author a history of the American Revolution—a challenge he imagined himself equal to in his letter to Jefferson—his *Writings of Washington* would help others do so.

Sparks depended on epistolary relationships to gather materials about Spanish American history, but in pursuit of papers for US history he also took to the roads and waterways. Over the following months, he managed to access record offices in Delaware, Maryland, Virginia, the Carolinas, and Georgia, where he extracted originals or copies of revolutionary records from public and private collections before moving onward to the northern states. Sparks gravitated to the offices of secretaries of state, where he hoped to uncover the neglected correspondence of political and military

FIGURE 7. Portrait of Jared Sparks, ca. 1829. (From *Memoir of Jared Sparks*, by Brantz Mayer [Baltimore: Maryland Historical Society, 1867]; image from Archive.org)

elites during the Revolution. He became a regular in these rooms, seeking the traces of governors, generals, and famous individuals, sifting through the papers of sundry officers and officials. As in his study of the Spanish American republics, his bias toward these American records reflected the common belief that history was made—and made most compelling—by the most powerful actors. Along the way Sparks also interviewed aged veterans and battlefield tour guides, whose accounts he integrated into his growing collection of historical materials.

To governors, secretaries of state, clerks, and other officials in each state, he made the case that his project was "wholly of a public and historical nature"—consequently, they had a responsibility to facilitate it. One by one, they acceded to his request. As in his correspondence with consuls and diplomats in Spanish America, Sparks leveraged his access to one record office as a precedent to peruse the next.[49]

His hope to gather a comprehensive archive of the Revolution confronted the reality of records offices, "particularly at that deranged period of the commencement of the Revolution," he reported to Jefferson.[50] He condemned or complimented the relative disorder or completeness of each state's revolutionary documents. The forces of war, displacement, and natural disaster had left an uneven archival landscape, especially in the southern states ravaged in the later years of the war. Sparks recorded which offices could furnish enough material to recount their respective histories and which could not. In Virginia, the British had either absconded with or destroyed colonial records during Benedict Arnold's campaign there, leaving the most valuable papers lost. In South Carolina, it was worse. "After an hour's toil in tumbling dusty folios," Sparks recounted of his visit to the secretary of state's office, "we found nothing whatever bearing on the period of the revolution. There are a few musty volumes of colonial matter . . . but nothing in the nature of a journal, nor any facts whatever of historical value. During the whole period of the Revolution no single paper or record of any description was found, nor does the secretary know, that any such are contained in his office."[51] These absences troubled him, but he moved briskly, even mechanically, through these spaces. At the same time, he could be deeply moved by archival breakthroughs. One unearthed letter from Lafayette seemed to "breathe the author's spirit and enthusiasm," almost as if Sparks sat again before the man with whom he had dined at George Ticknor's home the previous year.[52]

To properly archive the nation's history, Sparks believed, Washington's writings were the essential element. Many of these were scattered in state records offices, but the major storehouse was Washington's home on the Potomac River: Mount Vernon. In early 1826, Sparks wrote to Supreme Court Justice Bushrod Washington, nephew of the president and inheritor of his personal papers, home, and plantation. Sparks insisted on the importance of bringing before the public Washington's writings, which would do more than document Washington's exceptional attributes and role in important historical events. Rather, in Washington's writings one could read the nation's exceptional history, including "the controlling influence of his opinions and character in gaining the independence and establishing the free government, which are now the glory and happiness of his countrymen, and the admiration of the world," Sparks argued to Justice Washington.[53] Washington's writings not only recorded the nation's history but made it.

Washington's papers had been curated, coveted, rummaged, and neglected for decades by the time Sparks sought them in 1826. During the Revolution and its aftermath, Washington was the first to undertake a comprehensive review of his private papers and attempt to fashion them for a national audience.[54] One biographer has written that "Washington could conceive of only one means of fixing his thumbprint in stone and ensuring some measure of true immortality: a written legacy."[55] He carefully transported his papers throughout his campaigns until 1781, when the Continental Congress approved his request for a team of editors to transcribe and arrange his revolutionary-era papers, which were subsequently stored at Mount Vernon. Washington worried not just about preserving his papers. He envisioned how his words would be preserved. He called for "a similarity and Beauty in the whole execution, all the writing is to be upon black lines equidistant. All the Books to have the same Margin, and to be indexed in so Clear and intelligent a manner, that there may be no difficulty in the references."[56] Washington understood that the aesthetic appearance of his preserved writings would reflect his character and the value of these materials to future readers.

The public would have to wait for Washington's writings, however. During his lifetime, many appealed to Washington for access, hoping to draw on materials without which, they were sure, a proper history of the new nation could not be written. In one of several requests, the historian William Gordon stressed, "I wait with earnestness for the period when I may be admitted with propriety to peruse your Excellency's papers."[57] Washington responded that he would wait until Congress opened its records to the public before making his own available, though he did permit Gordon to make several dozen volumes' worth of copies from his wartime correspondence and orders at Mount Vernon in 1784.

After his presidency, Washington devoted more time to emending and arranging his life's papers, a task that he left upon his death to his personal secretary, Tobias Lear. Bushrod inherited the papers, and he and Lear hoped to publish a history from them.[58] Writing to Judge Washington in 1800, the Marquis de Lafayette projected that the work would include a "great and wonderful part of the late Century and is fit to fix the ideas of Mankind on the events which for five and twenty years back have past not only in the United States but in both Worlds."[59] Though Washington and his admirers perceived a crucial link between these materials and the nation's history—indeed, as Lafayette remarked, the history of the broader Atlantic world—the project did not materialize. Washington's papers remained at Mount Vernon.

After Washington's death, the image that he had burnished during his own lifetime only brightened. He was quickly apotheosized and placed atop the new nation's pantheon of founding figures.[60] As published biographies boomed as a genre in the early United States, "only George Washington stood above the spate of collective biographies," receiving multiple book-length treatments in these decades.[61]

These authors included Chief Justice John Marshall, who helped to bolster the idealized image of Washington, first with an attempt to build a national monument to him in DC and then through a major publication about his life. Drawing on the many volumes of Washington's writing that he borrowed from Mount Vernon, Marshall quickly produced the five-volume *Life of George Washington* between 1804 and 1807.[62] Though its popularity as a biography paled in comparison to Mason Locke Weems's 1809 whimsical and widely read *Life of Washington*,[63] it remained the major historical work on Washington until Sparks's undertaking. After receiving the first volumes of Marshall's work in 1806, John Adams declared it an "Exegisti monumentum ære perennius": *A monument of durable bronze.* He went on, "As it is certainly a more rational, I hope and believe it will be a more glorious and durable Memorial of your Hero, than a Mausoleum would have been, of dimensions Superiour to the proudest pyramid of Egypt."[64] Adams, like Washington, sensed that the most enduring and significant monument to Washington would be text, not stone or metal.

Washington's major cache of writings was sought after but poorly preserved during these years. Avid autograph collectors, such as William Buell Sprague, visited Mount Vernon, and a range of correspondents in the United States and Europe wrote to Bushrod for a relic from Washington's papers, often in the form of a single page or clipped signature.[65] Washington's descendants also gifted fragments of his papers and other artifacts to correspondents in the United States and abroad. Martha Washington's eldest granddaughter, Eliza Parke Custis Law, sent John Lutz, who had served under Washington at Valley Forge, a piece of black velvet once worn by Washington along with a scrap of paper bearing the words "the Post Office," "written in his hand."[66] To the Polish Princess Czartoryska she sent another relic of velvet and text, which had once been "worn by General Washington—the words 'Mount Vernon' his favorite home, and where his sacred remains are entombed, written by his hand, in a letter addressed to me."[67] In this fashion, many documents dispersed from Mount Vernon. At no point in the three decades after his death did the federal government or the State of Virginia make a serious effort to acquire Washington's papers.

Fascination with Washington's writing reflected a broader popular desire to connect with the man through Mount Vernon, which became the nation's most popular tourist destination, almost a sacred site for many. An idealized historical image of it cherished by Americans and foreigners alike circulated in a range of printed material and other objects.[68] The romanticized perception of Mount Vernon only became more compelling to Americans, especially as the sectional crisis intensified. As one historian has put it, "in this desert of fractiousness, Mount Vernon seemed like an oasis of patriotism, a world apart. . . . Worshipping at Washington's tomb, Americans of all parties and stripes imagined a land free of turmoil."[69] During the years that Sparks labored over Washington's writings, thousands visited Mount Vernon annually, the ritualized pilgrimage appearing in myriad written accounts.

Yet the tattered state of Washington's legacy—from his material possessions to his physical remains—irked visitors. Many muttered at the conditions of the house and grounds. The state of Washington's vault seemed especially grievous. Year after year, Americans and Europeans alike heaped opprobrium on Justice Washington for letting it decline. In 1812, New Hampshire representative John Harper wrote home to his wife, Eliza Jane, in dismay: "It is a hole dug in the side of a hill, and lined up with bricks; but a little better than a good farm in New Hampshire would make, to keep his pigs from the storm, or his potatoes from the frost."[70] Mary Bagot, the wife of a British diplomat in DC, complained that "the grave looked exactly like an ice house with a wooden door and keyhole."[71] Such negative appraisals from foreigners especially troubled Americans who saw Mount Vernon as a symbol of their nation. In 1815, Andrew Jackson, newly famous from his triumph in the Battle of New Orleans, worried that this disregard of the nation's heritage was a distinctive feature of their republican government. "Why is it so!" he questioned, "must the charge of ingratitude forever rest upon Republicks?"[72] As much as the emotional outpouring that many experienced at the seemingly sacred site, the critique of its conditions became part of the tourist experience.

Since Washington's death, many had argued that his body belonged in the nation's capital, that the federal government should place it there, and that a fitting tomb and monument should mark it. Washington's will stipulated otherwise, and he and then Martha remained in their modest vault a short distance from their home. Blame was placed mainly on Bushrod for "not providing a more decent Vault of monument" for his uncle, as Benjamin Latrobe, the eminent architect and designer of the US Capitol, reported to him after meeting with senior government officials in 1810.[73] Such calls reverberated as frustration heightened with the "potatoe-hole" of a vault.[74] It fell further into dilapidation in the 1820s. "The despoliation, and sacrilege has been consummated by the profanum vulgus," one Scottish visitor sputtered, referring to the many pieces of wood that had been chipped away as relics, names carved into the door, and innumerable flowers, pebbles, and branches plucked from around it.[75]

At the same time, Americans after the War of 1812 increasingly castigated Congress for failing to build a vault and monument to Washington that would show the nation's appreciation for him. "The idea of ingratitude rushing on my mind," an editorialist in the *National Intelligencer* cried in 1818 about his visit to the site, "was gall and wormwood to my heart."[76] As increasing numbers of visitors treated Mount Vernon as public property, those critical of its poor preservation argued that the federal government had a responsibility to sustain it as a national memorial site. For these visitors, the worsening conditions of Mount Vernon undermined their narrative of Washington and corresponding beliefs about how his remains—architectural, mortuary, symbolic—should be preserved.

Sparks added Washington's texts to this broader conversation about how the nation should preserve and engage with his overall legacy. While others envisioned a worthier vault to enclose the Washingtons' remains or finer grounds to encompass their home, Sparks envisioned bound volumes holding Washington's writings. His work, Sparks promised Justice Washington, would be both "a tribute due to the name of Washington, and a repository for perpetuating the most valuable treasures of American History, which in their present scattered state, are subject to be swept into oblivion by every wind that blows; exposed to the mercy of accident, and the consuming power of the elements." He expressed his aim "to make a perfect edition of his writings, one that should stand as a perpetual monument, worth of his fame and of his country."[77] He repeated this vision of the project's monumental qualities to Lafayette the following year when he requested any correspondence from Washington in the Frenchman's possession. "It is intended that the work shall be such as to hold a place in the first rank of American

History," he announced, "and be a monument for posterity reared by the hands of our great hero himself."[78] In depicting Washington's writings as a monument, "reared by the hands" of Washington, Sparks of course occluded the influence of his own hands in crafting Washington's textual appearance, which some historians in his lifetime and many since have criticized. Yet he captured the desire of so many Americans to directly encounter their most famous founder.

In proposing that Washington's collective writings formed his monument, Sparks expanded on the claim made by many visitors who, distressed by the physical deterioration of Mount Vernon, concluded that the truest monument to Washington was not a physical site but his very name and memory. "I stood before the sepulchre," the Mississippi minister William Merce Green wrote in his diary in 1818, "of one, whose name needed not memento's of clay for it was eternal; whose trophies were worn by every freeman of our country; while his virtues were written in their hearts and themselves wept o'er his lowly tomb."[79] Others flattered themselves that Washington had bequeathed a monument superior to those that dotted Europe. Sarah Josepha Hale wrote in her 1823 poetry collection:

> Greece had her conqu'rers—and her warriors, Rome
> And some proud column, or some sculptured dome
> Each nation hallowed to her heroes' fame—
> But Washington thy monument's thy Name![80]

Finding that "nothing but a few coarse bricks and a mound of earth mark the grave of the Father of his Country," US Naval Agent Thomas Hayes similarly consoled himself during his 1826 visit that "he has a monument more precious more valuable than all the marble that could be erected[;] it is that that is inherent in the heart of every American and in the honest and true praise of a grateful nation."[81] Sparks's attempt to preserve and publish edited compendia of Washington's writings reflected such claims that the most significant legacy of Washington did not reside at a specific site but within Americans themselves. The writings of Washington could embody the attributes that Americans so admired in Washington and connect the larger national community, including those who could not visit his physical remains at Mount Vernon.

Bushrod was strained as an intermediary between Washington's legacy and this demanding public, which made him susceptible to Sparks's request to not only memorialize but turn a profit from Washington's writings. In practice, Mount Vernon continued to lose money, and Bushrod, when not traveling for his responsibilities on the Supreme Court, resented the intrusions of tourists.[82] He often refused to greet visitors who came to stroll about the grounds, shed a tear at Washington's gravesite, and meander through the house. Instead, the scores of enslaved people who maintained the estate dealt with the tourists, receiving tips and selling a variety of objects such as canes fashioned from the trees around Washington's vault.[83] Bushrod had already eked some value from Washington's writings and had envisioned more, which Sparks's undertaking promised to deliver.

Sparks convinced Bushrod that Washington's papers should be available to the nation and that publishing them as mass-produced volumes would yield a profit. In a letter to Supreme Court Justice Joseph Story, Sparks echoed Washington's own thinking in his later life. "Washington's public letters and papers," Sparks argued, "are the property of the nation. As such, they ought to be before the nation, and he, who brings them out, does a public service."[84] For the sake of effectively marketing them to the public, securing federal patronage, and maintaining the aesthetic and intellectual integrity of the whole, Sparks continued, they must be published together. Rather than dividing the papers into separate publications, "in a shape so broken and disconnected," Sparks projected that, "if the entire works of Washington were presented to the public, in a form suited to the dignity of the subject, a national interest and a national feeling would be excited, and a wide and honorable patronage might be expected."[85] To seal their support, Sparks made a "highly liberal" offer to Bushrod to evenly split with him and with John Marshall all profits from future publications derived from the papers. They signed, in March 1827, a deal that would add considerably to the profit they had already earned from publications based on Washington's papers.[86] By the spring of 1827 Sparks was in residence at Mount Vernon, ensconced among the volumes of Washington's correspondence, journals, military records, and other manuscripts.

Sparks's season at Mount Vernon placed him among the many seeking Washington's legacy there. He worked meticulously through the scores of volumes in the house. He wrote to Marshall that "the labor before me is prodigious, but I engage in it with a hearty zeal and good will, and despair not of seeing the end in due time."[87] Sparks observed as if from afar the tourists to Mount Vernon "on a sort of pilgrimage to the tomb of the father of this country."[88] Yet he was among these pilgrims, one of the many interlopers that season who made the trying trek overland from Alexandria or ascended from steamboats on the Potomac. He, too, depended on the estate's enslaved laborers, who curated many visitors' experiences and embodied the legacy of Washington.[89] Like these tourists, Sparks was eager for closer contact with Washington, anxious about the condition of what Washington had left behind, concerned with how the living related to it, and invested in what this meant for the future of the nation.

Weary and daunted by the scope of the materials, Sparks convinced Bushrod in May to let him remove all of Washington's papers to Cambridge, farther from the nation's capital but closer to Sparks's ambition to complete a project of national consequence. Boxes were shipped northward from Alexandria to Boston, those deemed of greatest value carted overland with Sparks. Justice Washington sent more in his wake, and Sparks made a final trip to gather additional papers the following year.[90] Insured at ten thousand dollars, this was likely the most dearly valued collection of papers in the United States. It would remain in Cambridge for nearly a decade as Sparks made the selections, expurgations, and editorial comments that would lead to the twelve-volume work that appeared between 1834 and 1837.

Before editing Washington's writings in earnest, Sparks immersed himself in his first major editorial project, editing the diplomatic correspondence of the American Revolution. Arriving in Washington, DC, in early 1827, Sparks found a White House and Department of State willing to support his research into revolutionary diplomatic correspondence stored in Secretary Clay's office.[91] Later that month, Sparks secured President Adams's endorsement to publish the diplomatic correspondence of the Revolution, for which a resolution had been passed in 1818 but neglected since. Sparks agreed to undertake the project so long as he received the copyright. Adams consented, provided that he could review selected papers before they went public. Sparks soon gained Clay's support as well as Webster's, who would steer the appropriation through Congress. In the spring of 1827, Sparks agreed to distill the twenty-two volumes of correspondence to a more manageable selection, for which he would be paid four hundred dollars per volume, and then $2.12 ½ for each of the one thousand copies printed.[92] This was the first substantial government investment in the preservation and publication of the nation's historical documents.

Sparks believed that this crucial period of American history could not be comprehensively told with the documents on American soil alone, which the gaps in state record offices had shown him. Over the following year, he looked to historical records in Britain and France to complement the archive of the American Revolution and Washington's life that he had spent two years gathering and analyzing in the United States. In one of his letters to Henry Dwight, chair of the House Ways and Means Committee, he wrote on 5 January 1829, "the single fact, that a history of no one of the old states can be written, without a free use of these papers is enough to show the importance of obtaining them at any reasonable sacrifice.... In no one are the old records and documents complete; in nearly all they are extremely deficient."[93] Sparks would continue to advocate for a congressional appropriation to make copies of *all* relevant papers in British archives before and during his trip. "Hence the best materials for our history were never, in fact, accessible here," he reflected to Edward Everett several years later, "and those that originated with ourselves have in some of the states, nearly all been lost. The Colonial papers in the British offices seem to be very complete, and I believe no accident has occurred to scatter or destroy them."[94]

Sparks believed that documents in the imperial record office in Britain would make it possible to reconstruct the nation's revolutionary record, including the diplomatic history of the war. Writing to James Madison in 1827, he explained his goal to counter European interpretations of the American colonial records stored in London. Only the British historian George Chalmers had analyzed them at length, Sparks wrote, and "with a very jaundiced eye," in preparing his *Introduction to the History of the Revolt of the Colonies* (1782).[95] Seeing himself as an arbiter of Atlantic historiography on the American Revolution, Sparks sought to use these same materials to revise the history of the Revolution. Access to these documents could bolster the nation's archival collections such that Americans would not need to depend on foreign repositories and historians to reconstruct their own nation's history.

Like the American readers who scrutinized the evidence and arguments about the Norse Atlantic emanating from the Royal Society of Northern Antiquaries at this time, Sparks depended on larger historical institutions, engaged with foreign scholars, and delved into denser archival collections in Europe. However, rather than incorporate the United States into a global frame of America's origins devised by a foreign institution, Sparks used these transatlantic exchanges to fill in a national frame that centered Washington and the emergence of the republic.

As in the United States, Sparks was convinced that this national project should inspire the cooperation of archive keepers wherever he went. In this first trip to Europe, he became the American most adept at using his social capital and the US diplomatic and consular corps to access and copy materials from European archives. He received endorsements from the Adams administration. Secretary of State Clay sent letters to US diplomats in France, Holland, and England to help Sparks, promoting him as "a gentleman of high literary attainments, and great worth and respectability."[96] Although Sparks leveraged the support of the federal government, his appeal to Clay that the United States should seek comprehensive copies of these documents for the Library of Congress never gained traction.

Through the intervention of US representatives, the relationships that he built with influential British and French officials, and his own arguments about how he would use their archives, European doors opened. To the Marquis de Marbois in Paris, Sparks made the case that he looked for "such particulars only, as are suited to the dignity and faithfulness of history, and as will help to give a more full and accurate account of the part acted by France."[97] Sparks encountered resistance to his requests for archival access during an era when the norms for scholarly access across national lines remained in flux.[98] Writing from France in the late summer of 1828 following his tour through Holland and Germany, he complained: "From Charlemagne down nobody had been admitted into the diplomatic archives; and I believe it is a maxim all over Europe, that what never has been done, never can be done, one would think the French Revolution would have taught them better."[99] Seeking to gain access to British colonial archives in 1829, he assured the skeptical British bureaucrats that "no person would be more unwilling than myself to gather up any thing from the events of former times, which should tend to perpetuate or revive unfriendly feelings in any quarter. My firm conviction is, that a full knowledge of facts, and a fair representation of them, will have a directly opposite effect."[100] Sparks pursued these papers by making a similar argument in both Britain and France that the historical record would vindicate the part that their ancestors had played in the American Revolution.

Having gained access to swaths of historical documents in the United States and western Europe, Sparks oversaw an extraordinary outpouring of documentary editions over the following decade, making public what he deemed crucial components of his nation's archives. Following his transatlantic trip, Sparks completed his federally sponsored, twelve-volume work titled the *Diplomatic Correspondence of the American Revolution*, which appeared between 1829 and 1830, earning him $2,525 per volume in compensation for his work and the publication of one thousand copies for Congress.[101] Sparks failed to secure the contract to continue editing and publishing the post-1783 diplomatic papers lying in disorder in the secretary of state's office, but his *Diplomatic Correspondence* further demonstrated his ability to activate the federal government as a force in building national archival resources.

He also coordinated another collection of texts that he hoped would preserve the nation's historical record and serve as a resource for constructing its history. Sparks's *Library of American Biography* enlisted a network of notable authors, including Bancroft, Prescott, Edward Everett, and John Quincy Adams, who contributed essays about pivotal figures in American history, in order to create a "history of the nation, told through biographies of its important characters." Though not published chronologically, the twenty-six biographies featured in the ten initial volumes between 1834 and 1839 formed a prosopography of American progress, spanning from European exploration and colonization, through the American Revolution, to the success of the independent nation.[102] Washington himself did not figure among them, but like the *Writings of Washington*, Sparks's *Library* compiled multiple texts into a larger resource that preserved America's historical record within a national frame. These could both stand collectively as a unified monument of the nation's past and serve as individual items referenced by curious readers and crafters of American history.

Writing Washington, Writing the Nation

During these busy years, Sparks's office became a site for preserving, memorializing, and commercializing Washington's legacy. As he ushered the final volumes through the press in 1835, he was visited by the novelist Catharine Maria Sedgwick, her teenaged niece, and her friend John Gorham Palfrey, then the editor of the *North American Review*.[103] After viewing Washington's writings stacked in Sparks's office, Sedgwick marveled in her journal at "the wonderful voluminous copies—journals, memos etc. of this most wonderful man."[104] In their midst, Sparks sat, "surrounded by the records of the Revolution," appearing to Sedgwick like a "rich country squire" with a private manuscript collection. Her transposition of an aristocratic European antiquarian onto an American citizen undertaking a historical publication intended for a national audience captured the contrast between Sparks, an individual collector and editor in Massachusetts, and the national scope of his undertaking.

Sparks's *Writings of Washington* received widespread acclaim upon release, becoming a vital source for such authors as Bancroft, Washington Irving, and Edward Everett as they, in the decades prior to the Civil War, constructed highly influential narratives of the American Revolution and Washington's life. A broader public also engaged with Washington's writings as a source for understanding the nation's history, including Sedgwick in her popular historical romance of the American Revolution, *The Linwoods* (1835), where Washington's written words came to life.[105]

Although Sedgwick never belonged to a historical society or received much recognition as a writer of history, by making her historical novel into an archival space where Washington wrote, she worked within the frame of Sparks's national project. Critics in her time and since have tended to diminish the historical value of the book. Her reviewer in the *North American Review* explained that a man writes a novel "as a means of effecting some, as he supposes, more important end," while the *The Linwoods* was further proof that "a female novelist gives up her whole work, with her heart and soul in it, to the distresses of the lovers."[106] But Sedgwick reflected in historical fiction the belief that animated Sparks's historical editing: Washington's writings not only embodied his exceptional character but brought into existence the exceptional nation. Over the course of the novel the author surrounds herself with the very type of historical documents that surrounded Sparks in his office.

By dramatizing the production of Washington's wartime archive and insisting on the intimate link between Washington, his writings, and the nation, she endorsed both the historical materials and the historical argument that Sparks was devoting such time and resources to preserving and publicizing. Like Sparks, Sedgwick also put these papers before the public's eyes, and in so doing used fiction to depict a version of the man and vision of his archive that aligned with the project that Sparks undertook as an editor and historian. Sedgwick hailed from a powerful family in Massachusetts, but

FIGURE 8. Silhouette of Catharine Maria Sedgwick, by Auguste Edouart, 1842. (National Portrait Gallery, Smithsonian Institution; gift of Robert L. McNeil Jr.)

as a woman it was all but impossible for her to actively fashion the nation's emerging archives as an equal with men like Sparks. Nonetheless, through her historical fiction she engaged with him at the threshold of the national archive he was building, displaying that women could actively shape its meaning for Americans.

The Linwoods is a family drama superimposed upon revolutionary New York and rural New England, the settings where Sedgwick spent her life.[107] Sedgwick aligned its plot with the fortunes of the Continental Army in the tenuous middle years of the conflict. The domestic dynamics of the Linwood family mirror the broader civil war portrayed in the book. The opposing political allegiances of the Loyalist Mr. Linwood, his daughter, Isabella, and rebel son, Herbert, nearly tear the family apart. In direct opposition to his father, Herbert's revolutionary sentiment swells. He joins the American forces alongside the virtuous New England hero Elliot Lee, who later saves Washington from a British scheme to capture him. In order to see his estranged family, Herbert surreptitiously accompanies Elliot on a special errand on behalf of Washington to Commander-in-Chief Sir Henry Clinton in British-occupied New York. Herbert is imprisoned, and amid the domestic turmoil that ensues, Isabella gravitates toward the American cause and away from both her father and her effete suitor, Jaspar Meredith. In a parallel plot, Meredith seduces Elliot's hapless sister Bessie in New England, "a gem fit to be set in a coronet," he writes, who recklessly seeks him in Manhattan too. Bessie is ultimately saved, Meredith wrecked, Elliot and Isabella wed, and the Linwoods reconciled by war's end. If still disdainful of the American rebels' cause, Mr. Linwood respects his children's commitment to it—and above all the man who led it. "I'll have one look at Washington," he tells Isabella during the American army's triumphal march through Manhattan at war's end. "By George of Oxford!" he exclaims, "a noble figure of a man!"[108]

Sedgwick had sought Sparks's guidance for background historical reading to inform her project, which he shared in a hefty, annotated reading list of sixteen secondary and primary sources. These items included Marshall's *Life of Washington*, which remained the preeminent biography of Washington, and the history of the Revolution published by William Gordon in 1788 (a "gossiping book," in Sparks's opinion). He suggested a range of other published sources, from memoirs to periodicals. "Tell your brothers not to laugh at me," Sparks joked, "for recommending to a lady to read old laws." Still, he urged her to look at the statutes from the period, the "very ones most valuable to the Historian." He assumed that she did not "intend to make pilgrimages or to turn antiquarian"—that is, visit physical archives or rustle up original documents herself. He understood rightly, however, that she meant to write "a work of fiction founded on facts," as he put it. But he also distinguished between what "factual" meant in her writing compared with his own. He viewed her project as "a historical novel, for which you desire to obtain correct impressions of the conditions, manners and feelings of the people, rather than an accurate statement of incidents."[109] The distinction would not be as simple as Sparks imagined.

Sedgwick engaged intricately throughout *The Linwoods* with the archival work that Sparks produced in his *Writings of Washington*. Fictionalized historical documents written by Washington and figures such as Lafayette waft throughout *The Linwoods*. These letters advance the plot and connect the far-flung and often mobile characters. Letters from Washington to the colonial governors in 1778 set the central plot line into motion, inspiring Elliot Lee's widowed mother to bless his enlistment in the Continental Army. The Lee family gathers letters of support on Elliot's behalf "from the best sources," which he bears to Washington, entwining the general with this American family. Elliot presents his letters of introduction from Massachusetts governor John Hancock and John Adams; soon, he receives a lieutenant's commission from Washington. This first connection to Washington—both for the characters and the reader—is epistolary. It leaves a written trace, which accumulates with others, making *The Linwoods* letter by letter a source of the very archival materials that appeared in the volumes published by Sparks.

These fictional historical documents penned by Washington aligned with the actual archive of Washington correspondence that Sparks was then publishing. Sparks's *Writings of Washington* documented the general's national network of correspondents during the Revolution, which Sparks organized into several classes: from Washington to Congress and American diplomats; to provincial governments and citizens; to officers in the Continental Army; to foreign ministers and nationals; to British officers, and to sundry private individuals. In Sparks's words, these were "the highest and purest fountains of history."[110]

In her novel, Sedgwick showed the production of or alluded to letters from each of these classes. For instance, following his performance at the Battle of Stony Point, Herbert proudly relates to Isabella that Elliot was promoted to captain and "received the thanks of General Washington, and got my name blazoned in the report to Congress."[111] In the recently published sixth volume, a reader could indeed survey Sparks's reproduction of numerous letters from Washington during the preparation for and success at Stony Point. In his 20 July 1779 report to Congress, Washington wrote, "It is probable Congress will be pleased to bestow some marks of consideration upon those officers, who distinguished themselves upon this occasion. Every officer and man of the corps deserves great credit; but there were particular ones, whose situation placed them foremost in danger, and made their conduct most conspicuous."[112] One could imagine—like Sedgwick—that the fictional names of Lee and Linwood were "emblazoned" alongside the factual names that followed in Sparks's printed version of Washington's report. In moving Washington's hand and dispatching these letters among the characters, Sedgwick dramatized the production and insisted on the influence of the same historical materials that Sparks was putting before the public.

In addition to showing how Washington's writings helped to forge a national community amid the Revolution, Sedgwick employed Washington's

FIGURE 9. *Le Général Washington*, engraved by Noël Le Mire, after Jean-Baptiste Le Paon, 1780. (Metropolitan Museum of Art; bequest of Charles Allen Munn, 1924)

fictional letters to reflect the character of the general. This becomes crucial to the plot and the outcome of the war. Throughout the book, honesty and commitment to one's principles are elevated as the general's supreme qualities. Sedgwick depicted the defense of Washington's reputation—especially through writing—as essential to the American cause. "No man that ever lived more jealously guarded against the appearance of evil than Washington," she wrote, in that "he was aware that his reputation belonged to his country, that it was identified with the cause he had espoused, the cause of liberty and popular government; and how has that glorious cause profited by it?" She continued, "heralded by his spotless name, [his reputation] has gone forth to restore the order of God's providence," advancing freedom in America and beyond.[113] As the American cause seems to depend on Washington's character, preserving his sterling reputation is vital, especially in the many letters that circulate throughout *The Linwoods*. Sedgwick's Washington is sensitive to the relationship between an individual's character and their writing. Upon receiving an anonymous letter written by Herbert, Washington burns it in the very candle by which he is writing his own letters. He explains to Elliot, "They are the resort of the cowardly or the malignant. An honest man will sustain by his name what he thinks proper to communicate."[114]

The link between Washington's writings, his character, and the course of the war appears again when the British assert that Washington has broken the law of war by dispatching a spy under a false passport. Secretly accompanied by Herbert, Elliot crosses enemy lines into New York with a passport and official documents produced by Washington for "important business to be transacted" with Sir Henry Clinton.[115] When Herbert is apprehended by British forces for disguising himself to fit one of these passports, Washington sees his own character under threat, for Clinton hopes "to seize every occasion to abate the country's confidence in Washington's integrity."[116] Washington defends himself through further correspondence with Clinton, "disclaiming all part and lot in Herbert's return," which Meredith then reads to the imprisoned Herbert "a la lettre" in an attempt to urge Herbert to renounce the American cause.[117] Like Clinton, Washington realizes the risk to his own reputation and, by extension, the American cause that this misuse of his name produces. Speaking to Isabella, Clinton elaborates, "We are bound, by the policy of war, to avail ourselves of the accident, if it be one, that enables us plausibly to impute to Washington an act held dishonourable in all civilized warfare."[118] Sedgwick's Washington has not used his correspondence to deceive anyone, but by making the authenticity of Washington's writing a key to the plot and the outcome of the war, Sedgwick argued both that Washington's character was legible in his letters and that this analogy between the man and his writing was historically significant.

She shared this understanding of the linkage between Washington's character and writing with Sparks, who claimed in *Writings of Washington* that "the pervading influence of one master-mind" was evident in all of Washington's letters.[119] Moreover, the fictionalized Washington letters that Sedgwick produced in this scene were tethered to actual letters reproduced in Sparks's volumes. Sedgwick wrote the drama of Herbert's capture into the historical context of Patriot soldiers captured by the British in occupied New York; she also wrote Washington's fictionalized correspondence with Clinton into the actual documents that Sparks was publishing when *The Linwoods* appeared. Washington's 1779 letters to Clinton were reproduced in Sparks's sixth volume of Washington's *Writings* along with an appendix of Clinton's letters concerning an agreement on the exchange of prisoners of war.[120]

Beyond the fictionalized production of such letters, Sedgwick also staged performances of Washington writing, which could only reinforce popular interest in Washington's archive and the appeal of Sparks's multivolume endeavor to collect and publish his neglected papers. Prefacing *The Linwoods*, Sedgwick confessed to the reader that "whenever the writer has mentioned Washington, she has felt a sentiment resembling the awe of the pious Israelite when he approached the ark of the Lord."[121] By placing readers in the very room and at arm's length from Washington as he composes, sends, and receives original letters, Sedgwick invited readers into a historical recreation of the war's administrative conduct.

She also accentuated the sacred quality that many Americans found in Washington's legacy, whether in his home, mortal remains, manuscripts, or mere name. The reader's first visual encounter with Washington interrupts the general in the act of writing. Glimpsing Washington writing within his tent, Elliot is escorted by a colonel into the room, where Washington bids him to sit while he finishes making copies of his outgoing letters: "The copies were before him, all in his own hand. 'Every *t* is crossed, and every *i* dotted,' whispered the colonel, pointing to the papers. 'He's godlike in that; he finishes off little things as completely as great.'"[122] In the introduction to his second volume of Washington's correspondence, Sparks had described Washington's writing process in a similar way. "Indeed he seldom suffered a paper of any sort to go out of his hands," Sparks explained, "even an ordinary letter of friendship or business, without first composing and correcting it with studious care, and then transcribing a fair copy."[123] Whether in Sedgwick's novel or Sparks's volumes, Washington, writing, literally impresses his moral qualities into the page: diligence, devotion, self-mastery.

Sedgwick's fictional depiction of an act that Washington performed many thousands of times throughout the war produced both a proof of his extraordinary personal qualities and a relic, which Elliot and the reader can marvel at. In a scene where Elliot is once again delivering dispatches to Washington, Sedgwick interjected, "it is well known that Washington's moderation and equanimity were the effects of the highest principle, not the gift of nature. He was constitutionally subject to gusts of passion, but he had acquired a power, almost divine (and doubtless from a divine source), by which he could direct the whirlwind and subdue the storm."[124] The aesthetic qualities of Washington's writings become a proof of the man's personal virtues that Sedgwick illustrated throughout the book.

Sparks celebrated the same qualities that Sedgwick attributed to Washington. In one of his 1834 lectures on Washington, Sparks praised him for "the power of applying his thoughts with intenseness for a long time to a single object—a self-possession, and control over his passions, that seldom forsook him—and inherent integrity of purpose, which impelled him to discharge every duty with the most scrupulous regard for justice and truth—a strong moral sense in every transaction of life."[125] By exhibiting these qualities in Washington as he writes and by making Elliot and the colonel venerate the act, Sedgwick modeled the reverence that Americans should feel toward both Washington and his written legacy. As Elliot's first encounter suggests, Washington's writing was the authentic expression of his extraordinary qualities. In contrast with Elliot's veneration of Washington writing, upon receiving a letter from Washington that confounds her plan to set a trap for him, the duplicitous character of Helen Ruthven "tore it into fragments and dispersed it to the winds."[126] Her disregard of the general's writing reflects her disdain for the American cause and exclusion from the national community that Washington was uniting. Such an act of documentary destruction was antithetical to Sedgwick's own praise of Washington as a writer and Sparks's painstaking salvage and editing of Washington's writings.

Sedgwick re-created and dramatized the production of Washington's writing, enabling a more intimate encounter between readers and this archive than Sparks's dense volumes could reach. Sparks remained an admirer of her intellect, inviting her to contribute an essay on the teenaged New York poet Lucretia Maria Davidson to the seventh volume of his *Library of American Biography* (1837).[127] Although she could not gather, edit, and publish historical documents in the same manner as men like Sparks, Sedgwick made her historical novel a site for accessing, working with, and encouraging others to explore the archival materials within the national frame in which Sparks had produced the *Writings of Washington*.

Washington's Archival Accessions

With the *Writings of Washington* bound, available to institutions and individuals throughout the nation, and circulating in novels such as Sedgwick's *The Linwoods*, Sparks's stewardship of the papers themselves was coming to a close. Although Sparks conducted much of this national archival project in his home, his contract stipulated that the papers had to be returned to Bushrod's heir and Washington's grandnephew, George Corbin Washington, then serving as a congressman from Maryland. Sparks parted reluctantly with Washington's writings. Rather than find a permanent home at Mount Vernon or another private residence, most of the documents from which Sparks had crafted a national archive were now sought by the federal government as the property of the nation.

Secretary of State Louis McLane made an overture to George Corbin in 1833 to express the federal government's desire of "rendering as complete as possible the archives of the United States, and especially those which belong to the most interesting portion of our history, the struggle for independence." McLane pointed to Washington as the precedent for the government's claim to the papers, citing his 1781 letter to the president of the Continental Congress in which he promised to donate his papers to the government once they had been edited. In fact, this very letter was reprinted in the seventh volume of Washington's Writings, in 1835.[128] Deploying the justification that historical societies had used for decades to motivate donations, the secretary continued, "It is presumed that it may be agreeable to you, as well on the grounds of public utility, as from a desire to preserve in so safe and suitable a depository the official papers and records of your eminent kinsmen."[129] McLane's proposal to deposit the full Washington papers in the secretary of state's office was an endorsement of the project that Sparks had started seven years earlier to secure Washington's papers, which could now become the foundation of a national historical archive based in the capital.

Learning of the offer, Sparks insisted to George Corbin that, "whatever form of transfer may be prescribed, it must leave me in precisely the same relation to the papers in which I stood before the purchase of Congress."[130] Sparks played for time, wanting to continue work on the papers and to benefit financially from them. In 1833, he had optimistically anticipated sales reaching six thousand in a few years and profits topping sixteen thousand dollars based on his printing contract with Boston's Hilliard, Gray, and Co. He boasted to Edward Everett that, "as a historical treasure to the nation, they are altogether invaluable. I have examined all the public offices in the country containing papers relating to revolutionary events, and I do not hesitate to say, that the manuscripts comprise a mass of materials for the history of that period, more authentic, rich, and important, than can be obtained from all the public sources combined."¹³¹ Nonetheless, as the first volumes were published, he became anxious that his high opinion of their value would not be reflected in sales. By 1835, he complained to George Corbin that "every dollar I have in the world is involved in the publication of Washington's Writings," and that, "as a pecuniary arrangement, the undertaking has been to me unfortunate."¹³² By the 1850s, Sparks tallied that some seven thousand sets had been sold, in addition to 8,500 copies of the *Life of Washington* that he authored to accompany the edited documentary volumes.¹³³

George Corbin would not part so lightly with the two hundred or so volumes in his and Sparks's possession. He estimated that these would yield some fifty to one hundred printed volumes, which he added in his response to McLane in early 1834 "was of great pecuniary as well as moral value." George Corbin's portrayal of the emotional and psychic experience of relinquishing the papers (even at a profit) echoed the language used by generations of Americans who had sought relics from Washington at Mount Vernon: "To part with these relics of the father of our country exacts no small sacrifice of personal feeling." Given Washington's own example of placing public duty over private interest, he went on, "I will consent to their being deposited in the Archives of the nation." Although the Washingtons had never conceded that his body, tomb, or home were the property of the nation, George Corbin called these papers just that: "These papers are distinctly national in their character, illustrative of the events of our glorious revolution, and of the rise and progress of all our political institutions, and, therefore, should be the property of the Nation. In the hands of an individual, they are also liable to casualties which might, in a moment sweep into oblivion this proud monument of the moral excellence and intellectual labors of one, who memory is cherished by his countrymen, and whose long life was devoted to their service." But they would come at a price to the public. Subtly, he suggested that if the federal government could not procure funds to buy them, then he suspected that "a liberal sum would be cheerfully given by citizens of one state of the union."¹³⁴ He may have had Virginia in mind, but the implication was an effective negotiation tactic because it raised the prospect that "one state of the union" would hold the nearly comprehensive record of the union's only unifying figure. By 1834, it was becoming clear that the federal government would never make a national monument of Washington's body and crypt or of Mount Vernon. However, Washington, DC, could preserve the written remains of Washington. George Corbin and McLane soon struck a deal to purchase the volumes for twenty-five thousand dollars, appropriated by the US Congress that summer.

It would take several years for Sparks to transfer all of the volumes in his possession to George Corbin, who came in person to Boston to transport the final volumes to Washington, DC. The new secretary of state, John Forsyth, repeatedly wrote George Corbin in 1837 and 1838 that the collected volumes were incomplete. The latter responded that he had indeed delivered all volumes of a public nature, as he saw them, keeping the private materials as his own.[135]

As Sparks finished the twelfth volume in July 1837, he looked back on "an undertaking, in magnitude and importance, vastly beyond what I had anticipated, but which I have executed in as faithful and thorough a manner as I was capable of doing it, and which I trust will not be without public benefit."[136] Sparks's archival work had helped establish the principle of government patronage of national history and the practice of acquiring historical manuscripts within a national historical archive. Between 1837 and 1853, the Washington, DC, mayor and influential printer Peter Force benefited from a government contract to gather a tremendous number early revolutionary-era documents for what became his nine-volume *American Archives*. Sparks's project and the federal acquisition of Washington's papers also initiated the practice of purchasing founders' papers. Between 1837 and 1848, Congress appropriated funds for the purchase of the papers of James Madison from Dolley Madison for thirty thousand dollars; Alexander Hamilton's papers from his widow, Elizabeth Hamilton, for twenty thousand dollars in early 1848; and Thomas Jefferson's for another twenty-five thousand dollars later that year. The elaborate process of gathering and publishing the papers of Washington that Sparks had undertaken through private contract with the Washington estate would be financed by the federal government for these other founding figures, further filling the national frame that Sparks had long worked within.

On the eve of the Civil War, Edward Everett praised Sparks's imprint on the nation's understanding of Washington over the preceding quarter century: "Since the appearance of the invaluable work, no one has had occasion to write or to speak of Washington, with out feeling himself under the highest obligations to Mr. Sparks."[137] When Sparks died in 1866, the literary elite of his age lauded him as having created the archival foundation they stood upon.[138] Critics had castigated the New England bias that they detected in Sparks's editions of Washington's writing, yet Sparks imagined an archive that transcended the particularities or exceptionalism of any one state. He broke new ground in the work of building an archive for the nation, in which he saw a monument grounded in no one corner of the American landscape or branch of genealogy, but in the unifying figure that he perceived in George Washington.

From initial fascination with the global phenomenon of revolutionary republics that he perceived in the Americas, Sparks narrowed the frame for his archival project to a national figure. In doing so, he worked within an institutional void between the global history explored by institutions like the Royal Society of Northern Antiquaries (discussed in chapter 2) and the state-centric archives produced across the United States (which chapter 4 examines). Sparks helped move the federal government toward constructing an archive framed around the nation's history, although this development paled in comparison with the projects to preserve and publish national historical records that Sparks and others encountered in Europe. As the following chapters show, throughout the antebellum United States, efforts at the state and local level, led by historical establishments and individuals rather than the federal government, remained the primary sites of salvaging and making sense of the nation's historical materials.

FOUR

State of the Archives

In 1846, the Swiss American statesman, scholar, and New York Historical Society (NYHS) president Albert Gallatin lobbied the state legislature to back the publication of New York's most important historical records, which included voluminous documents recently copied from national archives in the Netherlands, Britain, and France. According to Gallatin, these volumes, "when distributed to the various towns and counties in the state, will thus actually bring the sacred truths of our history to each man's own door and fireside." The prospect of New Yorkers reading by firelight these compilations of seventeenth- and eighteenth-century primary sources, many translated from the original Dutch or French, may seem doubtful. But Gallatin believed that such "sacred truths," when bound, could in turn bind New Yorkers to a shared belief in the state's exceptional historical significance—an imagined documentary community of sorts. Noting that Britain and France—European monarchies—had both made major investments in publishing crucial documents from their national archives, Gallatin asked New York's lawmakers why a republic would not "spread among her citizens, with a liberal hand, the lights of history which her archives now contain."[1] Rather than expect Washington, DC, to make available the nation's archival materials, the NYHS president implied that New York, a state, was as important as those foreign nation-states and could rival those European publishing projects by gathering and publishing its own archival heritage.

As historical societies multiplied and expanded between the 1820s and 1840s, their members increasingly directed their collecting aims and publishing plans toward their state's distinctive archival record and historical narrative. In contrast with early attempts around the turn of the century by historical societies in Massachusetts and New York to archive the history of the entire nation, over the course of the antebellum period most historical societies sought to elevate the historical record of their respective state within the nation.

Although framed around their state, these seemingly separate missions had national stakes. Historical establishments believed that the exceptional archive of their state could reveal critical aspects of the nation's, if not global, history. Their efforts to prove it, however, were bedeviled by a sense that their archival collections were deficient, that advocates lacked ample public and government support, and that the American public underappreciated the value of these archives. Colonial materials could appear like "a hoard of materially unsound, temporally fragmented, politically fraught, and endangered papers."[2] For many historical societies and their boosters, this only invigorated their work to gather and publish historical documents deemed vital to authenticating their state's history, especially its colonial period. To show both the range and similarity of these undertakings, this chapter spotlights the efforts that historical establishments in Pennsylvania, Maine, Kentucky, and—most active among antebellum states—New York undertook to confront these challenges.

Unlike those contemporary efforts in Europe that Gallatin admired, the federal government's investment in gathering and publishing the nation's historical record in the antebellum United States did not extend beyond backing publication projects like Jared Sparks's and acquiring papers like George Washington's. In this context, states became the main sites for the work of salvaging, ordering, and disseminating historical documents through curated publications. To the extent that historical societies succeeded in these efforts, they did so by leveraging popular interest, activating networks of sympathetic collectors and patrons, garnering support from their state legislature, and—especially in the case of New York—directing the US diplomatic corps to facilitate access to historical records in European archives. Indeed, without access to national archives in the Netherlands, Britain, and France, the archival collections and publications in New York could not have taken the form or sustained the narratives envisioned by its historical establishment. New York combined popular interest, state patronage, and federal power to surpass other antebellum states in building and promoting its archive, which set a new model for the role of government in determining what fell within and outside the threshold of American archives before the Civil War.

The Stakes of State History

In the 1820s, historical societies tended to shift from earlier attempts to gather and make sense of the nation's entire past toward building archives that could situate their individual state prominently within the nation's history of colonization, independence, and progress. By recognizing the mission of the Maine Historical Society (MEHS) in 1822 to "illustrate any department of civil, ecclesiastical, and natural history, especially of this State, and of the United States," the state legislature hinted at this new relationship between the history of their state and the history of the nation: archiving the former came first, but this archive could meaningfully inform the latter.[3] Impediments, however, made it difficult for historical societies to access coveted materials to build such an archive, mobilize state residents and the legislature to sustain this undertaking, and convince other states to endorse the narratives that emerged from it, as the cases of Pennsylvania, Kentucky, and Maine itself illustrate.

Pennsylvania

Historical institutions in antebellum Pennsylvania exemplified this aspiration to distinguish their state's past and place it prominently within national history, as well as the difficulty of gathering the materials deemed necessary to do so. William Penn was the seminal figure in the historical narrative promoted within Pennsylvania, making any historical material that he had touched a most prized source for archival collections. From 1815, the short-lived Historical and Literary Committee of the American Philosophical Society (APS) convened a cohort of powerful local men, including the French-born polymath Peter Stephen Du Ponceau, who became its corresponding secretary.[4] Du Ponceau lamented the especially sorry and scattered state of Penn's manuscripts to the prominent local merchant Samuel Coates. "No body had yet thought of collection with holy zeal the precious relicks of a man to whom Heathen, Greece and Rome would have raised Altars," he complained. "Many of the memorials he has left behind him are suffered to moulder away and perish scatered in the hands of various individuals."[5] The APS hoped to remedy this, placing Penn at the center of their state's history and locating Pennsylvania where, Du Ponceau argued, it "deservedly stands in the foreground" of the nation's history.[6]

Organized after the decline of the APS Historical Committee in 1825, the Historical Society of Pennsylvania (HSP) similarly organized its collecting goals and the narrative that it envisioned for the state around Penn. In presenting itself to the public, the HSP officers assured Pennsylvanians that "the Society does not undertake to compose a history; its desire is to collect materials for history."[7] In the preamble to its constitution, the HSP asserted that "to collect and preserve the evidence of its own history from the earliest date, is both the duty and interest of every political society, whether its progress has been prosperous or disastrous."[8] Such language implied that historical societies were disinterested assemblers of archives, but in practice the influential leaders of institutions like the HSP were convinced that their state had a distinctive historical significance that their archive would authenticate. The very constitution of the HSP depicted Pennsylvania as a scene in which "an honest, virtuous, and pious people, relinquishing their early possessions and enjoyments, laid in a wild and uncultivated country, the foundations of a State, now eminently great, successful, and happy."[9] Rather than a mass of individual papers and facts, Pennsylvania's archives would support this special history of the state.

Even when near at hand, the materials to authenticate this vision of the state's exceptional history were not always easy to archive. This was on display in Deborah Norris Logan's management of the historical correspondence between Penn and her husband's grandfather, James Logan (1674–1751), a leading figure in colonial Pennsylvania and "the companion of Penn and the friend of the Indians," as her contemporaries saw him.[10] In 1781, she married the physician, diplomat, and politician George Logan and moved to Stenton, his family's suburban mansion in Philadelphia.[11] Perusing the family library in 1815, she "discovered in a very old box a treasure of—Old Papers—many Books of Letters. James Logan to William Penn, Folios of Letters. From Hannah Penn, and many others!"[12] Logan spent years transcribing and editing these documents, which she was reluctant to relinquish fully to the historical institutions that coveted them.[13]

For the APS and then the HSP, the Logan household held essential materials for illuminating Pennsylvania's colonial period and Penn's life in particular. "Biography of James Logan WANTED," the APS Historical Committee emphasized from its earliest meetings.[14] Word reached the APS about the "treasure of historical documents" that Logan had in her hands. Initially, she imagined a "a Cabinet of [documents] which might be of great advantage to elucidate the early history of Pennsylvania," where the "Gentlemen forming the Committee" could consult these archival materials and make copies.[15] In response to their entreaties, however, she agreed to arrange the mass of disorganized papers, transcribe selections, and annotate these documents.[16] The committee sent representatives and regular correspondence to Stenton to check on her progress. In late 1817, she shared her annotated transcriptions of John Logan's correspondence with Penn and other founding figures, original manuscripts of proceedings from Pennsylvania's colonial council, and a cash book kept by Penn.[17] Between 1817 and 1820, she produced three more volumes of transcriptions and an appendix, which her husband, George Logan, also conveyed to the APS committee. In all, it amounted to around one thousand pages. The committee's recording secretary made a copy of each volume for the APS to retain before returning the original transcriptions to Stenton.[18]

Logan mediated between these precious documents and the men who hoped to draw them across the archival threshold. In the process, her reputation as a historian grew. She noted, gratified, in her diary that "the historical committee of the P. Society have mentioned my work with much approbation."[19] They repeatedly sought permission to publish these materials "in pursuance of their general design of throwing light on the Hist. of Pennsylvania," which they imagined filling two eight-hundred-page volumes and selling well.[20] Logan hesitated, especially as her husband, George, declined and died in 1821, leaving her bereft. "There seems to be nothing in store for me in this world, but what will loose [sic] by comparison with the Past," she recorded to her diary in a "Memoranda of the desolate state of my mind."[21] With this grief she also inherited the Logan family papers, placing her in the company of the many widowed women and daughters who became the primary curators of household history in this period.[22]

As the APS Historical Committee dissolved, the HSP emerged in 1825 as the major institution for gathering the state's historical materials and soon turned its gaze to Stenton. Delivering his inaugural address at the University of Pennsylvania to a packed audience, President William Rawle announced, "There is still reason to believe that many private documents are still in existence, which would present to us, in colors strong and true, the enlightening, vivifying, and chastening power of [the founder of Pennsylvania's] genius on all around him."²³ The officers of the newly founded historical society quickly appealed to Logan for the manuscript correspondence in the hope that it could be archived and published.²⁴ She thought otherwise, confiding to her diary that, "now, unprotected, and conscious of my own deficiencies, for the share which I may take in the work, I dread to come before the publick, and had rather the Publication were deferred. I dread blame, and I want not praise."²⁵ As a widowed editor facing the prospect of public judgment, she viewed her relationship between personal historical materials and a public archive in a different light. Despite this impasse, the HSP nominated Logan as one of its first few honorary members in 1826—the first woman nominated to any historical society.

While papers such as Logan's remained out of reach, Penn and the exceptional state narrative that he embodied remained at the center of the archival aims of the HSP. Over the years, papers and artifacts related to Penn were donated to its archive. A silver coin depicted the Walking Treaty of 1737, Penn shaking hands with a Delaware Indian leader, the words "By Deeds of Peace" engraved on it, from which the HSP derived its emblem.²⁶ In 1845, the society's officers received a lock of Penn's hair encased in a ring from one of his descendants, which the president was required to wear at all future meetings, as if to entwine the president with Penn himself.²⁷ Beyond these clubby rituals, the HSP orchestrated larger public celebrations of Penn, such as his bicentennial birthday in 1844 and a 170th anniversary of his landing in Philadelphia in 1852. To the large crowd gathered that evening at the United States Hotel for an eight-course meal, one orator marveled, "In the short space of eighty years, Penn's woodland was converted into a cultivated country, rivalling, in some districts, the husbandry of Belgium. Savages were made to yield their land *willingly*, for a fair equivalent, to the industrious settler. And civilization (with brotherly love) was established in all our borders, solely by the mild influence of Quaker rule."²⁸ The figure of Penn symbolized this gratifying interpretation for the historical society, which hoped to distinguish Pennsylvania's origins and progress from other states'. The claim that Pennsylvania's settlers expanded civilization by engaging honorably with Delaware Indians made it possible "to paper over the violent eighteenth-century clashes between Penn's descendants and indigenous populations throughout the region."²⁹ Throughout this period, the society placed Penn and the larger historical trajectory that he represented at the center of its archival frame. However, the very effort to distinguish the state's origins resembled archival projects across the country, which, in seeking separately to enshrine their distinctive colonial origins, produced archives that collectively vindicated the nation's imperial expansion westward.

Kentucky

Even when states benefited from widespread public support of the history that they aimed to archive, these undertakings could languish in the absence of sustained backing by influential figures and state government. The early Kentucky Historical Society (KHS) bustled briefly and left few archival traces. Such a fate was common throughout the United States, where dozens of historical societies formed and disbanded in the decades prior to the Civil War. Of the fifty-eight documented historical societies organized in this period, almost half did not survive it.[30] However, in contrast with long-lasting historical societies like the HSP and MEHS, those in the western states of Illinois, Indiana, Iowa, Kentucky, Michigan, and Ohio found it especially testing to motivate members, generate public support, build an archival and library collection, and solidify as institutions.

In 1838, a cohort of elite Kentuckians and newly arrived New Englanders formed a historical society in Louisville designed to document the conquest, settlement, and development of Kentucky, which they believed would represent the nation's broader history of westward expansion.[31] The society's founding librarian and most zealous booster, the Massachusetts physician Edward Jarvis, explained that "the principal objects were the gathering of the records printed and written, manuscripts, letters, traditions—everything that could illustrate the early and recent history of Kentucky and the Western country."[32] Although Kentucky men endorsed the society, served as officers, and formed most of its membership, Jarvis and several fellow New England transplants drove the bulk of the society's efforts, hoping to re-create an institution that resembled the ones they knew back east.

Among them was the Massachusetts newspaperman and local historian Leonard Bliss, who in 1838 wrote from Louisville to James Savage, president of the Massachusetts Historical Society (MHS), for his help.[33] Bliss asked Savage for a copy of the MHS constitution, which he hoped might serve as a model for their own, and for copies of MHS publications. The letter reflected the clear power imbalance between an inchoate archive in a western state and the nation's oldest historical society. At the same time, Bliss let Savage know how the new western institution aimed to set itself apart. "Our Society will devote itself to Western history in the widest sense of the term," he explained.[34]

To archive this expansive historical terrain, the society drew on the support of prominent Kentucky men and the widespread veneration of the pioneer period as its last members faded away. In May 1840, Clark and Madison Counties organized a sixty-fifth anniversary celebration of "the first settlement of Kentucky" to recognize the building of Fort Boonesborough in 1775, a three-day commemoration bringing together Kentucky military companies, religious leaders, an eager public, and men and women of the pioneer generation and their descendants.[35] The *Kentucky Gazette* reported, "The true moral beauty of the celebration consisted in the grey haired band of pioneers who have survived to behold this day," including a daughter of Colonel Richard Calloway, who had built the fort alongside Daniel Boone.[36] "Every one was anxious to behold this noble relic of a noble race," who was placed prominently in the procession to the fort, according to the newspaper.[37] This event displayed the outpouring of popular interest in the white Euro-American historical narrative of conquest of Indigenous lands, settlement, and progress that the KHS sought to document.

Despite such widespread interest in the state's historical narrative, the KHS encountered major impediments to building an archive that could authenticate it. "Much was found in attics, in by-places, in sheds, some in damp, basement rooms," Jarvis recollected, "where they mildewed and moulded, and some were rotten."[38] Moreover, with the late introduction of printing presses and Kentucky's relatively brief history as a colony and state, there was simply less text to collect.[39] Jarvis explained that the state's pioneer generation, "eye-witnesses of those intense struggles, between the white and the red man, for possession of the bloody ground," was swiftly disappearing. He continued, "They have left to their children the legacy of the tales of their thrilling adventures. These traditions are sacredly treasured in their families, and transmitted as heir looms from father to son."[40] Although some committed these oral traditions to paper, these could not rival the many texts that historical societies in eastern states could archive. Meanwhile, a rapidly growing but relatively young and busy population was not easily mobilized to build the historical archive envisioned by these KHS officers.[41]

To stir public interest, Bliss published especially important manuscript items from this growing archive. Unable to produce the full-length publications regularly emitted by older historical societies, KHS members turned to this more ephemeral genre to promote their undertaking. As the new editor of Louisville's *Literary News-Letter*, Bliss published a series of eleven "Scraps of Western History" over the course of 1840. Introducing the series, he was at pains to distinguish the remarkable qualities of these historical materials from those in other states:

> These documents, consisting of letters, journals, memorandums, etc., show the "very age and body of the time, his form and pressure," better, perhaps, than learned essays or stately harangues. The pictures which they present of the toils and sufferings of the early pioneers, are vivid and to the life; for they are drawn by the real actors of the scenes they describe. We have found them scattered here and there; often in a very mutilated state, and frequently so difficult to decipher that nothing but the most eager curiosity with regard to all documents of the kind—a sort of historical mania—could have induced us to persevere in mastering their contents.[42]

Bliss praised the perseverance of the KHS in recovering these materials, which in their "very mutilated state" seemed to embody the physical hardships endured by their pioneer authors. In doing so, he also promised readers proximity to those "toils and sufferings," as if the reader could encounter these historical actors and conditions through the documents that they left behind. Publicizing these "scraps" was designed to inform, to show off, to stimulate donations of seemingly mundane historical materials, and to build the civic bond between the Kentucky public and their archive.

Despite popular interest in attending events and reading periodicals that celebrated the pioneer period, the state government in Frankfort did little to bolster the new institution beyond furnishing a small number of donations. Having failed to secure government support the previous year, the KHS successfully petitioned the state legislature in January 1841 to supply it with newly published state documents as well as copies, when available, of past publications.[43] For 1842, the one year when the KHS seems to have received a donation of books from the state librarian, Jarvis documented these accessions and returned the thanks of the society. The donation included, by the librarian's count, seventy-three volumes comprising US executive documents, US congressional reports and papers, and state legislative papers. Jarvis, however, complained in a letter to Governor Robert Letcher that the donation did not meet his expectations. Fewer volumes of published state papers arrived than promised, Jarvis charged, some of these were duplicates, and in transit to Louisville "one volume was spoiled, being thoroughly saturated with linseed oil, on the boat."[44] The destruction by fire twice over in 1813 and 1824 of most printed and historical materials held in the state capital buildings did not help.[45] But Jarvis's influence within the legislature was lacking, too.

These meager acquisitions revealed the limits of the KHS's ability to gather and preserve historical resources. Although incorporated by the state and counting several politicians among its members, the KHS did not secure meaningful public support from the community for which it was building the archive. The society lacked basic resources enjoyed by larger historical societies. The members most eager to meet, archive, and publish through the society did not have deep roots in the state. Meetings rotated among their households. Lacking institutional space, Jarvis turned his medical office—already serving as his bedroom most nights when he did not return to his boardinghouse—into a makeshift archive. "It had no other home," he wrote simply.[46] Jarvis concurred with KHS president John Rowan, one of the state's longest-serving politicians, who reportedly told him that he would need to ask men in northern states for help gathering documents, "for they, not the Southern men, were accustomed to save."[47]

By the early 1840s, Jarvis had returned to Massachusetts, Rowan and recording secretary Daniel Chapman Banks had died, corresponding secretary Bliss was murdered in the street by a rival newspaperman, and vice president George Mortimer Bibb relocated to Washington, DC, to become US secretary of the treasury. Missing its most active members and buy-in from the community it intended to serve, the society soon lost momentum, and its swiftly built collection began to disperse.[48] "At his removal from the city and his return to Boston," Jarvis recorded in a third-person account, "the Society began to languish, and languishing it became extinct. The library was scattered or destroyed."[49] The KHS had hoped to replicate a state-centric frame for its history and, like the historical establishment in Pennsylvania, distinguish the role of its founding and progress within the larger trajectory of the nation. However compelling this narrative to people in Kentucky, with neither sustained support from the state nor a coherent community of collectors, the society disbanded.

Maine

Even when its own historical establishment, broader public, and state government were committed, the attempt to archive and argue for a state's distinctive past could encounter resistance or indifference beyond its borders. Following its belated statehood in 1820, Maine's historical establishment hoped to recast the coast and territory of Maine as an important site in the nation's history that could, like Pennsylvania's settler generation or Kentucky's pioneers, distinguish it—especially from Massachusetts. The historical society was swiftly founded after Maine's statehood and incorporated enthusiastically by the state legislature with this goal in mind. The crafters of Maine's historical record sought to depict Maine as an early site of exploration and colonization and a crucial space in the imperial wars for North America, but this narrative met the skepticism of outside readers.

As in most other states, the men of Maine's historical establishment wanted to build an archive that documented the generations who conquered and settled its territory, employing the state's distinctive resources and their own attributes to advance what they perceived as civilization within the state.[50] This left Maine within the shadow of Massachusetts, however, where for years archival institutions and historians had insisted that their state was preeminent within the arc of American history. Daniel Webster's well-known Plymouth Oration in December 1820 was a potent articulation of this. "We feel," the famed orator projected that day, "that we are on the spot where the first scene of our history was laid; where the hearths and altars of New England were first places; where Christianity, and civilization, and letters made their first lodgement, in a vast extent of country, covered with a wilderness, and peopled by roving barbarians."[51] From the vantage point of Maine, this meant that their state's influence on the nation's history could only be marginal to the historical significance of Massachusetts.[52]

It took nearly a decade for the MEHS to gather the documents, secure the funds, and develop the network of members necessary to issue its first *Collections* in 1831. Some documents in that volume depicted Maine as a pivotal site of American history, such as an account of American Indian linguistics and French missionaries by deceased Maine governor Enoch Lincoln, which broadened the scope of the state's history well beyond its borders. "It may be observed," the editor introduced Lincoln's work,

> that the field of these researches, to an intelligent investigator, is not strictly confined to the original, or even the existing, geography of Maine; but that it may be considered as extended in some measure over the whole surface which once formed the scene of contest between the French and English titles in this quarter.... The large tract of territory embraced by this bold, and vague, and somewhat irregular outline ... forming the subject of fierce conflict, upon the debatable ground, between the national arms of France and England ... may be termed the *Flanders,* or in more modern phraseology, the *Belgium,* of America.[53]

By publishing these papers in its *Collections*, the society claimed that Maine was a meaningful part of the much larger scene on which the defining struggle in colonial North American history played out: the wars for the future of the continent between the French and British empires. In doing so, it cast Maine within an imagined geographic context far greater than its contemporary boundaries—at a moment, moreover, when the contemporary US-Canadian border remained undefined and tensely contested, leading to the Aroostook War and widespread sympathy for Maine's territorial claims by the end of the decade.[54] "No scope less ample" could explain Maine's role amid the historical change in the colonial and revolutionary period, the editor continued. The analogy between Maine and Flanders or Belgium would have evoked the Dutch war of independence against Spanish rule (1568–1648), or the decisive British victory at Waterloo over French forces in the Napoleonic Wars, both instances—many antebellum readers would have understood—where progressive Protestant forces triumphed over oppressive Catholic foes.[55]

In subsequent publications and public events, the society also aimed to distinguish the first colonists of Maine, however ineffectively. The second *Collections* appeared after a long delay in 1847, as was often the case as historical societies secured funding and prepared a new volume. It featured a number of documents that illuminated Maine's earliest colonial history, including "A Brief Narration of the Original Undertakings of Plantations in

America" by Sir Ferdinando Gorges, the Lord Proprietor of early Maine, "A Voyage to New England, in 1623" by Christopher Levett, and the 1846 annual discourse to the society from historian George Folsom, who examined the failed attempt to establish the Popham Colony in 1607, the ephemeral settlement at Sagadahoc under Sir John Popham.

This emphasis on England's first plantation along the Kennebec River in the fierce winter of 1607 placed the origin of New England history on Maine's coast more than a decade before the Pilgrim landing in Massachusetts. However, even Folsom—born in Maine but by that point a well-established historian and historical society member in New York— questioned the character of those transient settlers who departed prematurely the following year. By contrast, he apostrophized, "how superior was the spirit exhibited twelve years after by the Pilgrim emigrants at Plymouth."[56] Despite such ambivalence toward Maine's first English settlers, the narrative of Maine's founding was compelling because it predated the later settlements in Massachusetts. George Burgess, Maine's first Episcopal bishop and soon vice president of its historical society, noted in his 1854 address to the society that "colonial enterprise was earlier here than in any other Northern State."[57]

The Popham colony reappeared in MEHS meetings, publications, and nowhere more prominently than in Burgess's own address before a large crowd assembled at the newly constructed Fort Popham at the mouth of the Kennebec River on the 256th anniversary of the colony's founding in 1862. Built in defense of a nation at war with itself, this large garrison of sandstone also gave Maine the chance to position the original settlement of Popham within a historical arc that linked that first enfeebled settlement to the modern military and industrial heft of the United States.[58] The completion of a major federal fort at the mouth of the Kennebec River seemed to retroactively vindicate Popham, suggesting a trajectory between a wilderness fort's defense of its first settlers and the defense of the nation during the Civil War.[59]

Yet the celebration of Maine's first colonial settlement was muffled by a more critical discourse that very day, by John Wingate Thornton, a fellow Mainer and leading New England historian and genealogist based in Boston who had been invited by the society to expound on the settlement's legacy. Before the crowd, he cast Sir John Popham's first attempt and Sir Ferdinando Gorges's subsequent settlement scheme as ill-conceived and morally vacant. Gorges, he argued, wanted only to conquer land with the surplus of idle military men in England, rather than institute pious, civil government. In contrast to the Plymouth plantation, which set into motion the course of national history, Thornton suggested that this first settlement was predestined to fall by the wayside. Evoking the popular belief that the Pilgrim Mary Chilton had been the first English settler to set foot on Plymouth Rock, Thornton waxed, "There is a pleasing tradition that Plymouth Rock was first pressed by the feet of a woman, the pioneer of our colonization, the central figure in the Christian home; her gentle presence was a surer pledge of success than were the stalwart soldiers under Popham's charge."[60] It surely shook the confidence of the many listeners to hear that neither the ground they stood on nor the founders who claimed it were a stable historical sediment for the formation of the state's historical identity. "His speech is rather keeping with truth and fact," the *North American Review* summarized, "rather than with the expectations of those who invited him."[61] In the large memorial volume of the event that MEHS secretary Edward Ballard published afterward, Thornton's address was jettisoned; the Popham skeptic would publish it separately.[62]

Moved perhaps by this struggle to distinguish Maine's colonial history, the MEHS collaborated with the state government in the years after the Civil War to gather and publish materials that emphasized the significance of Maine within the imperial contest over the continent. In 1867, society leaders successfully lobbied the state legislature to appropriate funds for the publication of a documentary history of records gathered from private collections in Europe related to Gorges and Popham, as well as "treasures of ancient time preserved in English archives" and other national repositories in Spain, Holland, and France. They hoped to document all early European exploration along Maine's coastline and meaningfully place the state within a far larger Atlantic history that could be traced back to the medieval voyages of the Norse.[63] Struggling to frame the history of their state in a way that would have significance for the nation's larger history, Maine's historical establishment ambitiously sought archival material that might place its origins within a wider global frame.

Leonard Woods, former Bowdoin College president and longtime society member, undertook the task during what he had intended as a retirement tour of Europe. Arguing for the significance of these papers to the leading British antiquary Sir Thomas Phillips, he explained, "The state of

Maine was for more than a century the principal battleground between the French and English. . . . [T]here more than anywhere else, it was decided that English Protestantism should be the governing power." Woods continued, "It is a constant allegation of our publications that had it not been for Sir Ferdinando Gorges and . . . Popham, the founders of our state, the Western Continent must have fallen under . . . Roman Catholic France, and that if not by these colonies in Maine, more than by everything else, that North America was saved not only for England but for Protestantism."[64] In Europe, Maine sought the archival materials to authenticate the state's distinctive history, whether as a site for colonization since the time of the Norse or a critical borderlands in the struggle between French and English empire from which the United States emerged. In venturing to archives across the Atlantic to fill in the frame for its state's history, Maine followed in the wake of New York, where a committed historical establishment and state government had succeeded in amassing and publishing archival materials that impressed Americans beyond its borders.

Archives of the Empire State

Reclaiming

Perhaps no residents felt as anxious about the state of their archives as New York's. Destroyed, moldering at the state capitol in boxes, or held across the ocean, materials for the state's Dutch colonial chapter seemed deficient, indecipherable, and vulnerable to mischaracterization in the eyes of the state's historical establishment. The rest of the colonial period following the English conquest in the 1660s also seemed patchy compared to colonial archives in other states, undermining New York's historiography of this period. "The truth is," Jared Sparks bluntly observed to Catharine Maria Sedgwick in 1833 as she worked on her historical romance of the Revolution, "there is no such thing as a history of New York during the Revolution, nor any account of the military operations in that state." One Massachusetts resident to another, Sparks indicted the "literati of New York" for their general disregard of their history: "Neither patriotism, ambition, the love of doing good, nor the shame of insignificance, will kindle the spirit, prompt the resolution, or move the will. The Atlas is left to rest on the shoulders of posterity."[65] Similar to the criticism that Alexis de Tocqueville leveled against the United States as a whole, Sparks questioned the capacity of New York to tell its own history.

Powerful New Yorkers agreed with Sparks. They sensed that a deficient archival collection undermined their ability to document New York's triumphant rise from its Dutch founding, through revolutionary upheaval, toward its booming nineteenth-century growth. To gather and promote an archive that could authenticate this history, they took action. By the eve of the Civil War, the NYHS had secured unprecedented support from the state government, an enthusiastic public, and the diplomatic arm of the federal government to this end, surpassing by far efforts in other states.

In the early nineteenth century, the NYHS feared that Washington Irving's sensational and wildly popular account of New Netherland under Dutch colonial rule had elbowed out their effort to distinguish the state's history. In Irving's *History of New York, from the Beginning of the World to the End of the Dutch Dynasty* (1809), the fictive narrator Diedrich Knickerbocker delighted readers as an affable, hapless, Dutch-descended chronicler of New York.[66] Beyond the walls of the historical society, New Yorkers "claimed Diedrich Knickerbocker for their mascot and muse, as never before."[67] As Boston's leading periodical explained, "The meagre annals of this short-lived Dutch colony have afforded the ground work for this amusing book, which is certainly the wittiest our press has ever produced."[68] The appraisal had some truth to it, given that the manuscripts from New Netherland stored in Albany were untranslated and in a seventeenth-century Dutch script, making them nearly as indecipherable to nineteenth-century Americans as Old Icelandic.

Members of New York's historical establishment were aggrieved that Irving's work had caused a rupture between the state's colonial origins and nineteenth-century New Yorkers, subverting the whole enterprise of comprehensively archiving the state's distinctive history.[69] Indeed, Irving's popularity diminished interest in a historical account of New Netherland based on the manuscripts that the NYHS aimed to archive and publicize. It upended the progressive narrative imagined by NYHS leaders, in which a modest settlement infused with virtuous attributes rose majestically along the Hudson River. Irving's *History*, in contrast, featured "placid Dutch burghers" who "do little but eat, sleep, and pull on their pipes in ever obscuring clouds of smoke."[70] While the NYHS attempted to adorn the Hudson with compelling historical associations, Irving's work vacated this setting of serious history, creating space for his caricatures to frolic.[71] Knickerbocker was a charismatic lampoon of the collectors who might donate materials to the NYHS archive or the historian who would craft them into a meaningful narrative of the state. His "researches among the family chests and lumber garrets of our respectable Dutch citizens" were precisely the materials that the NYHS hoped New Yorkers would donate to its archive; such accessions might be announced at a historical society meeting and recorded in its minutes, listed in a society's published library catalogue, or reprinted in its *Collections*.[72] Knickerbocker's satisfaction in the "host of well authenticated traditions from divers excellent old ladies" made archival accession seem an indecent, rather than a reverent, civic act.

In a jeremiad before the NYHS, the Dutch-descended civic leader Gulian Crommelin Verplanck crystallized the consternation of New York's historical establishment.[73] Verplanck tried to recast the significance of New Netherland within the larger history of not only the state's but national and global history. "We have no cause to blush for any part of our original descent, and least of all for our Dutch Ancestry," he reassured his audience. Their colony, he recalled, had been founded by the United Provinces as it entered its age of remarkable accomplishments, "after a long, bloody, and most glorious struggle against civil and religious tyranny, during which all the energies of patriotism, courage, and talents, had been suddenly and splendidly developed."[74] Alone against contemporary European monarchies, the Dutch republic represented a bastion of political liberty, commerce, and intellectual advances in science, law, literature, and art, he claimed. Verplanck depicted this Dutch Golden Age as both a historical antecedent to "the wisdom and equality of our own institutions." He suggested that the spirit behind the Dutch struggle for liberty against Spanish oppression could be traced to the colonial period of New Netherland, through the transfer of power to English rule, and into the eventual independence of the United States and growth of the new republic.

To seize control of this narrative required seizing control of New York's archival materials both within the state and in national repositories in Europe. In 1814, NYHS vice president and New York City mayor DeWitt Clinton issued a memorial from the NYHS to the New York state legislature warning that "documents that may illuminate the obscure, explain the doubtful, and embalm the memories of the good and the great, may now be drawn from their dark abodes, where in a few years they will be forgotten or lost."⁷⁵ The scattering of the state's colonial records vexed him in particular: papers from the Dutch period strewn among New York, neighboring states, and the Netherlands; transactions of New York's Indian commissioners "conveyed away" by Loyalist Sir John Johnson during the Revolution; copious colonial materials held in London's Plantation Office and the British Museum.⁷⁶ Clinton called on the liberal support of its "enlightened" legislators, hoping to flatter the state government to assume a role supporting a scholarly institution that was more common of European nation-states than states in the US republic.

Clinton's ambitious goal of retrieving materials from Europe exceeded the capacity of the early NYHS or the will of the state at that moment, but as governor between 1817 and 1828 he directed unprecedented state resources toward its colonial materials.⁷⁷ During these years, the Dutch expatriate and polymath Francis Adrian van der Kemp, a radical republican leader in the Dutch Patriot movement and champion of the American Revolution, delved into the "Albany Papers," the collection of Dutch-language documents from the West India Company stored in the New York State House. Van der Kemp regarded translation as a civic duty to his adopted nation.⁷⁸

Yet as the project dragged on and his vision deteriorated, Van der Kemp echoed NYHS concerns about the state's treatment of its compelling Dutch past. He complained that "all New Yorkers . . . who dare to consult the translated Dutch record must blush with shame and confusion when they reflect how ignorant this State is of what it owes" to the early Dutch leaders.⁷⁹ Writing to his long-standing correspondent Thomas Jefferson, he found certain Dutch colonial petitions "So bold So provoking—considering the association—in this state—and N. Engl—I See the Embryo—Seed of Revolutionary principles—which in time were to be developed."⁸⁰ Like Verplanck, Van der Kemp saw in the Dutch colony the qualities and principles that distinguished their state within the larger trajectory of American history. Although Van der Kemp did not publish these records, in translating some twenty-four folios containing more than ten thousand pages under the aegis of the state, however imperfectly, he began the work of aligning these archives with the historical vision of the state espoused by its historical establishment (while reaping some eight thousand dollars for his services along the way).⁸¹

At first, due to wobbly finances and wavering support from the state in the 1820s and 1830s, the NYHS and its advocates in the state government struggled to build the archive that would sustain their vision of the state's history. By the late 1830s, however, the NYHS had steadied its finances, found new accommodations, enhanced its public image, and secured an unprecedented degree of state support for its work; it had "gained a new existence," in one officer's words.[82] After years of declaring the deficiency of their current archives and the promise that their full colonial record held, the NYHS set into motion not only the machinery of the state but the diplomatic power of the federal government.

Repatriating

In 1839, a NYHS committee led by the popular travel writer John Lloyd Stephens petitioned the state's governor, William Seward, to finance the search for American colonial papers in major European archives that Clinton had proposed a quarter century earlier, without which "no true and perfect history of this state can ever be written." New York, the committee flattered, "stands as a wonder in the history of the world; and in a few years will almost surpass human belief, and then, the smallest scrap which illustrates its former condition will be regarded as a precious memorial."[83] Seward was a receptive audience, having vocally supported the project for almost a decade.[84] He did them one better by adding France to the proposed itinerary of the Netherlands and Britain, reasoning that the century of French and British combat along colonial New York's borderland was among "the most interesting and important particulars of our history."[85] Steward encapsulated the broader aim that "every important circumstance connected with the rise and progress of our free institutions should be recorded and illustrated."[86] Since the 1820s, a handful of states had urged the federal government to support such a project and even undertaken their own limited efforts to do so.[87] Steward's support catapulted New York into this undertaking. He quickly ushered the bill before the legislature, which allocated four thousand dollars in initial funding for a state agent to visit Dutch, British, and French archives. Over the following three years, the state would funnel an additional eight thousand dollars into the project.

Among the numerous applicants who vied for the coveted position, Seward selected the twenty-seven-year-old New Yorker John Romeyn Brodhead, an unlikely choice who very well could have failed this mission to repatriate, as many saw it, these vital documents.[88] Writing to Brodhead with instructions for the post, Seward explained grandly that, "in recommending those objects to the Legislature, I observed that their successful accomplishment would advance the cause of free government throughout the world, and that it was due to ourselves and to the memory of our predecessors, and to a just regard for the respect of posterity, that every important circumstance connected with the rise and progress of our free institutions should be recorded and illustrated."[89] Like many advocates of America's archives, the governor perceived a direct link between enshrining historical evidence of this exceptionalism and ensuring its future—not only for New York, but "throughout the world."

Brodhead had just returned from a stint in the Netherlands, where he was the secretary to US Minister Harmanus Bleecker's legation to the Hague, one among the cast of young, aspiring American men who landed such foreign sinecures in the expanding US diplomatic corps. Unlike Washington Irving in Madrid or Henry Wheaton in Copenhagen or correspondents of Jared Sparks such as Joel Poinsett in Mexico, Brodhead was a tepid diplomatic representative, remaining at arm's length from his foreign environs. "I do not find that I am doing any good here," he sighed as the new year turned, "and wish that I were far away."[90] Brodhead, relieved, returned home in 1840. But after winning the archival commission that winter, he returned to Europe the following year with more wind in his sails, emboldened with the confidence that his three-country mission could serve the higher aims outlined by Seward.

Compared to the previous decades, by the 1840s the capacity of the US diplomatic corps in western Europe had strengthened substantially, facilitating Brodhead's mission. Moreover, US ministers sympathetic to his accessing and copying documents were positioned in the Netherlands, Britain, and France. Brodhead's former boss, Bleecker, a longtime Albany lawyer and close friend to President Martin van Buren, remained as chargé d'affaires at the Hague until 1842. When Bleecker arrived in Europe in 1839, he saw himself as the "representative of the descendants of the Dutch in Albany."[91] He met positive press and a warm reception from the Dutch monarch, who had met Van Buren, a Dutch-speaking descendent of New Amsterdam colonists, several years earlier.[92] Bleecker participated in the tradition of elite Americans perceiving a transatlantic, transhistorical link between the seventeenth-century United Provinces and his own nineteenth-century republic.[93] As New York historians had espoused since the founding of the NYHS at the turn of the century, the Dutch colony was the first page of an epic state history culminating in the metropolis of New York. Reflecting on Brodhead's project, Bleecker shared with an old friend in New York: "In contemplating the history of our State, we, naturally, dwell on its marked successive periods: when it was a Dutch colony; when it was subject to Great Britain; when it had emerged from the colonial State;—and then . . . the crowning epoch . . . the blessed union!—dear to the wise and good of our common country, and interesting the enlightened philanthropists of all other countries."[94] Viewing his state's history in this light, Bleecker was quick to champion Brodhead's search for relevant records in the Royal Archives. In the spring of 1841, he arranged for Brodhead to meet King William at the royal palace as well as the Dutch foreign minister and interior minister, who was responsible for the state records.[95] With Bleecker's advocacy of the project and the generally positive disposition of Dutch officials, Brodhead was soon cheered by the "generous and liberal policy" of access to the Royal Archives that summer and autumn.

Brodhead depended on the enthusiasm and discretion of the commissioner Johannes De Zwaan and other employees of the Royal Archives to detect and copy relevant colonial papers. Parcel by parcel, he received these copies from De Zwaan and began to catalogue them. By October, this had amounted to 1,700 pages, and the following month he received the "tremendous bundle" of all remaining documents copied by De Zwaan. "Thanks be to god," he exhaled in his diary, "who has given me the victory!"[96] As Brodhead traveled to Amsterdam in August in search of West India Company papers, Bleecker again gained approval for him to visit the state archives there, this time from the Dutch minister for the navy and colonies.[97] Brodhead proceeded to London that autumn, and De Zwaan continued to ship small collections of copied documents to him there.

Across the Channel in England, Brodhead confronted the geopolitical tension due to the ongoing dispute with Britain over the US and Canadian border, but he also benefited from the presence and sympathy of the newly arrived US minister and former Massachusetts governor Edward Everett. Everett became a well-liked member of London's diplomatic and literary scene, which included the Earl Stanhope, then in the midst of writing his major history of eighteenth-century England.[98] Similar to Bleecker, Everett understood himself as an interlocutor between records in Britain and Americans seeking to access archival evidence about their past. In London, he pursued historical records for himself and Massachusetts visitors such as the MHS president James Savage and historian George Bancroft while disputing tariffs and British naval searches of American vessels suspected of slave-trading.[99]

Brodhead and he initially struggled to pry open what seemed the rigidly guarded State Papers Office, the "Sovereign's own Private Library," as Brodhead later described it.[100] Brodhead bristled at the ongoing impediments to the British archives that he encountered into 1842. "It is very singular," the *New-York Tribune* censured back home, "that such narrow-minded policy should prevail in relation to a subject purely literary."[101] A half century after the resolution of the American Revolution, the Northeast Boundary between British Canada and Maine remained disputed. The British Foreign Office feared that American interlopers in the State Papers Office might serve not as "purely literary" researchers but also as government agents seeking documents to bolster US land claims. The NYHS had indeed already sought to assist US negotiators by sharing materials from their own collections, and men like Everett, Sparks, Irving, and others were all hopeful to uncover favorable proof in European archives before formal negotiations opened between Secretary of State Daniel Webster and British emissary Lord Ashburton in 1842. Brodhead, however, unswerving from his task, disregarded the apparent evidence in favor of the US claim that he came across.[102]

By the spring of 1842, Brodhead benefited from Everett's skill at easing access to the State Papers Office, which coincided with the relaxation of tension around the Northeast Boundary Dispute. To aid Brodhead and other American researchers, Everett leveraged the gradually emerging norm of international access to foreign historical archives, which Sparks had advanced in the 1820s. To allay fears that the United States would exploit this access, he explained that Brodhead's request was "made on behalf of the State of New York exclusively; nor has the United States Government any interest in the result, beyond that which it must take in every enterprise designed to illustrate American History." Whereas earlier US ministers had requested a privilege to access British archives, Everett recast New York's request as a principle that advanced the production of knowledge rather than any nation-state's self-interest. Holding up the Dutch monarchy's openness to Brodhead as a standard, Everett suggested that the principle of open archives was a broader international ideal. And "her Majesty's government," he cajoled Lord Aberdeen, the British secretary of state for foreign affairs, "has never permitted itself to be surpassed by any other, in the Countenance which it has, at all times, extended to every judicious effort for the promotion of useful knowledge." By calming British anxiety that the United States would use evidence gathered by American researchers, Everett enabled the State of New York to produce "useful knowledge" toward its own ends.[103]

When, in March 1842, Everett recounted a positive conversation with Aberdeen about their request, Brodhead felt his "heart overwhelmed at the sudden change of my affairs.... Joy, gratitude, sorrow for my having been 'dis' contented and ungrateful before, overcame me by turns, and I had to lock my door, but anyone should interrupt my flood of tears.... I do not remember when ever before I felt such overwhelming emotion of such a peculiar kind. If I ever thanked God fervently and sincerely for his goodness, it was this day. I consider this hour *the brightest in my whole life.*"[104] Brodhead's nearly sublime moment in the archives reflected the stakes he perceived in his mission to repatriate his state's colonial record. Those archived papers and the gates guarding them were a source of great strain on Brodhead, who, stymied for months in an unfamiliar country, came to see access to the British records as an almost existential undertaking in service of his goal to repatriate crucial documents for New York's history across its archival threshold.

From another vantage point, Brodhead remained a typical political appointee, fretting over the accomplishment of his task, exasperated by the administrative hurdles imposed by the British gatekeepers. "The dear knows I have been unfortunate in respect to this English business," he fussed in his diary.[105] His securing access to the British records eventually facilitated a routine process that would help to close the gap between American researchers and the foreign records going forward.[106] Initially, Brodhead was permitted to peruse just three of the many volumes cataloguing New York records. A State Papers officer monitored him as he inserted slips of paper next to records he wished to be transcribed. The list was forwarded to Aberdeen, who would approve or cross out documents with a red line. Finally, a copyist of the State Papers Office's choice would make a transcription of the acceptable documents.[107]

At Everett's urging, Brodhead came to receive access to a larger array of volumes in 1842, and the Foreign Office's review process became more perfunctory. When MHS president James Savage arrived that summer eager to examine British records in the State Papers Office, Everett could ask Aberdeen on behalf of Savage "for the continuance of the liberality, for which we are already under great obligations to your Lordship."[108] Brodhead became so pleased with his access that he enthusiastically nominated the State Papers Office chief clerk, Robert Lemon, for NYHS membership, "persuaded that the State [of New York] is greatly his debtor."[109] Lemon applauded in return the "wisdom and energy to procure to consolidation and to transmit to posterity those authentic stores of information in which alone the undoubted source of history can be sought and obtained."[110]

As Brodhead worked his way through the former Board of Trade papers at the State Papers Office, he prompted General Lewis Cass, US minister to France, to see if the French would be amenable to a similar request. As with Bleecker and Everett, Cass arrived at his post with a distinct interest in his host country's imperial history in North America and the archival materials from that period. As territorial governor of Michigan, Cass had also founded its historical society in 1828, where he was especially intrigued by the history of French exploration and settlement in the region.[111] But it was above all the century-long contest for supremacy between the French and British that authenticated Michigan's historical significance in his eyes.

In France, Cass was well-placed to support Brodhead's work inscribing the French and British imperial contest into America's archive and history, the very topic that had moved Seward to include France in Brodhead's archival itinerary in the first place. On Brodhead's request, Cass applied directly to François Guizot, the renowned historian then serving as King Louis Philippe's foreign minister. Guizot was an eager student of American history, having recently published his flattering "Essay on the Character and Influence of Washington," part of the abridged French edition of Jared Sparks's *Writings of Washington*.[112] Arriving in Paris in the early summer of 1842, Brodhead was assisted by a French archivist in his search through the archives of the Navy Department, which he found voluminous but in disarray. Still, Brodhead returned to London in the fall satisfied with his collection of copies from the French archives. When he settled back in Paris the following autumn, he was even more successful, benefitting from the help of the American journalist Benjamin Perley Poore, whom Massachusetts would later appoint as its archival agent in France. Looking back from New York, Brodhead praised "His Majesty's Government" for granting access "in the spirit of broad and liberal courtesy, for which the French Government has become almost proverbial."[113]

Brodhead's mission to these three European capitals promised to make good on the New York historical establishment's decades-long, uneven attempt to authenticate their vision of the state's history. Although presented to Europe's archival gatekeepers as a disinterested desire to examine America's history, it served New York's interest to elevate the significance of its historical record and place within the nation. Awaiting the arrival of Brodhead's materials, the legal scholar and NYHS member William Lawrence Beach pronounced at the 1842 annual meeting that "we cannot too emphatically declare, that the history of New York is not yet to be written."[114] When Brodhead's resources wobbled in mid-1842, halfway through his archival work, he and the NYHS argued successfully against cutting off state funding. Writing to Bleecker, Brodhead insisted that continuing the research "is demanded by the *honor*, as well as by the *interest* of the state."[115] At their January 1843 meeting, the NYHS stressed the importance that "an immense and invaluable mass of historical documents be added to our archives, supplying the gaps and deficiencies that have heretofore prevented the full illustration of our annals, and enduring to all time, a splendid and worthy monument of the enlightened forecast, liberality, and patriotism of the State."[116] Though some legislators argued that it was a wasteful investment, Albany approved an additional three thousand dollars that spring. As Brodhead completed his research, the NYHS began to voice a new confidence that their archive and history could finally validate "the patriotic design of the founders of the institution." As the volumes were about to ship from Europe, the legal scholar James Kent announced, "they have been redeemed from confusion and made conveniently accessible to the scholar and the antiquary; and can now, with great satisfaction, be presented to the view of our citizens, and of intelligent strangers."[117] In this light, Brodhead had not simply procured copies of important documents but "redeemed" them, restoring their value within the frame of New York's history.

Once Brodhead was back in Manhattan in 1844, his work was celebrated in one of the largest spectacles ever organized by a historical society—the evening when John Quincy Adams pronounced that historical societies "must be regarded as among the most useful Institutions upon earth."[118] Two hundred fifty influential Americans converged for the fortieth anniversary of the NYHS to fete Brodhead, who described himself in his address that evening as "the child of the society."[119] As Brodhead told the audience in Manhattan, "every old Document rescued, every memorial preserved, every scrap added to our Records, is an additional link in the chain that binds us to our country."[120] Brodhead's return was recognized in other states as a distinctive success for New York, which spoke "nobly for the liberality of New-York, and of her proper sense of what is due to herself and the future."[121] These texts, salvaged in their copied form from European archives, could be placed both within the security of New York's archives and within the arc of its progressive history, as the attendees perceived it.

At the same time, New York's successful repatriation of these materials had national stakes. The legal scholar and Supreme Court Justice Joseph Story complimented the New York Historical Society's contribution upon Brodhead's return in 1844 as a national success: "I look upon the efforts of your Society as of great importance to our common country, and, in connection with the other Societies of a like nature in other States, as destined to furnish an ample means for a true and worthy history of the foundation and progress of the Colonies which so gloriously achieved the independence of the Republic."[122] Much impressed by the archival cargo, George Bancroft wrote that "by exciting the emulation of other States, and of the country collectively, [they] will not fail to stimulate inquiry, till we shall have among ourselves all that remains in European archives, commemorating the wisdom or the heroism of our fathers."[123] Bancroft had recently returned from his own archival research in London. In 1846, he would depart again to serve as the nation's lead diplomat there. For the following three years, he kept one hand always in the British archive. That night, he imagined his and Brodhead's Atlantic transits as part of a state-by-state endeavor to extract and reclaim all American manuscripts from European archives until copies or originals of every document related to their colonial forebears had been brought west.

New York's archival accomplishment also resonated beyond the United States, Brodhead and others argued. Reporting to the New York legislature upon his return, Brodhead observed, "It has been made a subject of reproach to this country, by enemies of republican institutions, that no care is taken among us to preserve our ancient records, a charge implying a semi-barbarous condition of society." A shift was under way, however, "for public attention is beginning to be more and more directed to the importance of rescuing from destruction whatever may tend to illustrate the rise and progress of our institutions, and exhibit, in bolder relief, the character and labors of the pioneers of civilization upon the shores of the new world." Repatriating these materials vindicated not just New York's but America's reputation. Brodhead applauded that New York "has been among the foremost of the confederation to vindicate her self-respect to the world."[124] By leveraging public enthusiasm, state funding, and federal diplomatic support, Brodhead's mission served not only to fill in the frame for New York's distinctive historical record. The extensive attention to this project—surpassing efforts in states such as Pennsylvania, Kentucky, and Maine—distinguished New York's historical records and narrative within the broader frame of the nation and, as Brodhead and others saw it, elevated America's archives in the eyes of the world.

Republishing

New York's transatlantic archival mission made possible an unprecedented series of publicly funded publications that documented the state's exceptional historical trajectory from Dutch settlement to national independence. Soon after Brodhead's return, Edmund Bailey O'Callaghan emerged as the unlikely steward of this project. For decades he had crossed borders, learned new languages and skills, and enmeshed himself in diverse networks. O'Callaghan spent a childhood influenced by "The Liberator" Daniel O'Connell's Catholic emancipation movement against British rule, joined university opposition to the policies of the Bourbon Restoration that shuttered his medical school in Paris, and provided medical care to the impoverished community of newly arrived Irish immigrants in Quebec. There he waded into politics, editing the *Irish Vindicator* and partnering with Canadian Patriote leader Louis-Joseph Papineau. When the Lower Canada Rebellion against British imperial rule misfired in 1837, its leaders scattered, and he took refuge in New York with his young family, settling once again into a new life in the Atlantic world.[125]

O'Callaghan quickly took a keen interest in American history, and in New Netherland in particular. While writing for *Northern Light*, a periodical edited by John Romeyn Beck, head of the State Library, O'Callaghan began examining the past of his adopted state where, it was later reported, he was disturbed to find "a lapse of more than half a century in the connected

FIGURE 10. Portrait of Emund Bailey O'Callaghan, "the Archivist of New York." (Frontispiece of Catalogue of the Library of the Late E. B. O'Callaghan [New York, 1882]; image from Archive.org)

history of a people not yet two centuries and a half old!"[126] Encouraged by Beck and other influential historians, O'Callaghan mined the State Library, the NYHS, and Brodhead's unpublished volumes of documents as he undertook his two-volume History of New Netherland; or, New York under the Dutch (1846–48), the first major historical account of the state's Dutch colonial period since Washington Irving's History in 1809.[127]

O'Callaghan turned to both federal and state government for support as he delved into archival research and writing. Then Secretary of the Navy Bancroft procured him a clerkship at the US dry dock in New York, where O'Callaghan sifted through Dutch colonial documents in Long Island and Manhattan. Like Bancroft during his diplomatic appointment in London, O'Callaghan used political patronage to subsidize private historical research, which he thought would redound to the public's benefit. By O'Callaghan's reckoning, however, the six hundred dollars was pitiable, as he explained in 1847 to New York senator John Adams Dix. Having failed to negotiate a higher salary, he now had a better post in mind: the New York Custom House. The 1846 Warehousing Act, pushed by Senator Dix, helped propel New York's rise as the nation's most important port, and O'Callaghan hoped to turn federal support for commerce into support for his book project. By nudging national politicians who might prove sympathetic to his research into the state's past, O'Callaghan—like Brodhead abroad—made a case that his state-based historical research merited national support: "I trust, Sir, that the honorable and commendable object which I have in view—to rescue from the obscurity and oblivion in which they have too long lain the records of the infancy of our State—will be a sufficient apology for this application. Under no other circumstances, I am sure, would I be an applicant for office."[128] At a moment when the United States did not formally support the writing of history, this back channel of political patronage was as close as O'Callaghan could get to publicly funded historical research.

O'Callaghan completed his *History* in 1848, and with the help of prominent figures in Albany he generated a subscription base in both New York and neighboring states. Solomon Alofsen, a Dutch-born diplomat fascinated by the region's history, wrote to O'Callaghan, "Really you have put every lover of the early history of New York under many obligations, and the Hist. of N. Neth. Has been much admired by some of my friends in Holland."[129] O'Callaghan's narrative went to considerable lengths to laud the virtues of these Dutch founders as the foundation for the history of New York and to present them as the ideological forebears of the United States.[130] Like Verplanck thirty years before, O'Callaghan believed that important institutions and qualities had been transmitted from the seventeenth-century Dutch republic to New Netherland. With this in mind, O'Callaghan gifted a copy of his *History* to the Dutch chargé d'affaires in 1848, which he hoped would be passed on to the king and placed in the royal library in the Hague. "Two centuries ago the seeds of Civilization were planted in this coast by the Dutch Nation," he wrote to the Dutch chargé d'affaires. "The territory which they then discovered embraces now four Sovereign States of the Republic and contains a population of nearly five Millions of Souls." In this fashion, he inscribed the Dutch into not only the state's narrative but a larger frame of the nation within global history.[131]

Federal appointments helped him complete his first historical project, but it was fickle patronage, leading O'Callaghan to look to the State of New York as a more stable backer. In 1848, the new State Library at Albany was completed. It featured a record office that would require a historical clerk, O'Callaghan learned, to sift through, arrange, and translate the state's colonial manuscripts in the secretary of state's office. The legislature planned to distribute published volumes to state politicians, employees, and other state governments, libraries, and learned societies throughout the United States. O'Callaghan thought himself just the man for the job.

After securing the appointment, he developed the four-volume *Documentary History of the State of New York* (1849–51), combining colonial records in Albany, those obtained abroad by Brodhead, and sundry others accumulated by O'Callaghan. This only enhanced his reputation as the gatekeeper of New York's archives for the American public. Writing to O'Callaghan in 1852, the historian Francis Parkman applauded the *Document History*, which he had drawn on in his *Conspiracy of Pontiac and the Indian War after the Conquest of Canada* (1851), calling the fourth volume "a work which does honor to all concerned in it. I wish the example of New York might inspire all the legislatures with a similar spirit."[132] O'Callaghan willingly received the praise but remained upset about his salary. He lobbied Robert Pruyn, an influential New York state assemblyman, to push for a pay raise that compensated the extensive archival labor in English, Dutch, French, and Latin that the project required. O'Callaghan pointed out that Canada's government had recently provided more generous funding for the transcription of some of its historical manuscripts. In so doing, he pushed for a new relationship between his state and his archival work.[133]

The stakes mounted for O'Callaghan with the legislature's passage of a second law in 1849 that called for the arrangement, translation, and publication "for the use of the state" of the seventy-three volumes of copied manuscripts Brodhead had brought back from Europe. Thanks to his reputation and political connections, O'Callaghan secured this long-term position, which would continue beyond the Civil War.[134] Beginning in 1853, his ten-volume *Documents Relative to the Colonial History of the State of New-York* appeared, a sweeping archival panorama of the state's colonial period, printed in many hundreds of volumes for state politicians and employees in New York, as well as individuals and institutions across the United States. O'Callaghan became the best-paid state employee in the United States to focus exclusively on superintending the state's historical papers. By 1857, halfway through the project, the state's comptroller reported that O'Callaghan had been paid almost eleven thousand dollars since 1849 for his work on the state's historical papers, at a time when US senators received a three-thousand-dollar annual salary. This was in addition to the twenty-five cents he was paid for each folio page he translated in the Dutch and French volumes. All told, the state expenditures for the production of the

Documentary History and *Colonial History* had surpassed three hundred thousand dollars.[135]

O'Callaghan's continued appeal for better pay reflected the self-interest of a government employee, surely, but also his sense of the project's significance, which he shared with Parkman and the many other historians who used these volumes. In his annual reports to the state, O'Callaghan argued about the importance of translating and publishing the Dutch, British, and French documents in the State Library. In his eyes, these materials traced the rise of New York from humble origins as a Dutch colony through the epic contest between the British and French empires for the region to independence and prosperity. He imagined that these volumes would also inform the colonial histories of Ohio, Illinois, and Michigan, and that Americans as a whole would finally appreciate the preeminent place of New York's history within the nation's.

Closing his 1855 report to the state, when he was in the midst of the project, O'Callaghan wrote:

> If you desire its citizens to be justly proud of this state; if you wish the fact to be everywhere known that yours is a state not only older than Vermont, but actually planted before the Pilgrims landed at Plymouth, and that in point of antiquity it yields precedence only to the Ancient Dominion, you will concur in the propriety of completing this work, as originally designed; for it will afford a monument more permanent than brass, of the labor, the hardships, the suffering, and patience your ancestors endured in founding, fostering, and building up the noble structure beneath which we now enjoy life and Liberty and are protected in the Pursuit of Happiness.[136]

O'Callaghan echoed figures like Sparks who envisioned the archival record not as myriad manuscripts—carefully preserved and arranged, one by one—but as a unified monument, "more permanent than brass." This monument in fact crushed the many peoples whose history it did not represent, such as the Indigenous societies upended by the settlers of New Netherland or the many thousands of African-descended people enslaved during Dutch, British, and American rule. But for the citizens whom O'Callaghan had in mind, it could be gazed upon and celebrated. In New York, the work of historical preservation and the curation and publication of the state's archives had become absorbed by the state and institutionalized by the eve of the Civil War, a major shift in the relationship between government and the historical record. As historians such as Bancroft and Parkman had hoped, in the coming decades other states would follow New York's lead.

By gathering and publishing the records of their colonial period, influential New Yorkers positioned their state within a larger imperial conflict for the continent that was pivotal to the nation's history. This secured in archives and monumentalized in print the argument that individuals such as De-Witt Clinton, Gulian Verplanck, William Seward, and Harmanus Bleecker had envisioned over the preceding half century: the exceptionalism of their past derived from its ongoing "rise and progress," to quote Seward, which played out through the imperial contests for its soil.[137] The NYHS and state government succeeded in placing their past within a progressive history of New York State that could be foregrounded within a narrative of the entire nation, exceeding by far the efforts of states such as Pennsylvania, Kentucky, and Maine to do so.

In doing so, New York demonstrated that collecting and examining history within the frame of a state was the most effective means to build and make use of an archive in this period. It drew far more materials across its archival threshold, committed more resources to their examination and publication, and used them to influence historical consciousness to a greater extent than historical societies considering the global frame of Norse colonization or Sparks embellishing the national frame of Washington's writings, for instance.

New York did manage, as Gallatin envisioned in 1846, to "bring the sacred truths of our history to each man's own door and fireside," at least for those with the means and interest to access these volumes of historical documents. At the same time, many more Americans were moved in these years to collect and make sense of the historical materials already at their fireside and just beyond their door, the local past that could place their lives within history in a way that state, national, or global archival projects could not.

➤ FIVE ◀

All History Is Local

While researching the history of New London, Connecticut, in 1847, the local historian Frances Manwaring Caulkins told the Massachusetts Historical Society (MHS) president James Savage to "bear it in mind, my excellent Sir, that I am *prowling* quietly and slowly, but yet progressively, through the ancient precincts of this town."[1] After publishing her first major work of local history, *The History of Norwich*, in 1845, Caulkins had initiated a lively scholarly exchange with Savage as she undertook the plodding work to publish her second major local history, *The History of New London* (1852). In Savage, Caulkins found another tireless researcher who could help her unearth and untangle archival materials.

Over their years of correspondence, Caulkins mailed Savage letters brimming with genealogical details that she had gleaned from records offices, households, cemeteries, and oral testimony in her corner of Connecticut. Many of these facts came to populate the four-volume *Genealogical Dictionary of the First Settlers of New England* that Savage eventually published between 1860 and 1862, a massive undertaking that incorporated information furnished by local historians across the region. Drawing on MHS resources and his archival collection and network, Savage responded to Caulkins's claims and queries with his own questions, facts, and emendations about her local investigations. Though they never met in person, they cultivated a scholarly relationship and a friendship that entwined their respective undertakings: Savage's work to compile and publish a comprehensive dictionary of early New England colonists as a cornerstone of the nation's archive, and Caulkins's to write local histories that revealed far more than the story of their titular towns. Working within this archival frame, Caulkins demonstrated the special significance of local history, which produced materials and knowledge that could situate myriad individual lives and communities within the larger, overlapping frames of state, national, and global history, even as it excluded so many others.

As a graduate of Harvard, trained lawyer, successful merchant, founder of a savings bank, and active civic leader in Boston, Savage enjoyed considerable resources and privilege. Nominated to the MHS in 1813, he established his authority as a historian with his annotated edition of Massachusetts Bay governor John Winthrop's *History of New England*, which appeared between 1825 and 1826. Over the decades, he served on the society's publishing committee and as librarian, treasurer, and finally president between 1841 and 1855, becoming "a zealous maverick on many matters," in the words of the MHS historian Louis Leonard Tucker.[2] In 1842 he extended his examination of New England's founding generation across the Atlantic. In a voyage from Boston to England in 1842, he roved from the university archives and collections in Canterbury, Oxford, and Cambridge to the State Papers Office in London, thanks to US Minister Edward Everett and British Foreign Secretary Lord Aberdeen, the very helping hands that had enabled Jared Sparks and John Romeyn Brodhead to make copies of state papers for their national and state archival projects.[3]

By contrast, Caulkins "prowled" within the town borders where she had grown up. In the 1810s, she distinguished herself in the Norwich schoolhouse founded by that outstanding Connecticut woman of letters Lydia Sigourney, who helped expand the horizons of education typically available to girls to include subjects such as history. Caulkins used her education to become a popular teacher and then a director of a female academy in the 1820s and 1830s, which enabled her to support her siblings and twice-widowed mother. Relocating to live with extended family in New York City between 1835 and 1842, Caulkins wrote for the American Tract Society, which published editions of her widely read religious tracts, poetry, and other biblical commentaries. Returning to New London in 1842 and living in the household of her younger stepbrother, the prominent whale fishery businessman Henry Philemon Haven, she forged her own path as a historian, painstakingly gathering and reconstructing the historical record of Norwich and New London and crafting well-regarded accounts of the towns she called home.[4]

When Caulkins used a feline metaphor to describe herself "*prowling quietly and slowly, but yet progressively*" through her local research in her 1847 letter to Savage, this playful flourish reflected their rapport but also their unequal positions and the different scopes of history that each sought to gather and interpret. Savage was the hub of a community of far-flung genealogists and historians who helped him fill his four-volume *Genealogical Dictionary* of seventeenth-century New England; Caulkins labored at the periphery of that Boston-based scholarly community as she pursued her local research. In her letter, Caulkins seemed to diminish herself and excuse her slow progress as a woman collecting evidence to write local history. Yet, it was in fact due to, not in spite of, these local constraints that Caulkins could refine her meticulous research method and reputation for rigor and accuracy.[5]

In 1849, Savage nominated Caulkins as a corresponding member of the MHS, making her the first and only woman to belong to the society in their lifetimes.[6] After her death two decades later, MHS president Robert Winthrop observed that Caulkins was "the only lady, I believe, whose name has ever appeared on our rolls. I think it will be acknowledged by all that Miss Caulkins had fairly won this distinction."[7] At the end of her life, the society's leadership recognized that Caulkins had actively earned the MHS members' respect through her local historical labor, but how she did so has remained unexamined. "Just how this lady managed to crash the select masculine circle of the Society may never be known," the MHS editor and director Stewart Mitchell wrote in his 1949 *Handbook of the Massachusetts Historical Society*.[8] The answer lies in her correspondence with Savage—tucked within his voluminous genealogical papers—and with other like-minded students of history in her archival network.[9] These papers cast light on a largely neglected means by which women on the margins of historical societies could intervene in the work of building archival collections and mediating the relationship between Americans and their past.

Caulkins did so at a juncture when not only well-known national figures but many like-minded local historians were working to solidify and instill scholarly norms into the inchoate discipline of history. The burgeoning genre of local history provided a frame where researchers like Caulkins refined their critical analysis of archival evidence. Not only was the exacting research that Caulkins performed in the 1840s and 1850s integral to building the archival collections that could authenticate American history. She also collaborated with other local historians, who, collectively, inscribed and reinforced disciplinary norms for all writers of history.

As the previous chapters show, in the absence of meaningful federal investment and leadership, influential Americans working within antebellum historical societies examined archival materials in order to authenticate the global origins of America's history, the history of the nation as a whole, and the distinctive place of their states within the nation. Local archival work and historical writing was equally important. Readers across the expanding United States could situate their lives within local history in ways that state, national, and global histories did not so readily enable. This provided many Americans a medium for engaging with the historical record and locating their lives within not only their locality but the broader frame of their state, national, and even global history. Just as the collaborative research networks that produced local histories like Caulkins's sprawled well beyond any local historian's town of inquiry, the texts they produced transcended the local, too.

The Archival Sphere of Local History

When compared with the social capital and networks that historical societies could activate, the mobility and access to archival resources that influential men like Sparks enjoyed, or the authority and financial resources that states such as New York could harness, local historians generally had modest means to conduct historical research. Within their smaller sphere, however, distinctive opportunities opened. For Caulkins, the challenge to compile what she deemed comprehensive and authentic sources for her local history became the space where she refined the expertise and research techniques that enabled her and other local historians to sharpen standards for historical research and writing that had an influence well beyond their local frame.

Writing to Savage about her debut historical work in 1845, Caulkins hinted at the distinctive challenge of investigating local history. As she readied *History of Norwich* for publication, she explained, "I have had little assistance from either books or living antiquarians, but have rather felt my way among the old people and old records of the '9 miles square' [of the town], and gathered up the fragments that were left."[10] In the very years that influential collectors and historians such as Savage crossed the Atlantic to comb through private libraries and state repositories for historical records related to American history, Caulkins frequented the public records offices, parishes, households, and graveyards in her vicinity; Caulkins's archive lay along Connecticut's, not England's, Thames River. Savage, with his wealth and access to archival materials and collectors in the orbit of the MHS, was perhaps the ideal collaborator to help her gather details about Connecticut's colonial history within the larger history of New England and the Atlantic world.

Moreover, as a woman entering a field dominated by men, she faced additional constraints in gathering materials, publishing, and corresponding with other researchers who could support her project. Publishing as "Miss. F. M. Caulkins" (she would shed the "Miss" and fill in the initials in her subsequent local histories), Caulkins dedicated her 1845 *History of Norwich* "to the citizens of Norwich, Inhabitants of a beautiful and varied town" as a resource that her community could use to investigate their own families' pasts.[11] As scholars have analyzed in the work of women of letters such as Sarah Josepha Hale, this rhetorical posture was a common strategy for women writing into the public square in this period.[12]

Indeed, Caulkins figured among the many women who were integral to the preservation of historical materials and the crafting of historical narratives. In households, girls sewed samplers depicting family genealogy. Daughters, sisters, and widows such as Deborah Norris Logan inherited family papers, finding themselves the potential archivist, editor, or salesperson of those documents. In the public sphere, women wrote history within a range of genres, from local chronicles by Caulkins to national history textbooks by Elizabeth Palmer Peabody, and from popular poems about historical sites by the likes of Lydia Sigourney to historical novels such as Catharine Maria Sedgwick's.[13]

It is possible that Caulkins hoped to play for her community a role analogous to the household responsibility normally assigned to women "as stewards of family memory," but she was like other women writers of history who "found that their designated responsibility as custodians of the local past allowed them to perform the work of historical preservation, paid and unpaid, with authority, influence and social acceptance," as one scholar explains.[14] This is why Caulkins packaged her first major historical work not as a transgressive act that threatened gender norms but as an extension of the idealized feminine qualities of her domestic sphere into the collective

FIGURE 11. Bookplate for books purchased through a fund willed by James Savage to the Massachusetts Historical Society. (From October Meeting, letter of George P. Marsh, *Proceedings of the Massachusetts Historical Society* 14 [1875–76]; image from JSTOR archive)

households of Norwich. Although she presented her first book as a modest offering to her community, in building a relationship with Savage, Caulkins sought to integrate her herself and her research into a wider network and influential institutions that largely excluded women.

Laboring within this local frame offered Caulkins and myriad other local historians a space to participate in the vital work that historical societies had for decades implored Americans to undertake. Like the many members of the historical societies, Caulkins regarded the preservation of historical materials as an urgent civic duty. Deploying language commonly found in historical society meetings and publications, she explained to readers in her *History of Norwich* that she aimed "to give a more enduring form to a mass of local information, that would be lost if left much longer in the charge of mouldering paper, fading ink, and fast dropping age."[15] Caulkins joined influential male colleagues in their mission to preserve the imperiled traces of their historical communities before it was too late.

She also shared with leading historians and historical societies the conviction that the nation's entire past—as they conceived of it—could be comprehensively authenticated with historical documents. Preparing his

FIGURE 12. Portrait of Frances Manwaring Caulkins. (From her *History of Norwich*, 1874 edition; image courtesy of Cornell University Library)

Genealogical Dictionary of New England settlers, Savage labored letter by exhausting letter to document every child "born on our side of the ocean to a settler whose tent was pitched here before May 1692."[16] Savage included in this comprehensive research "*every* settler, without regard to his rank, or wealth," which Caulkins also sought within her towns.[17] In doing so, she showed that the vision of a comprehensive record of the nation's history could not be realized by historical societies, state governments, and federal allies alone. Rather, it was a collective undertaking that she and other local historians could take upon themselves and meaningfully advance.

Within the relatively small archival frame of local history projects, many obstacles hindered researchers. In southeastern Connecticut, natural forces and human choices had shaped the record that Caulkins could access. "Relinquish at once all expectations of finding a mine of genealogical ore at old Saybrook," she warned Savage in 1846 after one disappointing archival trip to the Connecticut town. "I was there a few weeks since and learned with bitter disappointment that the first book of records, i.e. all anterior to 1660, had perished in the flames which consumed the house of a former town clerk."[18] Daily, she confronted the incomplete and inconsistent archive that her generation had inherited from the colonial period. Records that she deemed essential to her research had been severely diminished over the years or simply did not exist. Seeking out evidence about New London's mid-seventeenth-century settler generation, Caulkins struggled to find certain vital records and deeds with complete and accurate information about residents.

This frustration irked local researchers and helped to unify them within a shared archival undertaking, passing advice to one another about the nature of the documents they found and how to access them.[19] In this spirit, Caulkins informed Savage that historic New London records—prior to the separation of adjacent towns such as Groton and Ledyard during the eighteenth and early nineteenth centuries—were collected by only one church and one town clerk. Settlers often did not deposit documents claiming title to Indigenous land in public records offices until years later, if ever.[20] She confessed to readers in her 1852 *History of New London* that, "in tracing the lines of genealogy, we find groups of names that can be traced no further than maturity. The records do not tell of their children; their graves are not found in our burial-places."[21] These archival conditions made it all the more arduous to comprehensively authenticate local history.

She also perceived a dearth of evidence for the region's Indigenous history. In her correspondence with the Northampton, Massachusetts–based minister, novelist, and keen genealogist Sylvester Judd, Caulkins described what she and Judd saw as its only textual traces: place-names, a common interest for local historians.[22] In doing so, she perpetuated the prevailing prejudice of her contemporaries that these scarce traces reflected the natural vanishing of Indigenous civilization in Connecticut rather than the ravages of settler colonialism, which by the eighteenth century had killed or displaced most of the Indigenous communities on lands claimed by the colony.

Indeed, for Caulkins, the alleged failure of Indigenous societies to document their history seemed to justify their decline. "The red race indeed," she wrote in *History of Norwich*, "seem to have lived and died from generation to generation, without ever passing out of themselves, and stamping an evidence of their existence, either upon the material forms around them, or the annals of time. They pass over the earth like the wind, or melt away like a dream, and leave no vestige behind, or if any, it is but the names that they bestowed on the hills and streams."[23] Caulkins borrowed this trope from popular portrayals of New England's Indigenous societies like the

1829 play *Metamora; or, The Last of the Wampanoags*, a fictional depiction of King Philip's (or Metacom's) War, the 1675–76 conflict that had devastating consequences for the Wampanoag and Narragansett at the hands of colonial forces supported by Caulkins's corner of Connecticut. Caulkins applied the trope of the "vanishing Indian" to the historical record of Connecticut, implying that, like the apparent disappearance of Indigenous communities, their seeming absence of historical traces was a natural process. Like many historians of her era, Caulkins hesitated to rely on oral testimony, or "tradition," which in her *History of Norwich* she relegated beneath town records, periodicals, and private documents. "But," she added in the preface to that work, "when tradition contradicts no authentic record, and when records fail, even history may be permitted to receive its aid."[24] By "tradition," however, she meant stories passed through white families. Her openness did not extend to Indigenous oral traditions, a tendency evident among local historians and communities across New England.[25]

To complement the papery sources for her history, Caulkins joined other historians in turning her gaze to the wider array of historical texts within arm's reach. Stone could prove a more durable medium than paper, as the American Antiquarian Society librarian Christopher Columbus Baldwin found. He envisioned a history of Sutton, Massachusetts, which he left unwritten when his overturned stagecoach crushed him in 1835 as he traveled to study Indigenous earthen architecture in Ohio. Like Caulkins, "he visited the gray haired inhabitants, inquired of their ancestors, traced the line of genealogy, and followed the stream of generations to its source. Every depository of information was carefully examined. The records of church and parish, the archives of the state, the dusty files and moulded volumes, were scrupulously searched." His eulogist added to the AAS that "his communion was with the dead as well as the living."[26] This included not only paper but stone. Visiting Hartford in 1831, for instance, he eagerly copied epitaphs from a nearby graveyard of Rebecca and Esther Hall, wives of former Sutton residents who had migrated to the area.[27] Baldwin left more than one thousand inscriptions from burial grounds that he had visited in his peregrinations around the region.[28]

Although Caulkins was less wide-ranging than Baldwin, her visits to records offices in Norwich, New London, Groton, Saybrook, Lyme, and other nearby Connecticut towns often included stops at burial grounds, where she examined deteriorated and overgrown gravestones with the same scrutiny that she applied to documents. Unlike her skepticism toward "tradition," she generally had confidence in text inscribed in any material, so long as she could decipher it. Despite her "bitter disappointment" that Saybrook's earliest records had been destroyed by fire, she turned to the gravestones in the local burial ground to locate the Backus family, perhaps the earliest English immigrants to the area.[29] The following year, she hoped to determine details about Elizabeth Winthrop, wife of the early Connecticut governor John Winthrop Jr. As she wrote to Savage, she had uncovered gravestones "lying head to head, a few inches apart. . . . [T]he turf has closed around their edges and one of them has sunk into an inclined position, and a considerable portion of it is covered with the earth. On removing this earth, we find that the covering has checked the disintegration of the stone in that place, and a few letters can be made out." Although unsure, she interpolated that the faded marks on the granite read: "IN MEMORY OF WINTHROP."[30] This poorly maintained outdoors scene seemed to reflect in three dimensions the conditions of many written documents. As she held worn and fragmented papers, she dirtied her hands deciphering these gravestones. Paper and stone could be equally valid and vexing sources in her attempt to comprehensively reconstruct the local historical record.[31]

Whether examining local text or tablet, Caulkins was a meticulous and highly disciplined researcher who often expressed anxiety that she might omit or mistake even one fact in her investigations. Writers of local history in this period "shared a reverence for data, for the publication of unexpurgated letters and documents, and for the straightforward presentation of events as they happened."[32] The intellectual, physical, and psychic toll of this local historical labor is easily obscured by the printed product, however. As Caulkins observed to Savage in the autumn of 1846, "It is only by amassing particulars and putting things together that a result is obtained. You will not be surprized therefore that I spend most of my time in correcting my own mistakes, and gathering materials which I cannot at present use."[33] In the early research for her *History of New London*, she chided herself for misreading at least, by her count, fifty times the name of Thomas Bolles, a New London settler who had migrated from Maine in the 1660s, for what was actually Thomas *Welles*. Having revisited two manuscript sources to find more details on Bolles for letter B of Savage's *Genealogical Dictionary*, she wrote quickly to Savage in 1846 to correct her error. "You would judge me leniently, however," she reasoned to Savage later that season, "were you to see the decayed state of both ink and paper," not to mention the penmanship."[34]

At other moments, records were in disorder or outright contradicted each other, leaving her in a quandary. "Here is a puzzle," she asked Savage and herself in one letter, "which of these records is wrong?"[35] This could lead to frustrating, sometimes futile encounters with the historical record. Early in her New London research in 1845, she complained to Savage that "the adventurers so quickly became numerous, and many of them so undistinguished, a mere populace, thrown upon the shore by the neighboring sea, and as fluctuating as its waves."[36] The Coit family, she grumbled the following year, "are all in confusion tangled together like the group of the Laocoön," referring to the ancient sculpture of the Trojan priest Laocoön and his two sons entwined in deadly battle with giant sea serpents.[37]

Uncertain of the evidentiary ground she stood on, Caulkins often doubted her own conclusions. Regarding her evidence about the Bushnell family, she asked in that same letter, "Is this house that I have built, founded upon rock or sand? Have you any whirlwind or flood to turn against it?"[38] These watery metaphors of Caulkins's depicted the historical record not as inert and stable but as a shifting, unsettled entity that she struggled to control or channel for the benefit of her communities. Navigating this confusion, Caulkins approached her local archival record not unlike the scientific historians of the later nineteenth and early twentieth centuries, when "the disciplining of the historian, along with the disciplining of historical confusion, was situated in the production, evaluation, and ordering of details, so that in their finished form they might serve as well-ordered facts."[39] Her expressions of uncertainty reflected the gendered deference to Savage that appeared throughout their correspondence, but they also attested to her persistent work to produce solid historical facts within her local frame.

To describe the challenge of making sense of such materials, Caulkins also employed metaphors of light and darkness that were familiar to collectors and historical societies throughout the United States. "Misty points and intricate mazes" appeared before her, she wrote in 1847.[40] On another occasion, she turned to Savage "in the hope that you will kindly stretch forth your sceptre and cause light to shine in upon the darkness in which I find myself involved relative to the contending claims of *Avery* and *Hempsted*."[41] Some figures seemed especially shrouded. She confessed to Savage in 1850 that "a doubt or rather thick darkness, hangs also over the origin of Mrs. Winthrop," wife to the colonial Connecticut governor.[42] Historians of global, national, and state history of course struggled to make sense of inaccessible, incomplete, and inconsistent records, and such murky metaphors would have felt familiar to them. But for Caulkins and her fellow local researchers who undertook projects outside the walls of major archival collections in US and western European cities, the darkness around the historical record could seem especially dense as they fumbled through, seeking clarity.

When successfully illuminated, each name, date, and life event recovered was a discrete fact that could be placed within the larger picture of town history that she was creating. This datum by datum gathering of the historical record defined local historical research. Finding the very first settlers of Connecticut's colonial communities was of particular importance. She was preoccupied with identifying the details of Margaret Lake—"my precious Lady of the Lake," an allusion to the Arthurian legend, Caulkins christened her in correspondence with Savage in 1850—because "as she is the first white female, that, so far as we know, ever set foot upon our shore, I have been naturally solicitous to learn who she was."[43] By the time she published *History of New London* in 1852, she could write confidently, "Honor Margaret Lake! The first European female that trod upon our fair heritage."[44]

Such proof could authenticate, step by step, the account of colonial conquest, expansion, and national triumph that she saw progressing through her local frame. Through the painstaking collection, analysis, and corroboration of papers, traditions, and artifacts, historians like Caulkins expanded the archival threshold to include these materials and the lives, places, and events that they encapsulated. While working within this local frame, historians made these materials and practice of historical inquiry available to a wider community of researchers and readers. In doing so, they supported a larger historical vision that transcended the borders of any one town.

Local Authority and the Historical Record

Local historical research was often more than a local undertaking, and writers like Caulkins were entwined in a network of genealogical and historical researchers that sprawled across local, state, and even regional lines. A scholarly community of leading historians emerged during this period, which included the likes of George Bancroft, Jared Sparks, and William Hickling Prescott. They circulated historical information, shared research advice, and offered criticism and mutual support. These practices "contributed to a nascent sense of identity among its members as historians with distinct concerns and expertise."[45] It is important to note that far more researchers entered the field of local history by the middle of the century, similarly sharing facts, bolstering standards for archival research, and forging a shared sense of purpose and identity that influenced the broader field. In fact, as the historian Jean O'Brien has emphasized, "the local historians of southern New England brought into being a practice of historical writing that historians from elsewhere drew upon, customized for their locality, and replicated across the landscape of the nation."[46] Although major publications from historical societies, individuals like Sparks, and state governments received more funding and attention in these years, local historical research and writing collectively influenced the discipline to a great extent.

For Caulkins and many others who actively contributed to this work, local history could rarely be gathered on one's own and only within the boundaries of the town they studied. Historical actors migrated, families dispersed, and traces of their lives scattered. In the 1820s, John Farmer first cultivated a collaborative network of local researchers who contributed a multitude of facts to his *Genealogical Register of the First Settlers of New England* (1829), a legacy and research model that Savage's own *Genealogical Dictionary* expanded upon in the following decades.[47] Likewise, between Connecticut and Boston, thousands of such facts moved between Caulkins and Savage during their years of correspondence, supporting each other's research. "I believe in *reciprocity*," Caulkins insisted to Savage in 1846 in recognition of his helpful information about a New London family, "and should be rejoiced if I could furnish a few pebbles towards the building of your immense pyramid."[48] Whenever possible, she proffered reliable facts about colonial Connecticut families, "crumbs of information which I might be able to add to his ample stores," she wrote Savage the following year.[49] Similarly, during a rare trip to Gloucester, Massachusetts, she worked closely with John Babson, who had inherited the project to write the maritime town's history from Gloucester Lyceum member William Ferson.[50] Caulkins in turn benefited from Babson's help identifying early Massachusetts settlers who had migrated to Connecticut. "Mr. Babson has been so indefatigable and thorough, that scarcely a grape of the vintage was left for me to glean," she concluded.[51]

"Pebbles," "crumbs," "grapes": Caulkins's many metaphors reflected the experience of local historians on the ground, often literally, as they gathered and processed evidence. As the famed German historian Leopold von Ranke accessed archives across national boundaries and exerted exceptional influence on the development of the discipline of history in the nineteenth century, he depicted archival documents as "so many beautiful princesses, possibly beautiful, all under a curse and needing to be saved," at once objectifying the archival source as feminine and depicting the historian as a masculine subject.[52] Caulkins did the inverse. Although the field of local research was largely in the hands of men like Babson, her depiction of the researcher as gleaner of grapes left behind by the harvest—the nonlucrative agricultural work traditionally performed by women—best captured Caulkins's collection of local evidence that was often discarded and close at hand. In turn, Savage picked this very metaphor for his own series of genealogical installments that appeared during the 1840s and 1850s in the *Collections of the Massachusetts Historical Society,* "Gleanings for New England History." For Caulkins's research and readers, this bore fruit.

Although Caulkins managed to produce her first town history mainly from materials in and around Norwich, in undertaking her more ambitious *History of New London* (1852), she sought materials in northern New England in order to tell the town's full history from colonization to the present. Caulkins saw the history of New London within a larger New England history of migration and settlement, beginning with the emigrants from Gloucester, Massachusetts, who peopled New London from the 1640s. Caulkins orchestrated an exchange in which she deferred to Savage's extensive knowledge and access to archives, libraries, and social networks as a means to pursue her own research into her local past. The Bostonian had become the hub for a large network of researchers who covered his desk with local facts about the first century of New England's colonization and petitioned him for information about their ancestors.[53] She also collaborated with her own network of genealogists and historians who shared sources and suggestions for her books. Fostering a collaborative relationship with Savage and other influential men helped her gain access to historical data beyond her sphere in southeastern Connecticut and earn credibility in their eyes.

However, she would also need to prove her ability as a woman to conduct rigorous historical research, a high standard to which she held herself and others. Conducting research in a field dominated by men, Caulkins positioned herself as a subordinate to Savage, which helped her to enter and gradually elevate her reputation as a researcher. In one early exchange of information with Savage in the spring of 1845, she closed, "with unfeigned respect and feeling even of acquaintanceship, permit me to subscribe myself yours, F. M. Caulkins."[54] She clearly recognized that the community of genealogists and historians was not egalitarian and that Savage exercised far more authority in it than she. By adopting this tone and cultivating this dynamic with Savage, she eased her entry.

Other women writers of history, such as Elizabeth Ellet, employed this tactic. Ellet undertook research for her prosopography *Women of the American Revolution* (1849) in the hopes of situating a range of American women within the dominant narrative of the nation's independence. As Ellet "redefined that realm to include women as fit subjects of inquiry as well as inquirers, she sought assistance from prominent male historians by presenting herself in the established feminine role of 'protégée,'", a tone that she modulated based on the prestige of her correspondent.[55] Caulkins likewise adopted a deferential tone with Savage to advance her research interests. "I hold myself subject to your orders in my little sphere, and am truly your sincere assistant," she wrote in 1847.[56] She regularly inquired which letter of his genealogical dictionary he was then working on so that she could send him information about colonial Connecticut linked with those surnames. Sometimes she filled pages with detailed information for him at the expense of her own research questions. "Like a true woman," she wrote on one such occasion in 1848, "I have left that for the last which most nearly concerns my own wants."[57] Such gendered self-effacement facilitated exchanges with correspondents like Savage.

At the same time, her ostensible deference could quickly turn more rhetorical—indeed, downright funny—than serious. A year into their correspondence in 1846, she promised Savage, "(a long, *long* time hereafter, I fear) to lay the History of New London at your august feet, *dread sire of genealogists!*" She called Massachusetts "that bishoprick over which you hold supreme genealogical sway."[58] Never content with just a single metaphor, she sent from New London "transmissions to head-quarters" in 1851, for instance.[59] Over time, these gestures of deference tended to fade as Caulkins built with Savage a sense of mutual scholarly respect and camaraderie in their entwined pursuits.

If a "subscriber" to Savage in 1845, she also subscribed him to her research agenda and, eventually, publishing aspirations over the following years. Caulkins managed a reciprocal exchange of genealogical facts that would prove instrumental to both their projects. Caulkins worked chronologically through New London's history, beginning with conquest and settlement. She sought precise information about the births, family relationships, major life events, and deaths of each individual she could identify; meanwhile, Savage worked alphabetically through the early settlers of New England, seeking information from the Abbots of New London onward. Each letter was answered, often dense with names and dates, minor corrections, and minute questions. "This letter has an extensive mission to perform—," Caulkins announced to Savage a year into their correspondence, "—to render thanks for favors received and favors expected—to ask any amount of questions and to answer not a few—let me therefore come at once to matters of moment, lest our 5 cents worth of paper be covered before I am aware of it."[60]

Caulkins contributed her local expertise to Savage's regional research project while directing his ongoing contributions to her own historical inquiries. In one 1847 letter, Caulkins both lauded the "richly freighted missives" that she received from Savage and needled him that "some shade of disappointment will mark every day's delay" of his response to her additional questions.[61] She even coordinated their work across state lines. Of one New England colonist who left Gloucester to settle in New London, she instructed Savage that, "where you leave him at Cape Ann, I will take him up, and bring him to this place." To do so, Caulkins made one trip to Cape Ann, which she named "my exploring tour of Cape Tragibizanda," playfully referring to John Smith's term for the peninsula, a tribute to a Turkish woman.[62] Collaboration with Savage and others across the region was essential to completing a comprehensive and authoritative local history as she envisioned it.

In building epistolary relationships with Savage and other researchers throughout the Northeast, Caulkins could share her knowledge about the region's colonial archive and collect information crucial to her own project. Local historians and genealogists corresponded with Caulkins and began to seek her help with their own research questions. After meeting at the MHS in 1848, Caulkins and Richard Frothingham shared questions and insights about their respective projects. Frothingham thanked Caulkins for her praise of his *History of Charlestown* (1845) but admitted that he was "just now full to the overflowing with Bunker Hill matter," which would appear the following year in his *History of the Siege of Boston*.[63] He then imparted his own praise for her *History of Norwich* and her ongoing research: "I remember with pleasure the brief conversation I had with you at our Historical Rooms and am happy to renew it by letter. Wishing you every success in your laborious investigations." Although he struggled to answer the historical questions posed by Caulkins, he asked if she could direct him to certain manuscript accounts of the Battle of Bunker Hill that he could not track down.[64]

During that same visit to the MHS, she also met Joseph Felt, formerly the Massachusetts state archivist and then MHS librarian, who had been charged with gathering copies of colonial records in England and France earlier in the decade. In addition, she corresponded with the novelist and historian Sylvester Judd, "the distinguished antiquary of Northampton," who was by Savage's reckoning far and away the most important contributor of genealogical data to his *Genealogical Dictionary* but would die the year it was published and before he could complete his own *History of Hadley* (posthumously released in 1863).[65] As Savage sought data for Connecticut towns in the 1846, Judd anticipated that Caulkins would "furnish you with what is necessary from Norwich and New London, and perhaps a few other towns in that neighborhood. Miss C. has many errors in her History of Norwich, but I should rather rely upon her for correct information than upon most men."[66] By building these relationships, local researchers like Caulkins gained access to archival information well beyond the geographic confines of their towns and reciprocally sharpened the standard for local research.

For Caulkins, these relationships also facilitated her publishing plans and reputation within the field. In 1849, Caulkins had secured Savage's assistance in publishing the seventeenth-century diary of the Reverend William Adams. The slim volume sketched the history of his descendants from Dedham, Massachusetts, to their arrival in New London, which had passed through the hands of the family's female descendants and eventually to those of the Reverend Robert Hallam of St. James Episcopal Church, where Caulkins worshipped.[67] She made an exact copy of the *"treasure"*—Latin phrases and all—that documented his daily life from 1670 to 1685. "You are aware," she confided to Savage, "that a female, alone in the world and hedged around with poverty and timidity has perplexities to encounter in the paths of literature, that lords of the creation, I suppose, know nothing about."[68] As in other exchanges with Savage, she positioned herself deferentially, writing to him as a patriarch of genealogical research who could help her not only gather information but share her work with the public.

Caulkins had in fact already published numerous texts through the American Tract Society and her own *History of Norwich*, but she still confronted a treacherous publishing industry that could exploit women historical writers in order to cut costs.[69] By eliciting Savage's interest in her project and his sympathy for her situation, she directed him toward the outcome that she desired: the use of his resources and status in Boston to steward her edited volume through the press. Although she diminished the considerable editorial work that she as *"the weaver"* had done on the volume, Caulkins was delighted when Metcalf and Company in Cambridge published the volume.[70] She also coordinated with the MHS's publishing committee to feature it as the lead item three years later in the 1852 *Collections of the Massachusetts Historical Society*, in the same volume that Savage published "More Gleanings for New England History."[71]

Just days after Savage received Caulkins's edited volume in 1849, he nominated her at a meeting of the Massachusetts Historical Society as a corresponding member, leading to her election the following month. Savage's decision to nominate her reflected his regard for her scholarship, the archival labor that she continued to contribute to his *Genealogical Dictionary*, and the rigor that she brought to the analysis of the historical record.[72] The nomination seems to have taken Caulkins by surprise. "I am assailed," she responded to Savage, "by the suggestion that you accord to *sex*, a degree of encouragement that *desert* could not claim." If flattered and moved by her nomination, she accepted it without hesitation. "Under your guardianship," she wrote Savage, "I consider myself safe, and I shall be inclined to esteem whatever you do as right."[73] Such deference toward Savage reflected her recognition that she was traversing a gendered boundary in the realm of archival research and historical writing. Yet, her nomination was an outcome of the professional relationship that she had built with Savage over the previous four years and the authority that she had earned as a local historian.

Through such mutual support of their research, historians developed not only knowledge but a shared professional identity—even friendship.

If gender seemingly distanced Caulkins from her correspondents, the experience of gathering, preserving, and making sense of their modicum of America's historical record thickened the affective bonds among them. Like any avid local historian, she could identify with Frothingham's sense of being "full to overflowing" with information on their subject. Payne Kenyon Kilbourn, a genealogist and local historian of Litchfield, Connecticut, who belonged to the MHS, reported to Caulkins having "*searched* and *read* myself sick" in preparing his publications by the early 1850s. He likened his decade-long research to struggling through a mire, from which Caulkins's guiding hand had hauled him.[74] Caulkins could surely identify with this feeling, shared by a virtual community of researchers who rarely stood in the same reading room or held the same document in their hands—decades before the centralization of professional historical practice within the university seminar room and archive.[75]

These personal bonds could sustain research projects that spanned years. Take, for example, Charles Miner, a Pennsylvanian politician who came of age in Norwich before relocating to the Wyoming Valley in Pennsylvania, where he published a local history in 1845, the same year that Caulkins's *History of Norwich* appeared. He was moved by her book, which connected him to his hometown, and he wished her good fortune for its reception. But, moving beyond formalities, he continued, "now, my Dear Miss Caulkins, will you allow me to draw my chair near you, a little less ceremoniously, and chat awhile."[76] When Savage confronted family tragedy in the late 1840s, Caulkins sent her condolences. She urged him to continue working, assuring him that "there is no better solace for the mind than constant occupation and a definite aim."[77] Engagement in research, by her reasoning, could offer consolation. They were not just researching olden times but working against time—before they became part of the historical record themselves.

This collaborative social context is essential to understanding the labor of local historical research and the production of historical knowledge during these formative years of the discipline of history in the United States. In such moments, Caulkins and her many correspondents sought a connection that was deeper than exchanging and arranging data. These personal, often sentimental, sometimes humorous exchanges among researchers, regularly corresponding but rarely meeting face-to-face, facilitated the interminable labor of gathering and interpreting the evidence of their subjects' place within history.

Within this community, local historians established their authority by demonstrating rigorous research methods and holding others to this same standard. Caulkins in particular did not hesitate to challenge the historical findings of Savage or anyone else, no matter their position in historical societies, state offices, or popular esteem. Eager to see historical records with her own eyes, confident only when she had fully sifted through them herself, suspicious of tendencies she saw in "what grave historians printed for truth," Caulkins called out published historians and took herself to task whenever these high standards were not met.[78] Though typically diminished as "antiquarians" or "amateurs," local historians such as Caulkins and Judd set standards that could appear just as rigorous as those associated with scientific historians decades later, when "scholars subjected themselves to innumerable hardships and inconveniences in order to pursue scientific knowledge."[79] Her critiques could be as minute as a misspelling of a New London resident's name in Farmer's *Genealogical Register* or a mistaken military rank in Benjamin Trumbull's *Complete History of Connecticut from 1630 to 1713* (1797), the first major history of the colony.[80]

Caulkins held Savage to the same exacting standard. She challenged him on small and large points of fact and historical interpretation. One was the resting place of the Narragansett sachem Miantonomoh, which had been marked by a monument in Norwich since 1841. The ally of the Connecticut colonists during the Pequot War in the 1630s, Miantonomoh was later executed for conspiring to form a pan-Indian alliance against the English colonists. "I cannot allow you, Sir, to meet me on any middle ground with respect to our old Narragansett Sachem," Caulkins wrote. "No. The mountain must come to Mahomet, or Mahomet must go to the mountain."[81] Caulkins often attempted to lighten her disagreements over facts with humor, but the core of her correspondence with other researchers was a commitment to finding the threshold between what archival materials could and could not authenticate.

She was particularly critical of Royal Ralph Hinman, a Connecticut politician and former secretary of state and member of various historical societies. Hinman had recently published *A Catalogue of the Names of the First Puritan Settlers of the Colony of Connecticut*, which drew on local historical records and histories.[82] "(Sub rosa)," she vented to Savage in 1848, "Hinman is so vague and loose in those items with which I am conversant, that I cannot confide in him upon any point[.] I should be afraid to trust to him *wholly* for *any fact*, without other corroboration, though of course he is often right by chance." Although she had heard he was "a worthy man," she observed that, "he throws off whatever comes in his way, chaff and wheat together, without separation. The antiquarian must winnow before using."[83] Caulkins's use of this agricultural metaphor—like Savage's own "gleanings"—reflected her belief that their research rigorously processed materials to produce a resource that would nourish other historians and a broader reading public. Caulkins was especially taken aback because Hinman, as secretary of state from the 1820s until the 1840s, was at arm's length from the largest repository of historical records in the state and wielded the resources and authority to consult local materials throughout Connecticut and beyond its borders.

In her research, correspondence, and publishing, Caulkins insisted that genealogical and local historical research must be a methodical practice that bit by bit built a foundation of knowledge that both researcher and reader could stand on. She may have felt particular pressure to determine the authenticity of materials and defend the precision of her research against the prejudice of male historians toward a woman working in the traditionally masculine realm of archival research. She criticized the popular historian John Warner Barber and others whom she found too careless in their analysis of historical records or too prone to infuse oral tradition or their own imagination into their findings. Barber's histories of Connecticut, Massachusetts, and other states combined historical data with his own detailed engravings of towns, landscapes, and notable historical sites. "He takes up with family gossip, instead of consulting records," Caulkins wrote to Savage in early 1849, explaining a mistaken detail that Barber published about Robert Hempstead, an original settler of New London.[84] Other researchers such as Judd, a major contributor to Savage's *Genealogical Dictionary*, shared Caulkins's concern with careless methodology. "There are some men," he protested to Savage, "who have a good deal of genealogical and historical knowledge, that are so credulous, so ready to believe all hearsays and traditions, and so inclined to jump at conclusions, that they mar all their work by mixing truth and fable together."[85] Caulkins was not one of those men, and like Judd she perceived the urgency of disentangling truth from fable, as they saw it, which their local expertise enabled them to do.

Caulkins, Judd, Savage, and others maintained this threshold in order to establish disciplinary norms that would outlive them. "The great point kept in view through the whole composition of the work, was *accuracy*," she assured readers in *History of Norwich*. "It was the aim of the author to be minutely accurate. Not a fact, name, or date has been given without careful inquiry and examination."[86] Caulkins constantly turned her critical eye not only at other researchers, but at herself. She was clear about the value of these painstaking research standards: "I only arrive at truth by inches, and therefore though I make mistakes today, I hope to be able to correct them tomorrow."[87] Toward the end of his decades of research, Savage recognized that, "one student in ten thousand will understand New England History better in its early days for my researches. How unimportant that he may be ignorant of the humble benefactor that smoothed the way by levelling obstructions or filling gaps."[88] Sharing this sense of responsibility to future generations, Caulkins worried about the historical knowledge that her contemporaries were producing. "There is so much crude genealogy published now-a-days," she observed, "that antiquarians of the next generation will sometimes be puzzled to reconcile authorities and ascertain the truth."[89] Such exchanges among often distant researchers allowed them to refine the disciplinary norms guiding their work.[90]

In local histories, authors could demonstrate their command of available archival materials and instill the importance of historical accuracy into their readers. To show this, Caulkins regularly brought readers within view of the physical conditions of the primary sources. In *History of New London*, she informed the reader that "the earliest records of the town were made in a loosely stitched book, which is now in a fragmentary state."[91] This authorial technique testified to Caulkins's close examination of the sources while serving as practical guidance for readers who might conduct their own examination of these sources. Regular footnotes throughout her editions of *History of Norwich* and *History of New London* refer to original documents, gravestones, and oral testimony that she consulted. One could imagine her turning the densely written pages of a book of minutes, deciphering the script, or carefully peeling back the overgrowth from gravestones. Her transcriptions of various primary sources appeared throughout her texts, such as minutes of town meetings, deeds bearing settler and Native signatures, and engravings on tombstones. All of this close analysis and documentation of primary sources made clear that Caulkins shared in the "desire" of antebellum historians seeking to establish norms within the discipline "for both originality and impartial truth."[92]

Beyond the local frame of these investigations and publications, local historians hoped that more ambitious historians could "transform into a grander, more poetic story" the hard-won facts drawn from their works.[93] Positively reviewing her 1852 *History of New London*, the *New England Historical and Genealogical Review* praised Caulkins's accomplishment: "Now what will our readers exclaim when we assure them that a very delicate lady, of very moderate physical abilities, possessing no very perfect health, has grappled with more old records and old books than would probably amount to two such libraries as that of Dr. [Samuel] Johnson; and out of that huge chaos has produced a beautiful history of one of the most interesting localities in all New England."[94] Beneath the condescension toward Caulkins as a female scholar, the review emphasized the physical and intellectual rigor that had allowed her to produce from the "huge chaos" of historical materials a work had both aesthetic and intellectual quality.

Ironically, there may have been more space for a local historical writer like Caulkins—a woman without formal academic training in history, laboring largely on the margins of scholarly institutions—to produce authoritative texts and influence disciplinary standards than historians working in the late nineteenth century. In the decades after her death, the formal professionalization of the discipline required participation in university seminars, archives focused on political and military affairs, and belonging within a masculine scholarly community that generally deemed women incapable of objective historical research.[95] In pushing against what she deemed substandard practices and emphasizing the importance of rigorous research, Caulkins was able to influence the historical field and community during its formative years.

Beyond Local History

Neither the materials nor the network of experts nor the scholarly practices needed to produce a local history were strictly local. In turn, the impact of "a beautiful history" such as the one authored by Caulkins could reverberate well beyond its locality, influencing the understanding and practice of history in other towns, states, and regions. Within the broader undertaking to examine America's archival materials and narrate its history in the antebellum United States, local history had the power to connect some Americans with not only the historical record and account of a given town but the full sweep of the nation's history, as these early historians imagined it.

"Miss Frances Manwaring Caulkins" stands out among the men listed as "Honorary and Corresponding Members" published in the 1852 *Collections of the Massachusetts Historical Society*, the first since her election in 1849. The recognition placed Caulkins alongside recently elected corresponding members such as the historian of Litchfield, Connecticut, Payne Kenyon Kilbourne (1848), and Connecticut assistant secretary of state James Hammond Trumbull (1850), who had just released the first edited volume of the *Public Records of the Colony of Connecticut*. But it also placed Caulkins and these experts of local history on the same page as George Bancroft, elected in 1850 while he was in the midst of writing his ten-volume *History of the United States* (1834–75).[96] Like them, Caulkins was sent a membership diploma from the society's corresponding secretary, signifying her place as a contributor and an authority within this virtual community of historians whose archival labor spanned from the local, to the state, to the national.[97]

Caulkins's local historical writing and expertise about archival materials diffused into research about other localities and states. Readers, including Sylvester Judd, admired Caulkins's *History of New London* as the best town history that they had encountered.[98] Notable collectors such as William Buell Sprague in Albany wrote Caulkins (Sprague later eulogized her as "a truly noble specimen of a woman," applying his collector's lexicon to her).[99] Men holding leadership positions in scholarly institutions reached out for facts and guidance, such as founding member of the New England Historic Genealogical Society John Wingate Thornton, and Harvard University librarian Thaddeus William Harris. As did a range of men working on their own genealogies and local histories in Connecticut, Massachusetts, New York, Pennsylvania, and beyond.

Typically, these requests came in the form of praise along with a request about a specific individual, family, or other historical fact. These male correspondents also imposed additional work on her. Most research requests would have been relatively light lifts for Caulkins. For instance, one author struggling with his history of Watertown, Massachusetts, urged her to put him in touch with any local descendants of Sir Richard Saltonstall, whom she discussed in her *History*. "If you have any such neighbor or personal acquaintance," he asked her, "will you do me the favor to ask him (or her) to furnish me as *full* and *minute* record of the descendants of Gov. G.S. as may be in his power."¹⁰⁰ Another correspondent from New York asked her in 1858 to check for details about his family in the New London cemetery.¹⁰¹ Charles Bushnell, who had undertaken to write a definitive history of American coins from the colonial period to the present, sought her help identifying Connecticut coins and suggested that Caulkins write a history of Saybrook, Connecticut, home of his grandfather. While she was at it, he suggested that histories of Coventry, Killingsworth, and New Haven would all be interesting.¹⁰²

Such requests made claims on Caulkins's time and unpaid labor, but they also reflected the confidence that Caulkins's readers had in her authority as a local researcher and writer who could support their own historical inquiries. Bushnell—who went so far as to request copies of her portrait to paste into his volumes of her two major histories—literally placed his local histories in a row in his New York City library. Bushnell assured Caulkins that eventually a superior history of the nation would "come forth from the press, stamped with the stamp of immortality, receiving its vitality, and deriving its freshness, its healthiness and its vigor from the local histories of our country."¹⁰³ In this way, local history could contribute to the grander goal of gathering and narrating the nation's history.

Caulkins's authority regarding local history and archival resources influenced histories of her broader region and the nation as a whole. Based on the meticulously detailed notes that she dispatched to Savage from New London, he would cite her some fifty times in his *Genealogical Dictionary* of New England's first century of colonists, which he and so many historians in the region saw as the foundation of the nation's archival materials and the start of its exceptional historical arc. Instances of her archival labor appeared throughout the text, too. Savage cited her histories and her correspondence with him to substantiate and corroborate—or verify the absence of—facts in the historical record. While sometimes disagreeing with her historical interpretations, he praised her work and recommended her books to his readers.¹⁰⁴ Meanwhile, references to her publications and other contributions appeared in the *New England Historical and Genealogical Register* in the 1850s and 1860s.¹⁰⁵

Collectors and authors of national history were eager to draw on local historical research such as Caulkins's. When Lyman Draper informed Caulkins of her nomination to the Historical Society of Wisconsin in 1855, he also prompted her to contribute whatever information or primary sources she could to their archive.[106] Given the society's focus on archiving and narrating the nation's history of westward expansion, this might have included materials about local individuals and families who had emigrated westward from Caulkins's region. Samuel Goodrich, the prolific author of national and universal history books for children—better-known to his many readers as "Peter Parley"—sought a copy of her *History of New London* directly from her after it sold out in Hartford.[107] Lorenzo Sabine, the leading historian of Loyalists during the American Revolution, whom he sought to integrate into the national narrative, contacted Caulkins about a local Loyalist mentioned in her *History of New London*.[108] From the corner of coastal Connecticut where she framed her historical inquiry, Caulkins had succeeded in using her expertise to influence networks and publications beyond it.

Institutions, researchers, and writers turned to local historians for their expert knowledge of local historical materials, but the local texts produced by people like Caulkins also had a distinctive power for readers. On a personal level, Caulkins's histories produced the pleasurable experience of recollecting historical associations at specific sites. For those drawn into the burgeoning study of family history, local history could helpfully direct them toward local archival materials and place their families within a larger historical context. In contrast with earlier perceptions that genealogy was an aristocratic practice at odds with American ideals, by the end of the antebellum period "a new genealogical regime dominated by middle-class, family-related, republican moral concerns while reinforcing many Americans' sense of self as individuals and citizens," such that examination of family history could bolster one's sense of belonging within the nation's history.[109] Writing from New Haven after the publication of *History of Norwich* in 1845, one reader thanked Caulkins for stirring "many very interesting reminiscences of former times and things which without such memorial would soon have been lost forever."[110] Such readers found in Caulkins's scholarship a deeply meaningful personal connection with minute details that she had painstakingly gathered.

Advocates of local history also argued that it had the capacity to cultivate a citizen's sense of belonging and identity in a way that state, regional, or global history could not.[111] Admiring readers moreover appreciated Caulkins's attention to a range of actors in Norwich and New London society rather than the elites who typically dominated historical narratives. One avid reader of local histories wrote from Cambridge, Massachusetts, to explain, "I value yours the more especially because you have not fancied the muse of history too nice to enter the dressingroom and the kitchen. For my own part I am glad to know how our ancestors dressed on Sundays, and what puddings they eat on special occasions."[112] These details—authenticated by documents, gravestones, and corroborating oral testimony—could bring the reader into closer contact with ancestors and the historical community with which the reader identified. Caulkins introduced her 1849 annotated edition of the Reverend William Adams's diary in these very terms, arguing that its value lay not in its evidence about critical events, but in "the sober, everyday variations in the life of the young student, and the domestic history of the minister, with the vivid, unexaggerated accuracy of a reflection."[113] By focusing her gaze on the materials within the modest boundaries of her towns, she could exhaustively examine its historical record within this plot and connect readers with the authentic details of life there.

From this vantage point, local history directed readers to view their town's trajectory spanning from its founding moment, through contests with Indigenous peoples and conquest of their lands, to colonial growth, revolution, and success within an independent nation. In her histories of Norwich and New London, Caulkins invited readers to envision the glorious future of these towns through the gaze of its first settlers. "It is not strange," she wrote early in her 1845 *History of Norwich*, "that a place possessed of such advantages by nature, when once known to the English, should have been highly prized by them; or that when obtained from the natives, it should be speedily settled; or that since its settlement, it should have grown and prospered more uniformly and extensively, than any other town in the eastern part of the state."[114] Seven years later, her *History of New London* cast readers in a similar sort of historical re-creationism, describing the town founder, John Winthrop Jr., "with knapsack and musket, under the guidance of some Indian chief." "How his heart would beat," she prompted her readers to imagine, "could he now stand upon that spot in the garb of mortality, with earthly feelings still yearning in his bosom, and survey the fair town which he first began to hew out of the wilderness!"[115] Through such rhetorical devices, Caulkins depicted these towns as microcosms of the region's and the nation's historical trajectory, a common technique in the antebellum United States for history writers who wished to idealize the virtues of the New England town and present it "as a model for the nation," especially as industrialization and the demographic change brought by immigration transformed the region.[116]

Caulkins's interest in documenting the lives of all settlers, regardless of status or accomplishments, reflected within her local sphere the approach that Savage took over the years in preparing his comprehensive *Genealogical Dictionary* of early European settlers in New England. Caulkins understood that traces of local history could bear national significance by authenticating the providential arc of progress from colonization to nationhood. In an essay on New London's old burial ground published in 1859, Caulkins argued that the simplicity of that "unadorned resting place of the hardy emigrants" actually served to remind the living of the "trials and deprivations of an infant settlement, planted as this was, far away from others and in the immediate neighborhood and companionship of savage tribes."[117] The physical qualities of the historical record—whether these deteriorated gravestones or the fragmentary paper record—attested to the exceptional historical circumstances and lives of the many modest historical actors who produced them, every trace of which was part of the exceptional history of the nation, as she viewed it. Within her local frame, Caulkins contributed to the larger historiographical project of vindicating American imperialism by celebrating the triumph of these "hardy emigrants" over "savage tribes," shared with historians like fellow MHS member George Bancroft.

Savage, like Caulkins, included "*every* settler, without regard to his rank, or wealth" within the scope of his topic. Savage saw the history of New England as an arc of progress emanating from this settler community. In the space of a few generations, he observed "descendants of the most humble (thank God we are all equal before the law) filling honorable stations and performing important services."[118] In their eyes, it was essential to gather every authenticating trace of this exceptional history.

Savage's archive of genealogical data on seventeenth-century New England settlers, to which Caulkins and so many others contributed, represented what he believed to be a people superior because of its cultural and racial homogeneity. Although Savage delved into English archives for evidence about his subject, he believed that between colonization and the outbreak of the American Revolution, "a purer Anglo Saxon race would be seen on this side of the ocean than on the other," which he calculated at 98 percent hailing from the Kingdom of England prior to the upheavals in England that "brought from the continent an infusion upon the original stock." Even if his genealogical data stopped in 1692, Savage used this palette to paint New England's enduring community as exceptional in the scope of global history: "A more homogenous stock cannot be seen, I think, in any so extensive a region, as any time, since that when the ark of Noah discharged its passengers on Mount Ararat, except in the few centuries before the confusion of Babel."[119] Within this distinctly white settler conception of history, each genealogical fact of an individual settler's life represented a vision of history that authenticated the region and every local community as exceptional.

In addition to the increasingly diverse immigrant populations moving to the antebellum United States, this racist historical vision and conception of authentic historical materials marginalized the complex Indigenous history of the region and demeaned historical knowledge that was not inscribed in documents. Surveying the field of local historical writing in this period, the historian Jean O'Brien explains that "the collective story these texts told insisted that non-Indians held exclusive sway over modernity, denied modernity to Indians, and in the process created a narrative of Indian extinction."[120] Local historians emphasized the archival traces left by settlers and their descendants who had displaced these Indigenous inhabitants in order to authenticate their own exceptional place within history—whether in their town, in New England, or the nation and its place in global history as a whole.

Some historians have attributed the new popularity of local history in Caulkins's time to "a new sense of the relationship between the present and the past," in which the living felt estranged from the past and sought to connect with it.[121] This was surely true to an extent, but the example of Caulkins shows that local history was as much about a relationship between the past and those in the present who would carry their community's legacy into the future. In the hands of historians like Caulkins, the significance of local historical materials was their very ordinariness. The extensive genealogical research that she conducted to authenticate the history of New England's towns was thus not an act of nostalgia but an ambitious archival pursuit to construct histories in which the local reader could read the entire course of history, even as this project excluded vast populations from belonging within this historical community.

Prefacing her *History of New London*, Caulkins claimed that, "the hand of God is seen in the history of towns as well as in that of nations."[122] Whether providing guidance to fellow historians for their own local, state, or national histories, furnishing facts for major archival resources like Savage's that would support researchers across the region, or tracing an arc of local history that could be mapped onto the nation as a whole, Caulkins's local writing filled these wider frames.

Savage preserved Caulkins's correspondence within his own extensive genealogical papers about New England history, in which he carefully noted responses to her questions, related facts, and questions between the lines and in the margins. Like so many surviving female family members in the nineteenth century, Emma Savage Barton, his daughter, came into the possession of these papers, which she donated to the MHS. Caulkins's local frame provided her the space to produce historical knowledge, establish her reputation, and influence the writing of history to an extent that otherwise would have likely found beyond her reach as a woman. In doing so, she wrote her way into Savage's archival collection and membership in one of the nation's leading historical institutions. Local historical labor like Caulkins's came closest to realizing the ideal of archival exceptionalism that institutions like the MHS had envisioned for decades: a comprehensive collection of a community's course through time, preserved for posterity within an archive, even as others denied belonging were left beyond its threshold.

Conclusion

Addressing the audience assembled by the Maine Historical Society at the state capital in Augusta in 1855, William Willis—who would serve as the society's president through the Civil War—explained the scope of their work to salvage its historical record. "The labors of the Society regard all parts of the State," he promised; "they are not sectional or partizan." This claim had echoed from older historical societies in eastern states to newer institutions across the nation's expanding continental empire. By envisioning a disinterested archive that would serve the entire state, Maine's historical establishment resembled others. Like archival advocates throughout the country, Willis agonized about the vanishing past while touting the promise of America's archives to show the exceptional history of his nation. Willis also shared the conviction that the evidence of America's history from colonization to the present could be amassed, published, and examined thanks to institutions like Maine's. "The origin of the old nations of the earth, is like that of our aborigines, hidden in obscurity or lost in myth and fable; while upon this continent, it is our privilege to be able to explore the foundations on which our empire is erected, and to follow its growth from its feeble beginnings, through all its gradations to its present imposing magnitude and beautiful proportions."[1] Along with other biases toward the past and present, Willis shared this conviction about his nation's capacity to save its entire record—America's archival exceptionalism.

Willis described the nation's history as a monumental edifice, its "foundations" produced by the colonists who claimed sites like Pemaquid on

Maine's southern coast, its "present imposing magnitude and beautiful proportions" reflected in the very presence of those attending his speech. By this point, it had become clear to people like Willis that no individual collector, historical society, state, or even the federal government could build this structure. "To his end," he applauded, "Historical Societies have been established in all the old States, which have drawn forth from obscurity a mass of materials not known, or imagined to exist, and have illuminated the whole track of the history of the country, from its earliest colonization to the present day."[2]

Like the archival actors who appear throughout this book, Willis and the Maine Historical Society perceived the historical record through overlapping frames: America's place within the expanse of global history, the exceptional history of the nation, the significance of each state within this nation, and the place of a state's many localities within each of these larger frames. The local history of the Pemaquid colony evoked in his speech, for instance, could signify the distinctiveness of the state, both within the nation's narrative and the larger global process of European exploration and colonization in the hemisphere. Evidence for these different frames of archival collecting and historical thinking were compiled in the very *Collections* where Willis's speech appeared: a memorial on the settlement of Kittery, Indian treaties struck with the government of Massachusetts (before Maine was a state), and a 1789 letter from George Washington to Secretary of War Henry Knox. In the following years, the historical society would seek evidence for medieval Norse exploration of its coastline.

Willis implied that the nation's exceptional historical record, once gathered, would coalesce into a magnificent monument of the nation's past. This book has shown that the process was far more complicated. Between the nation's founding and the Civil War, the many institutions formed and the myriad Americans mobilized to archive and interpret the nation's historical record regularly diverged. They disagreed about why certain historical materials were significant or not, as revealed in the transatlantic exchange of evidence with the Royal Society of Northern Antiquaries about America's place within global history. They disputed who was responsible for preserving the nation's historical materials and where these belonged, the uncertainty that Jared Sparks navigated as he collected, edited, and published *The Writings of George Washington*. They struggled over how to secure the support, recognition, and materials needed to illuminate the historical arcs that they envisioned, whether in Maine, Kentucky, Pennsylvania, or New York. And historians such as Frances Manwaring Caulkins scrutinized the meaning of local historical records and questioned the findings of fellow researchers. The historical edifice imagined by Willis and so many others remained unfinished, its threshold contested and contingent.

Building this edifice nonetheless enabled researchers and historical establishments, state and federal sponsors of archival collecting and publication, and international intellectual networks to not only expand archives but to develop practices that would shape the emerging historical discipline. Within their frame of archival collecting and historical analysis, researchers like New London's Caulkins, state officials like New York's Edmund Bailey O'Callaghan, national collectors like Sparks, and international correspondents such as Carl Christian Rafn and his American interlocutors all tirelessly pursued the evidence they deemed relevant and authentic.

Who, however, crossed the threshold of this archival structure? Which materials formed its foundation? What vision of history did they illuminate within? Gatekeepers like Willis envisioned the nation's exceptional archives, but this notion neglected so many other sources, as evidenced by his disparagement of Indigenous historical knowledge, and diminished both past and contemporary communities harmed by the "imposing magnitude and beautiful proportions" of the empire he celebrated. By narrowing their frame around the historical traces of European settlers and their typically elite descendants, these historical institutions, their networks of members, and the state and federal government that supported them simultaneously obscured or expelled the experiences of Indigenous societies, newer immigrant populations, and enslaved Africans and their descendants—archival losses that as much as archival accessions in this period bear today on our ability to decipher the past.[3]

However much they imposed their assumptions and prejudices about America's historical trajectory onto the historical record, these builders of archives carefully analyzed, interpreted, and reinterpreted this evidence, often within scholarly networks that circulated findings, shared guidance, and challenged conclusions. From self-trained researchers examining local tombstones to diplomatic agents exploring foreign archives, these many hands began to center objectivity in their archival collecting and historical analysis, the ideal "enthroned" by the professionalized discipline that emerged in the late nineteenth century.[4]

In doing so, they also contributed to the development of new archival norms. On the personal level, this included women winning greater access to archival sources and scholarly communities. Figures such as Sarah Josepha Hale, Lydia Sigourney, Deborah Norris Logan, Catharine Maria Sedgwick, and Caulkins engaged with scholarly communities and crossed the archival threshold in different ways, progress that women would build upon as the discipline professionalized later in the nineteenth century.[5] At the state level, the impetus to fill the nation's archives stirred a sense of civic responsibility and spurred many states to preserve and make public their historical records, which aided researchers and built administrative capacities that would expand even further in the cloven historical landscape after the Civil War. Internationally, even as the US government made only modest investments in the preservation and publication of the nation's archives, its diplomatic and consular officials regularly became cultural intermediaries and advocates of historical research and writing, arguing for researchers' right to access public archives in other countries.

Throughout the antebellum period, the belief in such a thing as a shared history moved these many actors to reinforce this imperfect, uncertain edifice. As late as 1858, South Carolina Historical Society president James Louis Petigru could announce: "Let us leave to [George] Bancroft, and the masters of the historic page, the ample roll of fame, and the honored task of inscribing a nation's gratitude on the tablet of memory. It is enough for us to have shown that our State has furnished some historic materials, and called attention to the objects of our Society."[6] Even on the eve of national disunion, it was conceivable that archives could sustain a historical narrative that transcended divisions not only within a state like Maine but across the nation's sectional rift. No matter how much had been committed to building such an edifice in the decades since independence, history became one of the many structures collapsed by the Civil War.[7]

NOTES

INTRODUCTION

1. *Report of the Committee of the New York Historical Society, on a National Name*, 31 March 1845, 1–3, reprinted in *Proceedings of the New York Historical Society for the Year 1845* (1846): 115–24.
2. *Report on a National Name*, 5.
3. *Report on a National Name*, 7. For nineteenth-century Americans' understanding of the Indigenous civilizations that had constructed earthen architecture in eastern North America, see Terry Barnhart, *American Antiquities: Revisiting the Origins of American Archaeology* (Lincoln: University of Nebraska Press, 2015); Edward Watts, *Colonizing the Past: Mythmaking and Pre-Columbian Whites in Nineteenth-Century American Writing* (Charlottesville: University of Virginia Press, 2020); and Christen Mucher, *Before American History: Nationalist Mythmaking and Indigenous Dispossession* (Charlottesville: University of Virginia Press, 2022).
4. *Report on a National Name*, 6–7.
5. For Adams's impact on US foreign policy and territorial expansion, see Samuel Flagg Bemis, *John Quincy Adams and the Foundations of American Foreign Policy* (New York: Knopf, 1956); William Earl Weeks, *John Quincy Adams and American Global Empire* (Lexington: University Press of Kentucky, 1992); and Charles N. Edel, *Nation Builder: John Quincy Adams and the Grand Strategy of the Republic* (Cambridge, MA: Harvard University Press, 2014).
6. John Quincy Adams to John Jay, 29 May 1845, Corresponding Secretary, Correspondence, 1st ser., vol. IV, MHS Pre-1900 Archives, Massachusetts Historical Society, Boston. He crossed out the second half of this sentence in the draft letter. The final letter was presented at the 28 May

1845 MHS meeting and reprinted in *Proceedings of the Massachusetts Historical Society* 2 (1835): 315–17.
7. For examinations of how Americans have perceived Christopher Columbus, see Claudia L. Bushman, *America Discovers Columbus: How an Italian Explorer Became an American Hero* (Hanover, NH: University Press of New England, 1992); and Elise Bartosik-Velez, *The Legacy of Christopher Columbus in the Americas: New Nations and a Transatlantic Discourse of Empire* (Nashville: Vanderbilt University Press, 2014).
8. *Report on a National Name*, 3.
9. *Proceedings of the New York Historical Society for the Year 1845* (1846): 209–29.
10. *Proceedings of the Massachusetts Historical Society* 2 (1835): 316.
11. "An Account of the Celebration by the New York Historical Society of Their Fortieth Anniversary, Wednesday, Nov. 20th, 1844," *Proceedings of the New York Historical Society for the Year 1844* (1845): 68–70.
12. The term "American Indian" will be used wherever relevant throughout this book in order to reflect the sovereign status of American Indian nations in accordance with treaties with the US government.
13. Many of the articles and books on America's early archives are recounted in the institutional publications commissioned by those very historical societies. Institutional histories are myriad, typically published within a given society's *Proceedings*, *Transactions*, or *Collections*, or in special anniversary accounts; for an excellent recent instance of the latter, see Philip F. Gura, *The American Antiquarian Society, 1812–2012: A Bicentennial History* (Worcester, MA: AAS, 2012). The traditional surveys of historical societies include Leslie Dunlap, *American Historical Societies, 1790–1860* (Madison, WI: Cantwell Printing, 1944); Walter Muir Whitehill, *Independent Historical Societies: An Enquiry into Their Research and Publication Functions and Their Financial Future* (Cambridge, MA: Harvard University Press, 1962); David Van Tassel, *Recording America's Past: An Interpretation of the Development of Historical Studies in America, 1607–1884* (Chicago: University of Chicago Press, 1960); and Clifford Lord, ed., *Keepers of the Past* (Chapel Hill: University of North Carolina Press, 1965). Recent works have begun to enrich our understanding of these institutions, but most studies have not explored the range of their social networks, the scope of their collections, and their imprint on American historical consciousness, such as Alea Henle's *Rescued from Oblivion: Historical Cultures in the Early United States* (Amherst: University of Massachusetts Press, 2020).

14. Forms of historical commemoration, preservation, and narration in this period are analyzed in such works as David Waldstreicher, *In the Midst of Perpetual Fetes: The Making of American Nationalism, 1776–1820* (Chapel Hill: University of North Carolina Press, 1997); Len Travers, *Celebrating the Fourth: Independence Day and the Rites of Nationalism in the Early Republic* (Amherst: University of Massachusetts Press, 1997); Sara Purcell, *Sealed with Blood: War, Sacrifice, and Memory in Revolutionary America* (Philadelphia: University of Pennsylvania Press, 2002); Susan M. Stabile, *Memory's Daughters: The Material Culture of Remembrance in Eighteenth-Century America* (Ithaca, NY: Cornell University Press, 2004); and Tom Wright, ed., *The Cosmopolitan Lyceum: Lecture Culture and the Globe in Nineteenth-Century America* (Amherst: University of Massachusetts Press, 2013).
15. Eileen Ka-May Cheng, *The Plain and Noble Garb of Truth: Nationalism and Impartiality in American Historical Writing, 1784–1860* (Athens: University of Georgia Press, 2008); François Weil, *Family Trees: A History of Genealogy in America* (Cambridge, MA: Harvard University Press, 2013); Lindsay DiCuirci, *Colonial Revivals: The Nineteenth-Century Lives of Early American Books* (Philadelphia: University of Pennsylvania Press, 2018); Henle, *Rescued from Oblivion*.
16. Mary Kelley, *Private Woman, Public Stage: Literary Domesticity in Nineteenth-Century America* (New York: Oxford University Press, 1984); Nina Baym, *American Women Writers and the Work of History, 1790–1860* (New Brunswick, NJ: Rutgers University Press, 1995); Julie Des Jardins, *Women and the Historical Enterprise in America: Gender, Race, and the Politics of Memory* (Chapel Hill: University of North Carolina Press, 2003).
17. Bonnie Smith, *The Gender of History: Men, Women, and Historical Practice* (Cambridge, MA: Harvard University Press, 1998).
18. For instance, the uses of historical materials to construct narratives about Indigenous North American history have been investigated in such excellent works as Jean O'Brien's *Firsting and Lasting: Writing Indians out of Existence in New England* (Minneapolis: University of Minnesota Press, 2010). The narratives that allege a medieval European colonization of North America have been intricately analyzed in Annette Kolodny's *In Search of First Contact: The Vikings of Vinland, the Peoples of Dawnland, and the Anglo-American Anxiety of Discovery* (Durham, NC: Duke University Press, 2012). The perception of the colonial period in the early United States has been traced in Edward Watts, *In This Remote Country: French Colonial Culture in the Anglo-American Imagination, 1780–1860* (Chapel Hill: University of North Carolina Press, 2006), and nineteenth-century Americans'

diverse interpretations of the Revolution in the anthology *Remembering the Revolution: Memory, History, and Nation Making from Independence to the Civil War* (Amherst: University of Massachusetts Press, 2013).

1. ENVISIONING AMERICAN ARCHIVAL EXCEPTIONALISM

1. Christopher Columbus Baldwin, *Diary of Christopher Columbus Baldwin* (Worcester, MA, 1901), 297-98.
2. "Of the Committee, Chosen by the Government of the Americas' Antiquarian Society, to Exhibit an Account of the Progress and Present State of the Institution, at the Annual Meeting in Boston," 23 October 1819, *Archaeologia Americana* 1 (1820): 47-48.
3. "Abstract of an Address to the Members of the American Antiquarian Society," *Archaeologia Americana* 1 (1820): 43.
4. "Records of the American Antiquarian Society, 1812-1849," 27 May 1833, 131, American Antiquarian Society, Worcester, MA.
5. Baldwin, *Diary*, 17 March 1834, 282.
6. Peter Fritzsche has made a compelling case for not just a shift in the perception of historical materials but in the conception of history itself caused by the Napoleonic Wars (Fritzsche, *Stranded in the Present: Modern Time and the Melancholy of History* [Cambridge, MA: Harvard University Press, 2004]).
7. "An Account of the Celebration by the New York Historical Society of Their Fortieth Anniversary, Wednesday, Nov. 20th, 1844," *Proceedings of the New York Historical Society for the Year 1844* (1845): 69-70.
8. Bernard Bailyn, *The Ordeal of Thomas Hutchinson* (Cambridge, MA: Harvard University Press, 1974) is the major account of Hutchinson's fate. Posthumously, Hutchinson's *History* was finally published in 1828 in Boston, an early example of American interest in Loyalist historiography (Thomas Hutchinson, *History of the Province of Massachusetts-Bay* [1767; Boston, 1828], ii-iii). For this turn, see Eileen Ka May Cheng, "American Historical Writers and the Loyalists, 1788-1856: Dissent, Consensus, and American Nationality," *Journal of the Early Republic* 23, no. 4 (Winter 2003): 491-519.
9. John van de Wetering, "Thomas Prince's Chronological History," *William and Mary Quarterly* 18, no. 4 (October 1961): 546-57.
10. Louis Leonard Tucker, *The Massachusetts Historical Society, A Bicentennial History, 1791-1991* (Boston: Northeastern University Press, 1995), 1-3; Louis Leonard Tucker, *Clio's Consort: Jeremy Belknap and the Founding of the Massachusetts Historical Society* (Boston: Northeastern University Press,

1990), 62–64. This belief in the providential significance of the Revolution has been analyzed in depth, such as in Ruth Bloch, *Visionary Republic: Millennial Themes in American Thought, 1756–1800* (New York: Cambridge University Press, 1985); and Donald Weber, *Rhetoric and History in Revolutionary New England* (New York: Oxford University Press, 1988).

11. Jeremy Belknap, *The History of New Hampshire*, vol. 1 (Philadelphia, 1784), iv. For Belknap's impact, see Agnès de la Haye, "Jeremy Belknap and the Origins of American Exceptionalism," *Transatlantica: Revue d'Études Américaines* (2020): 1–20.

12. "To John Adams from Jeremy Belknap, 18 July 1789," Founders Online, National Archives, https://founders.archives.gov/documents/Adams/99-02-02-0683.

13. For more on the creation of national archives, see Tom Verschaffel, "'Something More Than a Storage Warehouse': The Creation of National Archives," in *Setting the Standards: Institutions, Networks and Communities of National Historigraphy*, ed. Ilaria Porciani and Jo Tollebeek, 29–46 (Basingstoke, UK: Macmillan, 2012).

14. Tucker, *Clio's Consort*, 59–61. For the eighteenth-century British context, see Stuart Piggott, *Ancient Britons and the Antiquarian Imagination: Ideas from the Renaissance to the Regency* (London: Thames and Hudson, 1989); and Martin Myrone and Lucy Peltz, eds., *Producing the Past: Aspects of Antiquarian Culture and Practice, 1700–1850* (Brookfield, VT: Ashgate, 1999). On the Royal Irish Academy (RIA) in particular, see Joep Leerssen, *Mere Irish and Fíor-Ghael: Studies in the Idea of Irish Nationality, Its Development and Literary Expression Prior to the Nineteenth Century* (1986; repr., Cork: Cork University Press, 1996); and Clare O'Hallahan, *Golden Ages and Barbarous Nations: Antiquarian Debate and Cultural Politics in Ireland, c. 1750–1800* (Cork: Cork University Press, 2004). T. O. Raifeartaigh, *The Royal Irish Academy: A Bicentennial History, 1765–1985* (Dublin: Mount Salus, 1985) traces the institutional history of the RIA.

15. Isaiah Thomas, *An Account of the American Antiquarian Society, Incorporated, October 24th, 1812* (Boston, 1813), 6–7.

16. For broader explorations of this, see Elisa Tamarkin, *Anglophilia: Deference, Devotion, and Antebellum America* (Chicago: University of Chicago Press, 2008); and Kariann Akemi Yokota, *Unbecoming British: How Revolutionary America Became a Postcolonial Nation* (New York: Oxford University Press, 2011), 14.

17. Rosemary Sweet, "The Incorporated Society and Its Public Role," in *Visions of Antiquity: The Society of Antiquaries of London, 1707–2007* (London: Society of Antiquaries of London, 2007), 186.

18. T. Pownall, *A Treatise on the Study of Antiquities* (London, 1782), 2. See also Philippa Levine, *The Amateur and the Professional: Antiquities, Historians and Archaeologists in Victorian England, 1838–1886* (Cambridge: Cambridge University Press, 1986), 4.
19. Sweet, *Visions of Antiquity*, 75.
20. Levine, *The Amateur and the Professional*, 54.
21. William Smellie, *Account of the Institution and Progress of the Society of the Antiquaries of Scotland* (Edinburgh, 1782), 14.
22. *Collections of the New-York Historical Society, for the Year 1809* 1 (1809): 6–7.
23. *Transactions of the Historical and Literary Committee of the American Philosophical Society, Held at Philadelphia, for Promoting Useful Knowledge* 1 (1819): ix–xii.
24. "Preface," *Collections of the Rhode Island Historical Society* 1 (1827): 3. The nineteenth-century conviction about the pedagogical value of history, and of biography in particular, is examined in Scott Caspar, *Constructing American Lives: Biography and Culture in Nineteenth-Century America* (Chapel Hill: University of North Carolina Press, 1999).
25. Joseph Willard to John Farmer, 25 June 1826, Records of the Corresponding Secretary of the New-Hampshire Historical Society, NHHS Archives, Concord. For more on Farmer's work, see Francois Weil, "John Farmer and the Making of Antebellum Genealogy," *New England Quarterly* 80, no. 3 (September 2007): 408–34.
26. For an excellent discussion of this relationship between historical education and citizenship, see Linda K. Kerber, *Women of the Republic: Intellect and Ideology in Revolutionary America* (Chapel Hill: University of North Carolina Press, 1980), 185–232.
27. "Constitution," *Memoirs of the Historical Society of Pennsylvania* 1 (1826): 13.
28. *Collections of the Virginia Historical and Philosophical Society: To Which an Address Is Prefixed by Jonathan P. Cushing* 1 (1833): 14.
29. Annual Address by General Smith, 6 February 1845, Box 37, Ms. 2008, Institutional Archives, Maryland Historical Society, Baltimore.
30. For the relationship between spatial and temporal reasoning and national identity in the early United States, see Martin Brückner, *The Geographic Revolution in Early America: Maps, Literacy, and National Identity* (Chapel Hill: University of North Carolina Press, 2006); and Thomas M. Allen, *A Republic in Time: Temporality and Social Imagination in Nineteenth-Century America* (Chapel Hill: University North Carolina Press, 2008).
31. Correspondence and other loose papers, vol. 1, 1791–1813, Box 7, MHS.

32. Jeremy Belknap, "Plan of an Antiquarian Society, August 1790," *Proceedings of the Massachusetts Historical Society, 1791–1835* 1 (1879): xii.
33. Correspondence and other loose papers, vol. 1, 1791–1813, Box 7, MHS.
34. Louis Leonard Tucker, *The Massachusetts Historical Society, A Bicentennial History, 1791–1991* (Boston: Northeastern University Press, 1995), 25.
35. George Gibbs to MHS, Corresponding Secretary Correspondence, 1812–1833, Box 14, MHS.
36. "To the Public," *Collections of the New-York Historical Society, for the Year 1809* 1 (1809): 8.
37. *Address to the Members of the American Antiquarian Society*, March 1819 (Worcester, MA, 1819), 3.
38. *Proceedings of the Massachusetts Historical Society, 1791–1835* 1 (1879): 56.
39. "Introduction," *Collections of the Georgia Historical Society* 1 (1840): xi–xii.
40. Gouverneur Morris, "An Inaugural Discourse Delivered before the New-York Historical Society," 4 September 1816, *Collections of the New-York Historical Society for the Year 1821* 3 (1821): 30.
41. "Act of Incorporation," in *The Act of Incorporation, Constitution, and By-Laws of the New-Hampshire Historical Society* (Concord, 1823), 3.
42. "Articles on Which the Society Wish for More Information," *New-Hampshire Historical Society*, 19–21.
43. "Constitution," *Collections of the Rhode Island Historical Society* 1 (1827): 7–8.
44. Rawle, "Inaugural Address," *Memoirs of the Historical Society of Pennsylvania* 1 (1826): 39.
45. The "Table-Book of the Officers of the Maryland Historical Society" captures this standard meeting format (17 April 1845, Box 36, Ms. 2008, Maryland Historical Society).
46. *Proceedings of the Massachusetts Historical Society, 1791–1835* 1 (1879): 58
47. Lewis Cass to John Farmer, 25 July 1831, Records of the Corresponding Secretary of the New-Hampshire Historical Society, NHHS Archives.
48. Willis Papers, vol. O, Collection 175, Maine Historical Society, Portland.
49. Burnside to Du Ponceau, 26 March 1821, Letter Book, AAS.
50. No substantial biography of Warden exists. His extensive papers are held mainly by the Maryland Historical Society.
51. January 1819 quarterly meeting, *Proceedings of the Massachusetts Historical Society, 1791–1835* 1 (1879): 277–78.
52. Sarah Josepha Hale, *The Genius of Oblivion; and Other Original Poems. By a Lady of New-Hampshire* (Concord, NH, 1823). Hale's *Genius of Oblivion* became the first substantial fictional appropriation of the theories then

circulating about the origin and fate of the Mound Builders, which have been surveyed in Edward Watts, *Colonizing the Past: Mythmaking and Pre-Columbian Whites in Nineteenth-Century American Writing* (Charlottesville: University of Virginia Press, 2020), 23–53. I examine Hale's poem and engagement with this theory at greater length in "Borrowed Books and Scholarly Interventions in Sarah Josepha Hale's Genius of Oblivion (1823)," *Libraries: Culture, History, and Society* 6, no. 2 (2022): 304–32.

53. Terry Barnhart discusses this tendency in *American Antiquities: Revisiting the Origins of American Archaeology* (Lincoln: University of Nebraska Press, 2015), 159.
54. Sarah Josepha Hale to Jacob Bailey Moore, 24 January 1823, Jacob Bailey Moore Papers (MS Am 800.51), Houghton Library, Harvard University, Cambridge, MA. Subsequent citations of letters between Hale and Moore are found in this collection.
55. Hale to Moore, 24 January 1823.
56. Sarah Josepha Hale to Jacob Bailey Moore, 25 March 1823.
57. The volume is alluded to in Sarah Josepha Hale to Jacob Bailey Moore, 21 April 1823. "Description of the Antiquities Discovered in the State of Ohio and Other Western States," *Archaeologia Americana: Transactions and Collections of the American Antiquarian Society* (1820).
58. "Description of the Antiquities Discovered in the State of Ohio and Other Western States," *Archaeologia Americana*, 3–4.
59. For the ways in which women writers used footnotes, see Nina Baym, *American Women Writers and the Work of History, 1790–1860* (New Brunswick, NJ: Rutgers University Press, 1995), 86–87.
60. Hale, *The Genius of Oblivion*, 37.
61. Hale, *The Genius of Oblivion*, 62.
62. Hale, *The Genius of Oblivion*, 72.
63. Hale, *The Genius of Oblivion*, 141.
64. For a close examination of this, see Stephane Gerson, *Pride of Place: Local Memories and Political Culture in Nineteenth-Century France* (Ithaca, NY: Cornell University Press, 2003).
65. *Address to the Members of the American Antiquarian Society*, 8.
66. Frederic de Peyster, Jr. to David Hosack, 8 February 1827, Corresponding Secretary, New-York Historical Society general correspondence, NYHS-RG 2, New York Historical Society.
67. Kentucky Historical Society to MHS, 14 February 1847, Corresponding Secretary Correspondence, Box 17, MHS.
68. 15 June 1827, NHHS Minutes.

69. *Collections of the Virginia Historical and Philosophical Society: To Which an Address Is Prefixed by Jonathan P. Cushing*, vol. 1 (Richmond: Thomas W. White, 1833), 10.
70. *Rhode Island Historical Society, Sketch of Its History* (Providence, 1898), 6–7.
71. "An Act of Incorporation," *Collections of the Maine Historical Society* 1 (1831): ii.
72. Elizabeth Yale, "'The Manuscripts Flew about Like Butterflies': Self-Archiving and the Pressures of History," in *Sociable Knowledge: Natural History and the Nation in Early Modern Britain*, by Yale, 205–48 (Philadelphia: University of Pennsylvania Press, 2016).
73. Thomas Wallcut, 1791, Massachusetts Historical Society Archives, Correspondence and other loose papers, Box 7, MHS.
74. "The Address of the New York Historical Society," *Collections of the New-York Historical Society for the Year 1809* (1811): 7.
75. *Communication from the President of the American Antiquarian Society to the Members, October 24th, 1814* (Worcester, MA: William Manning, 1814), 5–6.
76. *An Account of the American Antiquarian Society* (Boston: Isaiah Thomas, 1813), 9–10.
77. Alfred F. Young, *The Shoemaker and The Tea Party: Memory and the American Revolution* (Boston: Beacon, 1999), depicts this popular response to aging veterans.
78. "An Account of the Rhode Island Historical Society," *American Quarterly Register* (May 1839).
79. "Annual Report of the Board of Trustees, 1823," Rhode Island Historical Society Archives, vol. 1 of Records, 1822–44.
80. Nathaniel Adams, *Collections of the New-Hampshire Historical Society for the Year 1824* 1 (1824): 2.
81. Ebenezer Clapp to John Pierce, February 1843, Dorchester Antiquarian and Historical Society, Ms. N-1128, MHS.
82. Ebenezer Clapp to Oliver Morris, 23 September 1843, Ms. N-1128, MHS.
83. For the history of this rhetorical form in the early United States, see Sacvan Bercovitch, *The American Jeremiad* (Madison: University of Wisconsin Press, 1978), 132–75.
84. Thomas Speed to John Rowan, 13 July 1841, Speed Family Papers, 1780–1905, Mss.A S742i, Filson Historical Society, Louisville, KY.
85. *Constitution and By-Laws of the New-Jersey Historical Society with the Circular of the Executive Committee* (New Jersey, 1845), 15, https://www.loc.gov/item/04007243/.

86. J. Proudfit to Corresponding Secretary of N.J. Historical Society, 7 May 1845, *Proceedings of the New Jersey Historical Society* 1 (1847; repr., 1968): 16–17.
87. *Collections of the Georgia Historical Society* 1 (1840): 4.
88. John P. Kennedy, *Discourse on the Life and Character of George Calvert*, 9 December 1845 (Baltimore, MD, 1845), 2.
89. See Malcolm Andrews, *The Search for the Picturesque: Landscape Aesthetics and Tourism in Britain, 1760–1800* (Stanford, CA: Stanford University Press, 1989); Stephen Bann, *Romanticism and the Rise of History* (New York: Twayne, 1995); and Susan Crane, *Collecting and Historical Consciousness in Early Nineteenth-Century Germany* (Ithaca, NY: Cornell University Press, 2000).
90. Arnaldo Momigliano explores the history of European antiquarianism in such works as "Ancient History and the Antiquarian," *Journal of the Warburg and Courtauld Institutes* 13, no. 3/4 (1950): 285–315. Concerning the culture of collecting in nineteenth-century Britain, Philippa Levine, *The Amateur and the Professional: Antiquities, Historians and Archaeologists in Victorian England, 1838–1886* (Cambridge: Cambridge University Press, 1986) is the classic work.
91. "Annual Report of the Board of Trustees," 19 July 1824, RIHS.
92. Thomas Day, *A Historical Discourse Delivered before the Connecticut Historical Society and the Citizens of Hartford*, 26 December 1843 (Hartford, 1844), 36.
93. Edward Everett, *The Mount Vernon Papers* (New York, 1860), 17.
94. John Pintard, "To the Public: The Address of the New-York Historical Society," reprinted in R. W. G. Vail, *Knickerbocker Birthday: A Sesqui-Centennial History of the New-York Historical Society, 1804–1954* (New York: New-York Historical Society, 1954), 452.
95. "Introductory Remarks," *Collections of the Maine Historical Society* 1 (1831).
96. William Law, "Oration Delivered before the Georgia Historical Society at the Celebration of Its First Anniversary," 12 February 1840, *Collections of the Georgia Historical Society* 1 (1840): 1–2.
97. *Proceedings of the New York Historical Society for the Year 1844* (1845): 61–62.
98. Chancellor Jack Kent, "An Anniversary Discourse Delivered before the New-York Historical Society," 6 December 1828, *Collections of the New-York Historical Society*, 2nd ser., vol. 1 (1841): 12.
99. John Romeyn Brodhead, *An Address Delivered before the New York Historical Society, at Its Fortieth Anniversary, 20th November, 1844* (New York, 1844), 49.

100. *The Charter of Incorporation and By-Laws of the Connecticut Historical Society* (Hartford, 1839), 3.
101. This sense of a vanishing documentary record of American history was expressed alongside anxiety about the loss of the natural environment and the culture of Indigenous peoples as westward expansion swelled. This led men like George Catlin and Colonel Thomas L. McKenney, superintendent of the Indian Trade Bureau, to build their own collections of Indian portraits, artifacts, and oral histories (see Lee Clark Mitchell, *Witnesses to a Vanishing America: The Nineteenth-Century Response* [Princeton, NJ: Princeton University Press, 1980], 102–17).
102. Willis, "Introductory Address before the Maine Historical Society, February 2, 1855, at Augusta," *Collections of the Maine Historical Society* 4 (1856): 4.
103. Jean M. O'Brien, *Firsting and Lasting: Writing Indians out of Existence in New England* (Minneapolis: University of Minnesota Press, 2010), 19.
104. Lyman Draper, *An Essay on the Collections of the Signers of the Declaration of Independence and of the Constitution*, Wisconsin Historical Collections 10 (1889): 15. John M. Mulder and Isabelle Stouffer, "William Buell Sprague: Patriarch of American Collectors," *American Presbyterians* 64, no. 1 (Spring 1986): 1–17, is the most reliable recent discussion of Sprague's life. They estimate his collection of autographs to number as high as one hundred thousand pieces.
105. Edward G. Lengel, *Inventing George Washington: America's Founder, in Myth and Memory* (New York: HarperCollins, 2011), 16.
106. William Buell Sprague to Thomas Raffles, 15 October 1828, Joseph E. Field collection of letters by autograph collectors, MS Am 1630, Houghton Library.
107. William Buell Sprague to Eliza Allen, 18 July 1845, MS Am 1630, Houghton Library.
108. This seems in contrast to the fascinating analysis of contemporary American handwriting in Tamara Plakins Thornton, *Handwriting in America* (New Haven, CT: Yale University Press, 1996), 81.
109. "Pickings of a Portfolio of Autographs," *Southern Literary Messenger*, 18 November 1856.
110. "Catalogue of Autographs in Possession of WB Sprague," Collection 623, Sprague Collection, Historical Society of Pennsylvania, Philadelphia.
111. Sparks to Sprague, 18 March 1838, MS Sparks 147a, Houghton Library.
112. Sparks to Sprague, 15 April 1832, MS Sparks 147a, Houghton Library.
113. Sparks to Forsyth, 13 January 1839, MS Sparks 147g, Houghton Library; Charles Moore, *A Biographical Sketch of the Rev. William Buell Sprague* (New York, 1877), 5.

114. 21 December 1791, MHS Correspondence and other loose papers, vol. I, 1791–1813, Box 7, MHS.
115. "Catalogue of Books, Pamphlets, Manuscripts, and Maps belonging to the Library of the Maine Historical Society," 5 February 1822, Entry 135, Institutional Records, Maine Historical Society.
116. "Preface," *Collections of the Rhode Island Historical Society* 3 (1835): 5.
117. Box 1, 1843, Sylvester Judd to Ebenezer Clapp, Ms. N-1128, MHS.
118. *Constitution and By-Laws of the New-Jersey Historical Society with the Circular of the Executive Committee* 16–17.
119. For more on Ludewig, see Alex Anderson, "Hermann Ernst Ludewig, 1809–56: Bibliographer," *Library Quarterly* 14, no. 2 (April 1944): 126–31; and Michael Winship, *Hermann Ernst Ludewig: America's Forgotten Bibliographer*, 1985 Sol. M. Malkin Lecture (New York: Columbia University, 1986).
120. Hermann E. Ludewig, *The Literature of American Local History; A Bibliographical Essay* (New York, 1856), vii.
121. "First Annual Report and Collections of the State Historical Society, of Wisconsin, for the Year 1854," in *Collections of the State Historical Society of Wisconsin*, vol. 1 (1855; Madison, 1903), 15, https://content.wisconsinhistory.org/digital/collection/whc/id/14911.
122. Reuben Gold Thwaites, "Lyman Copeland Draper, A Memoir," *Collections of the State Historical Society of Wisconsin* 12 (Madison, 1892), https://content.wisconsinhistory.org/digital/collection/whc/id/6751, 1–22.
123. Richard Magoon in 1845, quoted in Reuben G. Thwaites, "A Brief History of the Wisconsin Historical Society," in *The State Historical Society of Wisconsin*, ed. Thwaites (Madison, 1901), 95. See also "Objects of Collection Desired by the Society," *Second Annual Report and Collections of the State Historical Society of Wisconsin* 1 (1856; repr., State Historical Society of Wisconsin, 1903).
124. Benjamin Tappan, *Discourse Delivered before the Ohio Historical and Philosophical Society*, 22 December 1832 (Ohio, 1833), 7.

2. CONTESTING AMERICA'S GLOBAL ARCHIVE

1. Announced in a notice prior to the work's publication in 1837: "*Antiquitates Americanæ; Or a Collection of the Accounts Extant in Ancient Icelandic, and Other Scandinavian Manuscripts, Relative to Voyages of Discovery to North America*," *North American Review* 43, no. 92 (July 1836): 265.
2. See, for instance, Anthony Pagden, *European Encounters with the New World: From Renaissance to Romanticism* (New Haven, CT: Yale University Press, 1993).

3. Annette Kolodny, *In Search of First Contact: The Vikings of Vinland, the Peoples of Dawnland, and the Anglo-American Anxiety of Discovery* (Durham, NC: Duke University Press, 2012), 26–32.
4. Washington Irving, *A History of the Life and Voyages of Christopher Columbus*, 4 vols. (London, 1828), vol. 1, 1–2.
5. Irving, *Christopher Columbus*, vol. 1, 1–2.
6. Henry Wheaton to Dr. Levi Wheaton, 9 November 1830, Henry Wheaton Family Papers, John Hay Library, Brown University, Providence, RI.
7. Henry Wheaton Diary, 18 October 1827, Henry Wheaton Family Papers.
8. Henry Wheaton, *History of the Northmen; or, Danes and Normans, from the Earliest Times to the Conquest of England by William of Normandy* (London, 1831); Adolph B. Benson, "Henry Wheaton's Writings on Scandinavia," *Journal of English and Germanic Philology* 29, no. 4 (October 1930): 546.
9. Henry Wheaton, "*Danmarks og Hertugdommenes Statsret med stadigt Hensyn til dens ældere horfatning (The Present Public Law of Denmark, and of the Duchies, in Connexion with Its Past State)*, Vol. I by Joh. Fred. Wilhelm Schlegel, J. F. W. Schlegel," *North American Review* 27, no. 61 (October 1828): 285.
10. Wheaton, *History of the Northmen*, 24.
11. Irving, *Christopher Columbus*, vol. 4, 213–17.
12. Wheaton, *History of the Northmen*, 31.
13. "History of the Northmen," *Museum of Foreign Literature, Science, and Art*, December 1831.
14. Michael D. Hattem, *Past as Prologue: Politics and Memory in the American Revolution* (New Haven, CT: Yale University Press, 2020), 211.
15. George Bancroft, *History of the Colonization of the United States*, 2nd ed. (Boston, 1837), 5.
16. Alexander Hill Everett, "Irving's Columbus," *North American Review* (January 1829), republished in his *Critical and Miscellaneous Essays*, 2nd ser. (Boston, 1846), 176–77.
17. Irving, *Christopher Columbus*, vol. 1, 4; Elise Bartosik-Velez, *The Legacy of Christopher Columbus in the Americas: New Nations and a Transatlantic Discourse of Empire* (Nashville: Vanderbilt University Press, 2014), 82–86.
18. For Irving's complicated depiction of Columbus, see John D. Hazlett, "Literary Nationalism and Ambivalence in Washington Irving's *The Life and Voyages of Christopher Columbus*," *American Literature* 55, no. 4 (1983): 560–75.
19. Wheaton, preface to *History of the Northmen*.
20. Typically, *North American Review* articles were published anonymously, but it is often feasible to deduce their author from the content

or corroborating evidence. Henry Wheaton, "Scandinavian Mythology," *North American Review* 28, no. 62 (January 1829): 18–19.
21. Kim Simonsen, "Carl Christian Rafn," in *Encyclopedia of Romantic Nationalism in Europe*, http://show.ernie.uva.nl/CRa.
22. Announcement of works published by the Royal Society in the appendices to *Antiquitates Americanae, Mémoires de la Société Royale des Antiquaires du Nord, 1836–1839* (Copenhagen, 1839), 1; my translation.
23. *Mémoires de la Société Royale des Antiquaires du Nord, 1840–44* (Copenhagen, 1844), 23–24; my translation.
24. *Mémoires, 1836–1839*, 3–4.
25. Carl Christian Rafn to New York Historical Society, 19 August 1826, NYHS Correspondence, Institutional Archives, NYHS, New York; my translation.
26. John Farmer to Carl Christian Rafn, 31 October 1828, "Records of the Corresponding Secretary of the New-Hampshire Historical Society," NHHS Archives, Concord.
27. Benedikt Grøndal, *Breve fra og til Carl Christian Rafn, med en biographi* (Copenhagen, 1869), 42–46.
28. Kolodny, *In Search of First Contact*, 103–4. Kolodny's book should be the primary reference for anyone interested in these sagas and their influence on American culture and intellectual life in the nineteenth century, which this chapter seeks to complement with a focus on scholarly institutions and the transmission and reception of historical evidence.
29. Regarding France, see Philippe Boutry, ed., *La Province antiquaire: L'invention de l'histoire locale en France, 1800–1870* (Paris: Comite des travaux historiques et scientifiques, 2011); for Britain and the Low Countries, see Hugh Dunthorne and Michael Wintle, *The Historical Imagination in the Nineteenth-Century Britain and Low Countries* (Leiden: Brill, 2012); for Germany, see Susan A. Crane, *Collecting and Historical Consciousness in Early Nineteenth-Century Germany* (Ithaca, NY: Cornell University Press, 2000); Alice P. Kenney and Leslie J. Workman, "Ruins, Romance, and Reality: Medievalism in Anglo-American Imagination and Taste, 1750–1840," *Winterthur Portfolio* 10 (1975): 131–63.
30. "October 1829 Meeting," *Proceedings of the Massachusetts Historical Society, 1791–1835* 1 (1889): 425.
31. "Royal Society of the Northern Antiquaries of Copenhagen," *American Quarterly Register* 12, no. 1 (August 1839).
32. 29 January 1838 meeting, *Mémoires, 1836–1839*.
33. "Meetings of 1838," *Proceedings of the Massachusetts Historical Society* 2 (1880): 97–98.

34. Thomas Webb to Carl Christian Rafn, 22 September 1830, in *Antiquitates Americanæ* (Copenhagen, 1837), 356–61.
35. "Popular Poetry of the Teutonic Nations," *North American Review* 42, no. 91 (1836): 265–339.
36. *American Monthly Magazine* 10 (1838): 365–68.
37. Henry Wadsworth Longfellow to Carl Christian Rafn, 23 December 1835, in *Breve fra og til Carl Christian Rafn*, 178.
38. Carl Christian Rafn to George Marsh, 29 November 1834, in *Breve fra og til Carl Christian Rafn*, 297.
39. George Bancroft to Carl Christian Rafn, 27 December 1836, in *Breve fra og til Carl Christian Rafn*, 181.
40. "Antiquitates Americanæ; Or a Collection of the Accounts Extant in Ancient Icelandic, and Other Scandinavian Manuscripts, Relative to Voyages of Discovery to North America," 265.
41. Carl Christian Rafn to Charles Lowell, "Meetings of 1838," *Proceedings of the Massachusetts Historical Society* 2 (1880): 97.
42. "American Antiquities," *Boston Courier*, 21 July 1836.
43. Thomas Webb to Carl Christian Rafn, 30 December 1837, in *Breve fra og til Carl Christian Rafn*, 137.
44. "Scandinavian Literature and Antiquities," *Knickerbocker*, 10 September 1837.
45. George P. Marsh, *A Compendious Grammar of the Old-Northern or Icelandic Language: Compiled and Translated from the Grammars of Rask* (Burlington, VT, 1838), iii–v.
46. Carl Christan Rafn, *America Discovered in the Tenth Century* (New York, 1838). This had originally been published in French, it seems, for the sake of the 1836–39 proceedings of the Royal Academy of Northern Antiquaries as "Mémoire sur la découverte de l'Amerique au 10e siècle, par M. C.-C. Rafn, traduit par M.X. Marmier," *Mémoires de la Société Royale des Antiquaires du Nord, 1836–1839* (Copenhagen, 1839).
47. Kolodny, *In Search of First Contact*, 107–9.
48. Rafn, *America Discovered*, 31.
49. *Army and Navy Chronicle*, reprinted from the *Providence Journal*, 23 November 1837.
50. "Scandinavian Literature and Antiquities," *Knickerbocker*, 10 September 1837.
51. "The Discovery of America by the Northmen," *United States Magazine, and Democratic Review*, 2 April 1838.
52. Stephen Williams, *Fantastic Archaeology: The Wild Side of North American Prehistory* (Philadelphia: University of Pennsylvania Press, 1991), 189.

53. Kolodny, *In Search of First Contact*, 47–48.
54. For analysis of these archival and scholarly norms in the antebellum United States, see Eileen Ka-May Cheng, *The Plain and Noble Garb of Truth: Nationalism and Impartiality in American Historical Writing, 1784–1860* (Athens: University of Georgia Press, 2008).
55. "History of the Northmen," *Museum of Foreign Literature, Science, and Art*, 19 December 1831.
56. "Meetings of 1838," *Proceedings of the Massachusetts Historical Society* 2 (1880): 97.
57. Patrick J. Geary, *The Myth of Nations: The Medieval Origins of Europe* (Princeton, NJ: Princeton University Press, 2002), 15–40.
58. "Rapport des séances annuelles de 1838 et de 1839," *Mémoires, 1836–1839*, 1; my translation.
59. "A Memoir of Einar Sockeson, by Thorleif Gudmundson Repp," *Mémoires, 1840–44*, 81.
60. Laurent Etienne Borring, "Notice sur la vie et les Travaux de M. Carl-Christian Rafn" (Copenhagen, 1864), 4–7.
61. *The New-Yorker*, 31 March 1838; George Perkins Marsh, "The Origin, Progress and Decline of Icelandic," *The American Eclectic: or, Selections from the Periodical Literature of All Foreign Countries* (May 1841).
62. "Popular Poetry of the Teutonic Nations," *North American Review* (1836): 265–339.
63. Edward Everett, "Antiquitates Americanae," *North American Review* 46, no. 98 (1838): 170.
64. *North American Review* 45, no. 96 (1837): 150.
65. "America Discovered in the Tenth Century," *The Friend; a Religious and Literary Journal*, 13 January 1838.
66. "The Discovery of American by the Northmen, Article Second," *United States Magazine, and Democratic Review* (May 1838).
67. Henry Rowe Schoolcraft, "The Ante-Colombian History of America," *American Biblical Repository*, 1 April 1839.
68. George Perkins Marsh, *Life and Letters of George Perkins Marsh*, comp. Caroline Crane Marsh, vol. 1 (New York, 1888), 22; Richard Beck, "George P. Marsh and Old Icelandic Studies," *Scandinavian Studies* 17, no. 6 (1943): 198; George Marsh to Carl Christian Rafn, 21 October 1833, in *Breve fra og til Carl Christian Rafn*, 294.
69. Simon Halink, "A Tainted Legacy: Finnur Magnússon's Mythological Studies and Iceland's National Identity," *Scandinavian Journal of History* 40, no. 2 (2015): 243. Reginald Horsman places Marsh within the larger

intellectual context of American interest in Anglo-Saxon, Germanic, and Norse history in Horsman, *Race and Manifest Destiny: The Origins of American Racial Anglo-Saxonism* (Cambridge, MA: Harvard University Press, 1986), 180–82.

70. Carl Christian Rafn to George Marsh, 29 November 1834, in *Breve fra og til Carl Christian Rafn*, 298.
71. Marsh, *Compendious Grammar*, iii–iv. Marsh's Scandinavian collection was donated to the University of Vermont in 1883. His extensive collection of published Scandinavian literature, language books, and scholarship is listed in *Catalogue of the Library of George Perkins Marsh* (Burlington, VT, 1892).
72. "Literary," *London Athenaeum*, reprinted in *Daily National Journal*, 21 October 1831.
73. "History of the Northmen," *Ariel*, 7 January 1832.
74. See Ann Fabian, *The Unvarnished Truth: Personal Narratives in Nineteenth-Century America* (Berkeley: University of California Press, 2000).
75. Marsh, *Compendious Grammar*, ix.
76. Asahel Davis, *A Lecture on the Discovery of America by the Northmen, Five Hundred Years before Columbus*, 4th ed. (New York, 1839), 19; Wheaton, *History of the Northmen*, 50.
77. "Henderson's Iceland," *North American Review* (July 1832).
78. "America Discovered in the Tenth Century," *The Friend*, 13 January 1838.
79. Davis, *Lecture*, 15.
80. Kolodny, *In Search of First Contact*, 46–47.
81. Lydia Maria Child, "The Northmen," *Columbian Lady's and Gentleman's Magazine*, 6 December 1846.
82. David Levin, *History as Romantic Art* (Palo Alto, CA: Stanford University Press, 1959), 75.
83. Reginald Horsman, *Race and Manifest Destiny: The Origins of American Racial Anglo-Saxonism* (Cambridge, MA: Harvard University Press, 1986), 177–80. Ann Fabian's *The Skull Collectors: Race, Science, and America's Unburied Dead* (Chicago: University of Chicago Press, 2010) recounts the history of the construction of global racial categories in the antebellum period, which developed as the Norse theory met American readers.
84. *Massachusetts Quarterly Review*, 6 March 1849.
85. Kolodny, *In Search of First Contact*, 134.
86. For the racialized construction of Norse identity in the late nineteenth century, see Jørn Brøndal, "'The Fairest among the So-Called White

Race': Portrayals of Scandinavian Americans in the Filiopietistic and Nativist Literature of the Late Nineteenth and Early Twentieth Centuries," *Journal of American Ethnic History* 33, no. 3 (Spring 2014): 5–36. Robin Fleming presents the fascinating broader context of American interest in medieval aesthetics and history in "Picturesque History and the Medieval in Nineteenth-Century America," *American Historical Review* 100, no. 4 (October 1995): 1061–94; and Janet A. Headley discusses how New England's interest in Norse history related to the content of demographic change and racial anxiety in Boston in "Anne Whitney's 'Leif Eriksson': A Brahmin Response to Christopher Columbus," *American Art* 17, no. 2 (Summer 2003): 40–59.

87. Carl Christian Rafn, *Supplement to the "Antiquitates Americanae"* (Copenhagen, 1841), 4.
88. "Accounts of a Discovery of Antiquities Made at Fall River, Massachusetts," *Mémoires 1840–44*, 108.
89. *Mémoires, 1836–1839*, 372.
90. "Accounts of a Discovery of Antiquities Made at Fall River, Massachusetts," *Mémoires 1840–44*, 116.
91. *Mémoires 1840–1844*, 155–56.
92. *North American and Daily Advertiser*, 8 August 1840.
93. *Mémoires, 1840–44*, 8–9.
94. *Daily National Intelligencer*, 30 November 1838.
95. George Bancroft, *History of the Colonization of the United States*, vol. 3 (Boston, 1840), 313.
96. Henry R. Schoolcraft, *An Address, Delivered before the New York Historical Society, at Its Forty-Second Anniversary, 17th November 1846* (New York, 1847), 9–10.
97. Salma Hale, *History of the United States, from Their First Settlement as Colonies to the Close of the Administration of Mr. Madison in 1817*, vol. 1 (New York, 1840), 2.
98. Namely, through such works as *Evening Readings in History* (1833) and *Letters to Young Ladies* (1833). See Nina Baym, "Reinventing Lydia Sigourney," *American Literature* 62, no. 3 (September 1990): 385–404; and Sandra A. Zagarell, "Expanding 'America': Lydia Sigourney's *Sketch of Connecticut*, Catharine Sedgwick's *Hope Leslie*," in "Woman and Nation," special issue, *Tulsa Studies in Women's Literature* 6, no. 2 (Autumn 1987): 225–45.
99. Mrs. L. H. Sigourney, *Scenes in My Native Land* (Boston, 1845), 262, https://books.google.com/books?id=5DIfAAAAMAAJ&pg=PA262&

source=gbs_toc_r&cad=2#v=onepage&q&f=false. Sigourney was "a bold literary entrepreneur," as explained in Melissa Ladd Teed, "A Passion for Distinction: Lydia Huntley Sigourney and the Creation of a Literary Reputation," *New England Quarterly* 77, no. 1 (March 2004): 68. Her lengthy publication list and publishing and marketing techniques are surveyed by Gary Kelly, ed., *Lydia Sigourney: Selected Poetry and Prose* (Ontario: Broadview Editions, 2008).

100. Sigourney, *Scenes in My Native Land*, 208.
101. A discussion of possible Scandinavian voyages to North America appeared in an appendix to the last of Washington Irving's four-volume 1828 *History of the Life and Voyages of Christopher Columbus*.
102. Sigourney, *Scenes in My Native Land*, 77.
103. Joshua Toulmin Smith, *The Discovery of America by the Northmen in the Tenth Century* (London, 1839), iii.
104. Everett, "*Antiquitates Americanae*," *North American Review*, 162.
105. Irving, *Life of Columbus*, vol. 1, 2.
106. *Mémoires 1838–39*, 1.
107. *Carroll Free Press*, reprinted from *National Gazette and National Intelligencer*, 29 July 1836.
108. "American Antiquities," *Boston Courier*, 21 July 1836.
109. *Daily Commercial Bulletin and Missouri Literary Register*, 15 September 1836.
110. *New York Review*, 2 April 1838.
111. Davis, *Lecture*, 21.
112. *Alexandria Gazette*, 3 August 1836.
113. Schoolcraft, *Address Delivered before the New York Historical Society*, 10.
114. *The New-Yorker*, 31 March 1838.
115. Charles Goodrich, *Great Events in the History of North and South America* (Hartford, CT, 1851), 20–25.
116. Edward Larkin, *The American School of Empire* (Cambridge: Cambridge University Press, 2016).
117. *Christian Examiner and General Review*, 27 September 1839.
118. Bartosik-Velez, *Legacy of Christopher Columbus in the Americas*, 6.
119. Rev. Paul C. Sinding, of Copenhagen, *History of Scandinavia, from the Early Times of the Northmen and Vikings to the Present Day* (New York, 1860), viii.
120. Kolodny, *In Search of First Contact*, 146–47.
121. Henry David Thoreau, *Cape Cod* (Boston, 1865), 177–78.
122. Thoreau, *Cape Cod*, 229–30.

123. Everett, "*Antiquitates Americanae*," 194.
124. Thomas Cole, "Proceedings of the American Lyceum. Essay on American Scenery," *American Monthly Magazine*, January 1836, 12.

3. WASHINGTON'S NATIONAL ARCHIVE

1. Alexis de Tocqueville, *Democracy in America*, trans. Henry Reeve, ed. John C. Spencer (New York, 1841).
2. Tocqueville, *Democracy in America*, 228–29.
3. Tocqueville, *Democracy in America*, 228–29.
4. Charles-Olivier Carbonell, "La naissance de la Société de l'Histoire de France," *Annuaire-Bulletin de la Société de l'histoire de France* (1983): 111–27.
5. Jared Sparks to Alexis de Tocqueville and Gustave de Beaumont, 20 January 1832, MS Sparks 141h; Jared Sparks to Alexis de Tocqueville, 5 July 1837, MS Sparks 147g; Jared Sparks to Alexis de Tocqueville, 30 August 1833, MS Sparks 147f. All "MS Sparks" materials are to be found in Houghton Library, Harvard University, Cambridge, MA.
6. I discuss aspects of Sparks's work in "Jared Sparks and Constructing the American Archive," in *The Representation of External Threats: From the Middle Ages to the Modern World*, ed. Eberhard Crailsheim and María Dolores Elizalde (Leiden: Brill, 2019), 294–318. See, for instance, David Waldstreicher, *In the Midst of Perpetual Fetes: The Making of American Nationalism, 1776–1820* (Chapel Hill: University of North Carolina Press, 1997); Simon Newman, *Parades and the Politics of the Street: Festive Culture in the Early American Republic* (Philadelphia: University of Pennsylvania Press, 1997); Sarah Purcell, *Sealed with Blood: War, Sacrifice, and Memory in Revolutionary America* (Philadelphia: University of Pennsylvania Press, 2010), and, more recently, Michael McDonnell, Clare Corbould, Frances Clarke, and W. Fitzhugh Brundage, eds., *Remembering the Revolution: Memory, History, and Nation-Making from Independence to the Civil War* (Amherst: University of Massachusetts Press, 2013).
7. Jared Sparks, ed., *A Collection of Essays and Tracts in Theology, from Various Authors, with Biographical and Critical Notices* (Boston, 1823).
8. Sparks, *Collection of Essays and Tracts*, xi.
9. David Levin, *History as Romantic Art: Bancroft, Prescott, Motley, Parkman* (Stanford, CA: Stanford University Press, 1959), 23.
10. To raise money for his buy-out of *North American Review* shares, Sparks sold off 625 volumes, almost all theological, in late May 1824 for $657

(MS Sparks 161). Herbert Baxter Adams, *Life and Writings of Jared Sparks*, vol. 2 (Boston: Houghton, Mifflin, 1893), 605.
11. Levin, *Romantic Art*, 25–26.
12. Daniel Walker Howe, *The Unitarian Conscience: Harvard Moral Philosophy, 1805–1861* (Cambridge, MA: Harvard University Press, 1970), 174.
13. Scott E. Casper, *Constructing American Lives: Biography and Culture in Nineteenth-Century America* (Chapel Hill: University of North Carolina Press, 1999) provides an insightful survey of biographical writing in this period.
14. Jared Sparks Diary, 29 May 1824, MS Sparks 141d.
15. See Thomas A. Chambers, *Memories of War: Visiting Battlegrounds and Battlefields in the Early American Republic* (Ithaca, NY: Cornell University Press, 2012), 65–98.
16. In early 1831, when the Polish cause still seemed hopeful, Lafayette formed the Comité Central en faveur des Polonais, and with the help of James Fenimore Cooper and other Americans in Paris began to recruit American members—Lafayette even sent an official invitation to Washington's descendants: Lafayette to Washington Family at Mount Vernon, 10 February 1831, Box 55, Mount Vernon Historic Manuscript Collection, Washington Library at Mount Vernon. For more on the American response to the Polish Uprising, see Derek Kane O'Leary, "James Buchanan's 1832 Mission to the Tsar, the Plight of Poland, and the Limits of America's Revolutionary Legacy in Jacksonian Foreign Policy," in *Selected Papers of the Consortium on the Revolutionary Era, 1750–1850* (2021–22).
17. Daniel Webster, "The Revolution in Greece," in *The Great Speeches and Orations of Daniel Webster*, ed. Edwin P. Whipple (Boston, 1886), 58. Recently, American engagement with the Greek Revolution has been analyzed in Maureen Connors Santelli, *The Greek Fire: American-Ottoman Relations and Democratic Fervor in the Age of Revolutions* (Ithaca, NY: Cornell University Press, 2020).
18. D. F. Sarmiento, J. M. Gutiérrez, Jorge Ticknor, and Stuart Cuthbertson, "George Ticknor's Interest in Spanish-American Literature," *Hispania* 16, no. 2 (1933): 117–26. Ticknor was also already acquainted with Lafayette from his visits to La Grange, Lafayette's famous French residence (George Ticknor, *The Life, Letters, and Journals of George Ticknor*, ed. George Stillman Hilliard and Anna Eliot Ticknor, vol. 1 [Boston: Houghton, Mifflin, 1909], 344–45).
19. William Hickling Prescott, *The Historical Memoranda of William Hickling Prescott*, vol. 1, ed. C. Harvey Gardiner (Norman: University of Oklahoma Press, 1961).

20. Jared Sparks Diary, 27 May 1824, MS Sparks 141d.
21. Bolívar's popularity in the United States crested in the 1820s and declined as Americans objected to what they believed was his dictatorial turn (David Sowell, "The Mirror of Public Opinion Bolívar, Republicanism and the United States Press, 1821–1831," *Revista de Historia de América*, no. 134 [2004]: 165–83). For the book-length analysis of American responses to Spanish American revolutions, see Caitlin Fitz, *Our Sister Republics: The United States in an Age of American Revolutions* (New York: Norton, 2016). 23 October 1829 Meeting, "Records of the American Antiquarian Society, 1812–1849," p. 107, Institutional Archives, American Antiquarian Society, Worcester, MA.
22. James Lewis, *The American Union and the Problem of Neighborhood: The United States and the Collapse of the Spanish Empire, 1783–1829* (Chapel Hill: University of North Carolina Press, 1998), 186.
23. Sturgis E. Leavitt, "The Teaching of Spanish in the United States," *Hispania* 44, no. 4 (December 1961): 593.
24. Sparks Letter-book, 25 April 1824, MS Sparks 147b; María Ramírez Delgado, "La Biblioteca Americana y El Repertorio Americano," *América* 41 (2012): 113–21.
25. Jared Sparks to John Quincy Adams, 9 March 1824, MS Sparks 147c.
26. Sparks to Cesar Rodney, 28 June 1824, MS Sparks 147b; Sparks to William Tudor, 24 September 1825, MS Sparks 147c; Sparks to Robert Lowry and to Joel Poinsett, 27 September 1825, MS Sparks 147b. For an example of Poinsett's commentary on Mexico, see "Notes on Mexico Made in the Autumn of 1822," *North American Review* 20, no. 46 (January 1825): 77–99.
27. Sparks to William Tudor, 8 September 1826, MS Sparks 147b.
28. Sparks to Alamán, 27 September 1825, MS Sparks 147b. Alamán would later publish *Disertaciones sobre la historia de la república mejicana* (1844–49) and *Historia de México*, 5 vols. (1848–52). Luis Martin, "Lucas Alamán: Pioneer of Mexican Historiography: An Interpretive Essay," *The Americas* 32, no. 2 (October 1975): 239–56.
29. Sparks to Jose Manuel Restrepo, 10 August 1825, MS Sparks 147c.
30. Sparks to Heman Allen, 24 September 1825, MS Sparks 147b.
31. Sparks to Manuel de Salas, 24 September 1825, MS Sparks 147c.
32. Fitz, *Sister Republics*, 71.
33. Sparks to Jose Manuel Restrepo, 13 February 1826, MS Sparks 147b.
34. John Quincy Adams, "First Annual Message," 6 December 1825, in The American Presidency Project, ed. Gerhard Peters and John T. Woolley

(University of California, Santa Barbara), https://www.presidency.ucsb.edu/node/206789.
35. *The Memoirs of John Quincy Adams*, vol. 7, ed. Charles Francis Adams (Philadelphia, 1875), 102.
36. Sparks to Alamán, 27 September 1825, MS Sparks 147b.
37. Sparks to Alexander Hill Everett, 13 December 1825, MS Sparks 147b.
38. Alexander H. Everett, *America: A General Survey of the Western Continent* (Philadelphia, 1827), 15.
39. Sparks to Joel Poinsett, 10 March 1826, MS Sparks 147b.
40. "Ensayo sobre la Necesidad de una Federacion Jeneral entre los Estados Hispano-Americanos, y Plan de su Organizacion by H. Coronel D. Bernardo Monteagudo," *North American Review* 22, no. 50 (January 1826): 162–63.
41. Jared Sparks Diary, 20 May 1826, MS Sparks 147e.
42. As noted by Fitz, *Our Sister Republics*, 83. Also evident in reprintings of congressional debates such as "Negro Slavery," *Genius of Universal Emancipation*, 6 May 1826, 283.
43. *Register of Debates*, Library of Congress, 4 March 1826, Senate, 19th Cong., 1st Sess., 151–342. See Lewis, *The Problem of Neighbourhood*, 204.
44. Sparks to Manuel Moreno, 18 December 1826, MS Sparks 147d.
45. Sparks to Alexander Hill Everett, 12 September 1826, MS Sparks 147b.
46. Jared Sparks Diary, 7 May 1827, MS Sparks 141e.
47. "A Statistical and Commercial History of the Kingdom of Guatemala in Spanish America," *North American Review* 26, no. 58 (January 1828): 127–45.
48. Jared Sparks to Thomas Jefferson, 3 April 1826, MS Sparks 147.
49. Jared Sparks to Governor Tyler, 1 April 1826, MS Sparks 147b.
50. Jared Sparks to Thomas Jefferson, 13 May 1826, Founders Online, National Archives.
51. Jared Sparks Diary, May 1826, MS Sparks 141e.
52. Jared Sparks Diary, 28 May 1826, MS Sparks 141e.
53. Jared Sparks to Bushrod Washington, 16 January 1826, MS Sparks 147c.
54. On Washington's preoccupation with his papers, see W. W. Abbott, "An Uncommon Awareness of Self: The Papers of George Washington," *Prologue: Quarterly of the National Archives* (Spring 1989): 6–19.
55. Edward G. Lengel, *Inventing George Washington: America's Founder, in Myth and Memory* (New York: HarperCollins, 2011), 15.
56. Cited in Abbott, "Uncommon Awareness of Self." The longer history of Washington's papers is surveyed in *Index to the George Washington Papers*, s.v. "Provenance" (Washington, DC: Library of Congress, 1964).

57. The product of Gordon's research is discussed in George William Pilcher, "William Gordon and the History of the American Revolution," *The Historian* 34, no. 3 (May 1972): 447–64. "To George Washington from William Gordon, 2 October 1782," Founders Online, National Archives.
58. *Index to the George Washington Papers*, s.v. "Provenance."
59. Lafayette to Bushrod Washington, 20 June 1800 Lafayette Papers, Library of Congress, Washington, DC. (Thanks to Professor Cassandra Good for sharing this letter.)
60. Andrew Burstein, "Immortalizing the Founding Fathers: The Excess of Public Eulogy," in *Mortal Remains: Death in Early America*, ed. Nancy Isenberg and Burstein (Philadelphia: University of Pennsylvania Press, 2003), 105.
61. Casper, *Constructing American Lives*, 22–24.
62. Marshall would revise and reissue in different forms over the following quarter century, as discussed in William A. Foran, "John Marshall as a Historian," *American Historical Review* 43, no. 1 (October 1937): 57–60.
63. One the impact of Weems's *Washington*, see François Furstenberg, *In the Name of the Father: Washington's Legacy, Slavery, and the Making of a Nation* (New York: Penguin, 2006).
64. "From John Adams to John Marshall, 4 February 1806," Founders Online, National Archives.
65. Lengel, *Inventing George Washington*, 16; *Index to the George Washington Papers*, s.v. "Provenance." For more on the original documents taken from the Mount Vernon papers and William Buell Sprague's collecting practices, see Derek Kane O'Leary, "William Buell Sprague and the Trouble with Antiquarianism in the Early U.S.," *Archival History News* (Spring 2019), https://archivalhistory.news/2019/06/28/william-buell-sprague-and-the-trouble-with-antiquarianism-in-the-early-u-s/.
66. Eliza Parke Custis Law to John Lutz, 14 April 1828, Box 53, Mount Vernon Historic Manuscript Collection, Fred W. Smith National Library for the Study of George Washington at Mount Vernon, Mount Vernon, VA. Eliza's brother, George Washington Parke Custis, meanwhile acquired as much "Washingtonia" as possible, which he displayed for visitors in his nearby estate (see Seth C. Bruggeman, "'More Than Ordinary Patriotism': Living History in the Memory Work of George Washington Parke Custis," in *Remembering the Revolution*, 127–43).
67. Eliza Parke Custis to Izabela Czartoryska on April 26, 1828, Box 2, Washington Family Papers, Library of Congress.
68. Brandt, *First in the Homes*, 9–22.

69. Casper, *Sarah Johnson's Mount Vernon*, 32–33.
70. John Harper to Eliza Jane Harper, 29 November 1812, A-516, "Early Descriptions of Mount Vernon, 1800–1825," vol. 17, Washington Library.
71. Mary Bagot, August 18, 1816, in David Hosford, "Exile in Yankeeland: The Journal of Mary Bagot, 1816–1819," in *Records of the Columbia Historical Society of Washington, D.C.*, vol. 51, ed. J. Kirkpatrick Flack (Charlottesville: University Press of Virginia, 1984), 38.
72. Andrew Jackson, November 1815, in *Correspondence of Andrew Jackson*, vol. 2, ed. John Spencer Bassett (Carnegie Institute of Washington, 1927), 217.
73. Benjamin Latrobe to Bushrod Washington, "Early Descriptions of Mount Vernon, 1800–1825," vol. 17.
74. William Plumer, Jr., May 7, 1820, in "Mount Vernon of the Past," trans. Everett S. Brown in *D.A.R. Magazine*, February 1926, in "Early Descriptions of Mount Vernon, 1800–1825," vol. 17.
75. Journal of a "Scot recently come over," no. 40, 9 March 1823, in "Early Descriptions of Mount Vernon, 1800–1825," vol. 17.
76. "Tomb of Washington, From a Correspondent," *National Intelligencer*, 19 December 1818, in "Early Descriptions of Mount Vernon, 1800–1825," vol. 17.
77. Jared Sparks to Bushrod Washington, 16 January 1826; 12 September 1826, MS Sparks 147c.
78. Jared Sparks to Lafayette, 14 May 1827, MS Sparks 147d.
79. Diary of William Merce Green, 1818, in "Early Descriptions of Mount Vernon, 1800–1825," vol. 17.
80. Sarah Josepha Hale, "Washington," in *The Genius of Oblivion; and Other Original Poems* (Concord, NH, 1823), 87.
81. Thomas Hayes to Mrs. Patrick Hayes, 26 April 1826, RM-656, MS-4588, "Early Descriptions of Mount Vernon, 1826–1865," vol. 18.
82. Matthew R. Costello, *The Property of the Nation: George Washington's Tomb, Mount Vernon, and the Memory of the First President* (Lawrence: University of Kansas Press, 2019), 55.
83. Costello, *Property of the Nation*, 47–55.
84. Jared Sparks to Joseph Story, 14 March 1826, MS Sparks 147b.
85. Jared Sparks to Bushrod Washington, 16 January 1826, MS Sparks 147c.
86. That spring, Bushrod sold the copyright of Marshall's *Life of Washington* for seven thousand copies of the five-volume work at one dollar each, grossing thirty-five thousand dollars. He also sold the copyright for an English edition at two thousand dollars. Sparks to Marshall, 10 December

1826, *John Marshall Papers*, vol. 10, 316–17. Sparks Diary, 22 May 1827, MS Sparks 141d.
87. Sparks to Marshall, 3 April 1827, *John Marshall Papers*, vol. 11, 8.
88. Jared Sparks Journal, 16 April 1827, MS Sparks 141d.
89. Costello, *Property of the Nation*, 89–93.
90. *Index to the George Washington Papers*, s.v. "Provenance."
91. Jared Sparks to Henry Clay, 31 January 1827, MS Sparks 147d.
92. Sparks Diary, 19 May 1827, MS Sparks 141d.
93. MS Sparks 147e.
94. Jared Sparks to Edward Everett, 9 May 1836, MS Sparks 147f.
95. Jared Sparks to James Madison, 25 August 1827, MS Sparks 141b.
96. Henry Clay to William B. Lawrence, 18 January 1828, MS Sparks 147a.
97. Jared Sparks to Marbois, 21 July 1828, MS Sparks 147e.
98. I discuss the complications around access to foreign archives in Derek Kane O'Leary, "Archival Lines, Historical Practice, and the Atlantic Geopolitics behind the 1842 Webster-Ashburton Treaty," in *The Power of Maps and the Politics of Borders, Transactions of the American Philosophical Society* 110, no. 4 (Philadelphia: University of Pennsylvania Press, 2021).
99. Jared Sparks to William Lawrence, 15 September 1828, MS Sparks 147a.
100. Jared Sparks to John Hay, 10 January 1829, MS Sparks 147a.
101. Sparks's negotiations and the publication history are reconstructed in Adams, *Life and Writings of Jared Sparks*, vol. 2, 132–60.
102. Casper, *Constructing American Lives*, 141–52. Casper observes that the additional fifteen volumes published in the 1840s significantly expanded the range of authors, the subjects covered, and the scope of American history beyond the stark New England focus evident in the earlier volumes.
103. 10 August 1835, Journals, MS Catharine Maria Sedgwick Papers: Part I. Catharine Maria Sedgwick papers I, 1798–1897 Reel 7, Box 11, Folder 10, Massachusetts Historical Society, Nineteenth Century Collections Online.
104. 3 November 1835, Journals, MS Catharine Maria Sedgwick Papers.
105. I examine the dynamic between Sedgwick's and Sparks's depictions of Washington in Derek Kane O'Leary, "Washington Writing in the Archival Space of Catharine Maria Sedgwick's *The Linwoods*," *Harvard Library Bulletin* (2020).
106. "The Linwoods, or Sixty Years since in America," *North American Review* 42, no. 90 (January 1836): 160–61, 194.
107. Charlene Avallone, "Catharine Sedgwick and the Circles of New York," *Legacy* 23, no. 2 (2006): 115–31.

108. Catharine Maria Sedgwick, *The Linwoods, or, "Sixty Years Since" in America* (Hanover, NH: University Press of New England, 2002), 32, 358.
109. Sparks to Sedgwick, 28 October 1833, MS Sparks 147g.
110. As discussed in "*The Writings of George Washington; Being His Correspondence, Addresses, Messages, and Other Papers, Official and Private, Selected and Published from the Original Manuscripts; With a Life of the Author, Notes and Illustrations.* Vols. II, and III by George Washington and Jared Sparks," *North American Review* 39, no. 85 (October 1834): 471–76.
111. *The Linwoods*, 103.
112. George Washington to the President of Congress, 20 July 1779, in Jared Sparks, *The Writings of George Washington*, vol. 6 (Boston, 1834), 298–303.
113. *The Linwoods*, 204–5.
114. *The Linwoods*, 94.
115. *The Linwoods*, 104.
116. *The Linwoods*, 190.
117. *The Linwoods*, 187–89.
118. *The Linwoods*, 240.
119. Jared Sparks, *The Writings of George Washington*, vol. 3 (Boston, 1834), xv.
120. Sparks, *Writings of Washington*, vol. 6, 508–14.
121. *The Linwoods*, 5–6.
122. *The Linwoods*, 73.
123. Sparks, *Writings of Washington*, vol. 3, xv.
124. *The Linwoods*, 203–4.
125. Sparks, "Washington as a Man of Business," MS Sparks 132.
126. *The Linwoods*, 90.
127. Jared Sparks, ed., *Library of American Biography*, vol. 7 (Boston: Hilliard, Gray, 1837), 239–94.
128. Sparks, *The Writings of George Washington*, vol. 7 (Boston, 1835), 467–68, https://archive.org/details/writingsofgeorgew07wash/page/n9/mode/2up?view=theater.
129. Louis McLane to George Corbin Washington, 10 December 1833, Box 57, Mount Vernon Historic Manuscript Collection.
130. Sparks to George Corbin Washington, 5 September 1834, Box 58, Mount Vernon Historic Manuscript Collection.
131. Jared Sparks to Edward Everett, 3 March 1834, MS Sparks 147f.
132. Sparks to Mount Vernon, 7 January 1833, Bushrod Washington Family Papers; Sparks to George Corbin Washington, 11 May 1835, Box 59, Mount Vernon Historic Manuscript Collection.
133. Adams, *Life and Writings of Jared Sparks*, vol. 2, 280.

134. George Corbin Washington to Louis McLane, 3 January 1834, Box 57, Mount Vernon Historic Manuscript Collection.
135. George Corbin Washington to John Forsyth, 24 December 1838, Box 62, Mount Vernon Historic Manuscript Collection.
136. Jared Sparks Diary, 22 July 1837, MS Sparks 141h.
137. Edward Everett, *The Mount Vernon Papers* (New York: D. Appleton, 1860), 337. Sparks likely inspired Bancroft, an early contributing writer to the *North American Review*, to turn to history (Russel B. Nye, *George Bancroft: Brahmin Rebel* [New York: Knopf, 1944], 94).
138. Robert C. Winthrop, John C. Gray, Theophilus Parsons, Charles G. Loring, and Thomas Aspinwall, "Special Meeting. Tribute to Jared Sparks," *Proceedings of the Massachusetts Historical Society* 9 (1866–67): 157–76.

4. STATE OF THE ARCHIVES

1. Albert Gallatin to State Legislature, 3 February 1846, *Proceedings of the New York Historical Society for the Year 1846* (1847): 98–99. Comparative and transnational approaches to state archives in Europe include Ilaria Porciana, ed., *Setting the Standards: Institutions, Networks and Communities of National Historiography* (New York: Palgrave Macmillan, 2012); Michel Duchein, "The History of European Archives and the Development of the Archival Profession in Europe," *American Archivist* 55 (Winter 1992): 14–25; Pieter Huistra, "The Documents of Faith. The Centralization of the Archive in the Nineteenth-Century Historiography," in *From Early Modern to Modern Disciplines*, ed. Rens Bod, Jaap Maat, and Thijs Weststeijn, vol. 2 of *The Making of the Humanities*, 357–75 (Amsterdam: Amsterdam University Press, 2012); Philipp Müller, "Archives and History: Towards a History of 'the Use of State Archives' in the 19th Century," *History of the Human Sciences* 26, no. 4 (2013): 27–49.
2. Lindsay DiCuirci, *Colonial Revivals: The Nineteenth-Century Lives of Early American Books* (Philadelphia: University of Pennsylvania Press, 2019), 2.
3. State of Maine, "Act of Incorporation," 1822, reprinted in *Collections of the Maine Historical Society* 1 (1831): i.
4. 24 April 1815 meeting, Historical Committee Minutes, Archives, VIII, 4a, vol. 1, 1815–1820, American Philosophical Society (ASP), Philadelphia.
5. Du Ponceau to Samuel Coates, 12 March 1816, APS Letter book.
6. Du Ponceau to George Logan, 27 March 1816, APS Letter book.
7. *Memoirs of the Historical Society of Pennsylvania* 1 (1826): iii.
8. "Constitution," *Memoirs of the Historical Society of Pennsylvania* 1 (1826): 13.

9. "Constitution," *Memoirs of the Historical Society of Pennsylvania* 1 (1826): 13–14.
10. "History of Pennsylvania," *Saturday Evening Post*, 18 November 1826.
11. "Memoir of Mrs. Deborah Logan," in *Correspondence between William Penn and James Logan, Secretary of the Province of Pennsylvania, and Others, 1700–1750. From the Original Letters in Possession of the Logan Family, with Notes by the late Mrs. Deborah Logan*, edited with Additional Notes by Edward Armstrong, M.A. (Philadelphia, 1870), xli–xliv.
12. Deborah Norris Logan Diary, vol. 1, 3 April 1815, Historical Society of Pennsylvania (HSP), Philadelphia.
13. Deborah Logan Norris's unfinished memoir of her husband was edited by her granddaughter and published in 1899 under the auspices of the Historical Society of Pennsylvania (Deborah Logan Norris, *Memoir of Dr. George Logan of Stenton*, ed. Frances Logan [Philadelphia, 1899]). In addition to Susan M. Stabile, *Memory's Daughters: The Culture of Remembrance in Eighteenth-Century America* (Ithaca, NY: Cornell University Press, 2004), the scarce scholarship on Logan comprises a handful of short articles, including Terry L. Premo, "'Like a Being Who Does Not Belong': The Old Age of Deborah Norris Logan," *Pennsylvania Magazine of History and Biography* 107, no. 1 (January 1983): 85–112; Marleen Barr, "Deborah Norris Logan, Feminist Criticism, and Identity Theory: Interpreting a Woman's Diary without the Danger of Separatism," *Biography* 8, no. 1 (Winter 1985): 12–24; and Amelia Mott Gummere, "Her Contributions to History," *Journal of the Friends' Historical Society* (January 1905): 9–15. I discuss Logan's work on these papers and engagement with historical institutions in Derek Kane O'Leary, "Gender and the Archival Threshold in the Early U.S. Historical Society," *New Americanist* 1, no. 4 (Spring 2020): 29–57.
14. 30 October 1815 Meeting, Meetings of the Historical Committee, APS.
15. Deborah Norris Logan to John Vaughan, 1 April 1816, R. R. Logan Collection of John Dickinson Papers, 383, Box 6, HSP.
16. 22 May 1816 Meeting, Minutes of the Committee of History and Literature, APS.
17. 31 December 1817 Meeting, Minutes of the Committee of History and Literature, APS.
18. 3 November 1819 Meeting, Minutes of the Committee of History and Literature, APS.
19. Deborah Norris Logan Diary, vol. 3, 18 February 1818, HSP.
20. 16 May 1820 Meeting, Minutes of the Committee of History and Literature, APS.

21. 16 August 1820 Meeting, Minutes of the Committee of History and Literature, APS; "Memoranda of the desolate state of my mind," Deborah Norris Logan Diary, vol. 4, 18 November 1821, HSP.
22. This included prominent women such as Dolley Madison, who inherited James Madison's papers upon his death (see Mary Bilder, *Madison's Hand: Revising the Constitutional Convention* [Cambridge, MA: Harvard University Press, 2015]).
23. 5 November 1825, Society Minutes, HSP; "Inaugural Address," *Memoirs of the Historical Society of Pennsylvania* 1 (1826): 42–43.
24. 1 August 1825, Society Minutes, HSP.
25. Deborah Norris Logan Diary, vol. 8, 6 August 1825, HSP; Deborah Norris Logan Diary, vol. 8, 12 September 1825, HSP.
26. 13 May 1825, Society Minutes, HSP. The larger, complex context of oral tradition and documentary evidence related to Penn and the Walking Treaty is explored in Andrew Newman, *On Records: Delaware Indians, Colonists, and the Media of History and Memory* (Lincoln: University of Nebraska Press, 2012).
27. 3 February 1845, Council Meetings, 1844–48, HSP. The use of relics such as hair to connect antebellum Americans with the nation's past is explored in Keith Beutler, *George Washington's Hair: How Early American Remembered the Founders* (Charlottesville: University of Virginia Press, 2021).
28. "Celebration by the Historical Society of Pennsylvania of the Anniversary of the First Landing of William Penn," 8 November 1852, Correspondence, HSP.
29. DiCuirci, *Colonial Revivals*, 131.
30. This is based on the most recent compilation of data about early US historical societies in Alea Henle's *Rescued from Oblivion: Historical Cultures in the Early United States* (Amherst: University of Massachusetts Press, 2020), 193–97.
31. Edward Jarvis, "Some Account of the Kentucky Historical Society," *American Quarterly Register* 15 (1842–43): 72; William Wagner, "Location, Location, Location: Boosterism, Mobility, and the Market for Community in the Antebellum West," *Early American Studies* (Winter 2019): 120–46. I examine the early Kentucky Historical Society in detail in Derek Kane O'Leary, "'The Historical Society Has Removed to Massachusetts': Edward Jarvis and the First Kentucky Historical Society," *Register of the Kentucky Historical Society* 121, no. 1 (Winter 2023): 5–50.
32. Rosalba Davico, ed., *The Autobiography of Edward Jarvis (1803–1884)*, *Medical History* 12 (1992): 52.

33. For more historical context, see Lester F. Goodchild and David M. Wrobel, "Western College Expansion: Churches and Evangelization, States and Boosterism, 1818–1945," in *Higher Education in the American West: Regional History and State Contexts*, ed. Goodchild, Richard W. Jonsen, Patty Limerick, and David Longanecker (New York: Palgrave Macmillan, 2014), 3–37.
34. *Proceedings of the Massachusetts Historical Society, 1835–1855* 2 (1880): 113–14; "Circular Address," *Act of Incorporation, and Constitution and By-Laws of the Kentucky Historical Society* (Louisville, 1838), 11.
35. *Kentucky Gazette* (Lexington), May 7, 1840.
36. *Kentucky Gazette*, June 18, 1840 (quotation). For more on this topic, see Matthew Pearl, *The Taking of Jemima Boone: Colonial Settlers, Tribal Nations, and the Kidnap That Shaped America* (New York: HarperCollins, 2021).
37. *Kentucky Gazette*, June 18, 1840 (quotation); Herman, "The Other Daniel Boone: The Nascence of a Middle-Class Hunter Hero, 1784–1860," *Journal of the Early Republic* 18 (Autumn 1998): 429–57.
38. Davico, *Autobiography*, 52.
39. See Thomas D. Clark, "The Press," 234–55, in *A History of Kentucky* (repr., Lexington, KY: John Bradford, 1950).
40. Jarvis, "Some Account," 77.
41. Wagner, "Location, Location, Location," 134.
42. Leonard Bliss, "Scraps of Western History," *Literary News-Letter*, May 9, 1840, MIC 7104, Kentucky Historical Society.
43. *Acts of the General Assembly of the Commonwealth of Kentucky: Passed at Called Session, August, 1840, and at December Session, 1840* (Frankfort, 1841); Kentucky General Assembly, Senate, "Journal of the Senate of the Commonwealth of Kentucky, December 7, 1840–February 18, 1841," *Journals of the General Assembly of the Commonwealth of Kentucky* (Frankfort, 1840), 82.
44. Edward Jarvis receipt and letter to Robert Letcher, June 22, 1842, SC 699, Kentucky Historical Society.
45. Jarvis, "Some Account," 76.
46. Davico, *Autobiography*, 52.
47. Davico, *Autobiography*, 52.
48. Davico, *Autobiography*, 53; Stephens, "'A Glorious Birthright to Guard,'" 10–11.
49. Davico, *Autobiography*, 48.
50. "Introductory Remarks," *Collections of the Maine Historical Society* 1 (1831).

51. "Plymouth Oration," in *The Speeches of Daniel Webster*, ed. Reverend B. F. Tefft (New York: Chesterfield Society, 1900), 66; Lawrence Buell, *New England Literary Culture: From Revolution through Renaissance* (New York: Cambridge University Press, 1986).
52. Joseph A. Conforti, *Imagining New England: Explorations of Regional Identity from the Pilgrims to the Mid-Twentieth Century* (Chapel Hill: University of North Carolina Press, 2003).
53. *Collections of the Maine Historical Society* 1 (1831): 305.
54. Howard Jones, *To the Webster-Ashburton Treaty: A Study in Anglo-American Relations, 1783–1843* (Chapel Hill: University of North Carolina Press, 1977); Francis M. Carroll, *A Good and Wise Measure: The Search for the Canadian-American Boundary, 1783–1842* (Toronto: University Press of Toronto, 2001).
55. Richard L. Kagan, "Prescott's Paradigm: American Historical Scholarship and the Decline of Spain," *American Historical Review* 101, no. 2 (April, 1996): 423–46; *Going Dutch: The Dutch Presence in America, 1609–2009*, ed. Joyce Goodfriend, Benjamin Schmidt, and Annette Stott (Leiden: Brill, 2008).
56. Folsom, "Discourse," *Collections of the Maine Historical Society* 2 (1847): 31.
57. Burgess, "A Discourse," 67.
58. Burgess, *Memoire of Bishop Burgess*, 241–42.
59. John R. Weaver II, *Legacy in Brick and Stone: American Coastal Defense Forts of the Third System, 1816–1867* (McLean, VA: Redoubt, 2001).
60. John Wingate Thornton, "Colonial Schemes of Popham and Gorges," 29 August 1862 (Boston: Edward L. Balch, 1863), 4–6.
61. *North American Review* 97, no. 200 (July 1863): 288.
62. Rev. Edward Ballard, ed., *Memorial Volume of the Popham Celebration* (Portland, ME: Bailey and Noyes, 1863).
63. "Report of the Standing Committee, 1867," Standing Committee (Board of Trustees) 1861–1874, Coll. 110, Maine Historical Society; J. G. Kohl, *Documentary History of the State of Maine*, vol. 1, ed. William Willis (Portland: Bailey and Noyes, 1869); Standing Committee Meeting notes, 17 April 1863, Coll. 110, Maine Historical Society, 32–35.
64. Woods to Sir Thomas Phillips, 2 March 1868, Correspondence, Coll. 110, Maine Historical Society; Woods, *Documentary History*, vol. 2, xviii; John Poor to Leonard Woods, 15 June 1867, Correspondence, Coll. 110, Maine Historical Society.
65. Jared Sparks to Catherine Maria Sedgwick, 28 October 1833, MS Sparks 147f, Jared Sparks Personal Papers, Houghton Library, Harvard University.

66. Such as in *The Balance, & New-York State Journal*, 25 September 1810.
67. Elizabeth L. Bradley, *Knickerbocker: The Myth behind New York* (New Brunswick, NJ: Rutgers University Press, 2009), 28.
68. *Monthly Anthology, and Boston Review* 8–9 (1810): 123–24.
69. Paul Giles, *Transatlantic Insurrections: British Culture and the Formation of American Literature, 1730–1860* (Philadelphia: University of Pennsylvania Press, 2001), 151.
70. Robert A. Ferguson, "'Hunting Down a Nation': Irving's *A History of New York*," *Nineteenth-Century Fiction* 36, no. 1 (June, 1981): 27–32.
71. Judith Richardson, *Possessions: The History and Uses of Haunting in the Hudson Valley* (Cambridge, MA: Harvard University Press, 2009).
72. Washington Irving, preface to *History of New York, from the Beginning of the World to the End of the Dutch Dynasty* (New York, 1809), xvii.
73. Gulian Crommelin Verplanck, "An Anniversary Discourse Delivered before the New-York Historical Society, December 7, 1818," *Collections of the New-York Historical Society for the Year 1821* 3 (1821): 44.
74. Verplanck, "An Anniversary Discourse," 83–86.
75. DeWitt Clinton, "Memorial to the Legislature of New York," 11 January 1814, *Collections of the New-York Historical Society* 2 (1814): ix; Mary Weatherspoon Bowden in "Knickerbocker's History and the 'Enlightened' Men of New York City," *American Literature* 47, no. 2 (May 1975): 159.
76. Clinton, "Memorial to the Legislature of New York," 11 January 1814, viii–ix.
77. Van Cleave, "Rescuing the Albany Records," 359–60.
78. Accounts of this project include Arnold Johan Ferdinand van Laer, "The Translation and Publication of the Manuscript Dutch Records of New Netherland: With an Account of Previous Attempts at Translation," *Education Department Bulletin, New York State Library Bibliography* 46, no. 462 (1 January 1910): 5–28; Vivian C. Hopkins, "The Governor and the Western Recluse: De Witt Clinton and Francis Adrian Van der Kemp," *Proceedings of the American Philosophical Society* 105 (June 1961); and Vivian C. Hopkins and Louis C. Jones, "The Dutch Records of New York: Francis Adrian van der Kemp and Dewitt Clinton," *New York History* 43, no. 4 (October 1962): 385–405. The most recent account of Van der Kemp's work is in Peter D. Van Cleave, "Rescuing the Albany Records from the Fire: Redeeming Francis Adrian van der Kemp's Notorious Attempt to Translate the Records of New Netherland," *New York History* 96, no. 3–4 (Summer/Fall 2015): 354–73.
79. Francis Adrian van der Kemp, *Francis Adrian van der Kemp, 1752–1829: An Autobiography*, ed. Helen Lincklaen Fairchild (New York, 1903), 179–81.

80. "Francis Adrian Van der Kemp to Thomas Jefferson, 10 December 1818," Founders Online, National Archives, https://founders.archives.gov/documents/Jefferson/03-13-02-0427. (Original source: *The Papers of Thomas Jefferson*, Retirement Series, vol. 13, *22 April 1818 to 31 January 1819*, ed. J. Jefferson Looney [Princeton, NJ: Princeton University Press, 2016], 479–83.)

81. The expert on the history of these materials is Charles Gehring, which he surveys in Gehring, "Documentary Sources Relating to New Netherland," in *Colonial Dutch Studies: An Interdisciplinary Approach*, ed. Eric Nooter and Patricia U. Bonomi (New York: New York University Press, 1988), 33–51.

82. William Beach Lawrence, "Anniversary Address," 1 November 1842, Orations, NYHS.

83. "To the Assembly of the State of New York," xi, reprinted in Edmund Bailey O'Callaghan, ed., *Documents Relative to the Colonial History of the State of New York* (Albany, 1856), xii.

84. In Frederick W. Seward, *Autobiography of William H. Seward, 1801–1834* (New York, 1877), 84.

85. Edmund Bailey O'Callaghan, *Documents Relative to the Colonial History of New York; Procured in Holland, England, and France, by John Romeyn Brodhead, esq., Agent* (Albany, 1856), 13.

86. O'Callaghan, *Documents Relative to the Colonial History of New York*, 12.

87. Van Tassel, *Recording America's Past*, 104–7.

88. Accounts of Brodhead's work include Nicholas Falco, "The Empire State's Search in European Archives," *American Archivist* 32, no. 2 (April 1969): 109–23; Paul W. Becker, "The Colonial Documents of New York," *New York History* 28, no. 3 (July 1947): 304–12. I discuss this case at some length in "New Netherlands, Archival Deficiency, and Contesting New York History in the Antebellum U.S," *Dutch Crossing*, 43, no. 3 (2019): 252–69.

89. John Romeyn Brodhead, *The Final Report of John Romeyn Brodhead, Agent of the State of New-York, to Procure and Transcribe documents in Europe, Relative to the Colonial History of Said State* (Albany, 1845), 11.

90. John Romeyn Brodhead Diary, vol. 3, 2 January 1840, John Romeyn Brodhead Papers, Archibald Alexander Library, Rutgers University.

91. Bleecker to John V. L. Pruyn, 1 March 1839, in Harriet Langdon Pruyn Rice, *Harmanus Bleecker: An Albany Dutchman, 1779–1849* (Albany, NY: William Boyd Printing, 1924), 111.

92. Harmanus Bleecker to John Forsyth, 30 August 1839, RG 59, NARA II.

93. Harmanus Bleecker to John Forsyth, 28 January 1841, RG84; Wim van den Doel, "From Distant Images to Closer Relations: The Netherlands and the United States during the Nineteenth Century," in *Four Centuries of Dutch-American Relations, 1609–2009* (New York: SUNY Press, 2009); Mark Peterson, "A Brahmin Goes Dutch: John Lothrop Motley and the Lessons of Dutch History in Nineteenth-Century Boston," in *Going Dutch*, 113.
94. Bleecker to Robert Pruyn, in *Bleecker*, by Rice, 139.
95. Brodhead Diary, vol. 4, 27 May 1841; Foreign Minister to Harmanus Bleecker, 3 June 1841, RG 84.
96. Brodhead Diary, vol. 8, 9 April 1841.
97. To Bleecker, 16 August 1841, RG 84.
98. Edward Everett to Earl Stanhope, 22 January 1842, "Letters from Distinguished Americans," U. 1590 C.363/3, Kent History and Library Centre, Kent, Great Britain. Earl Stanhope, Philip Henry (1805–1875) correspondence, Kent History and Library Centre, Kent, Britain.
99. I discuss Everett's diplomatic work at more length in Derek Kane O'Leary, "Repatriating the American Archive in the Antebellum U.S.," *Archival History News*, Spring 2018 newsletter, https://archivalhistory.news/2018/05/23/repatriating-the-american-archive-in-the-antebellum-u-s/, and the relationship between archival access and the US-British dispute over the Canadian border in "Archival Lines, Historical Practice, and the Atlantic Geopolitics behind the 1842 Webster-Ashburton Treaty," in *The Power of Maps and the Politics of Borders, Transactions of the American Philosophical Society* 110, no. 4 (Philadelphia: University of Pennsylvania Press, 2021). For more context for Everett's diplomatic work, see Matthew Mason, *Apostle of Union: A Political Biography of Edward Everett* (Chapel Hill: University of North Carolina Press, 2016).
100. John Romeyn Brodhead, *An Address, Delivered before the New York Historical Society, at Its Fortieth Anniversary, 20th November, 1844* (1845), 5–12, reprinted in *Proceedings of the New York Historical Society for the Year 1844* (1845).
101. "From the Hague," *New-York Tribune*, 6 October 1841, Chronicling America.
102. Brodhead Diary, vol. 4, 16 December 1842.
103. Edward Everett to Lord Aberdeen, 23 December 1841, State Papers Office Records, FO83 222, National Archives, Kew Gardens, UK.
104. Brodhead Diary, vol. 8, 6 March 1842.
105. Brodhead Diary, vol. 7, 28 February 1842.

106. Lord Aberdeen to Hobhouse, 18 April 1842, FO83 223; Hobhouse to Addington, 18 May 1842, FO83 223.
107. Foreign Office to Hobhouse, 30 March 1843, FO83 223.
108. Everett to Aberdeen, 10 December 1843, FO83 223.
109. John Romeyn Brodhead to George Folsom, 10 January 1843, "Correspondence," NYHS Archives.
110. Robert Lemon to George Folsom, 7 November 1843, "Correspondence," NYHS Archives.
111. Lewis Cass, *A Discourse Delivered at the First Meeting of the Historical Society of Michigan* (Detroit, 1839), 6–9.
112. Translated into English and published in the United States as M. Guizot, *Essay on the Character and Influence of Washington in the Revolution of the United States of America* (Boston, 1840).
113. Brodhead, "Address," 5–12.
114. Lawrence, "Anniversary Address," Orations, NYHS.
115. Brodhead to Bleecker, 8 March 1842, in *Harmanus Bleecker*, by Rice.
116. 21 January 1843, *New World*, Miscellanea, Brodhead Papers.
117. Jack Kent, "Discourse," in *Proceedings of the New York Historical Society for the Year 1844* (1845): 11.
118. *Proceedings of the New York Historical Society for the Year 1844* (1845): 70.
119. Brodhead, "Address," 3.
120. Brodhead, "Address," 46.
121. "Documents of American History in Europe," *Southern and Western Monthly Magazine and Review* 2, no. 2 (August 1845): 138.
122. "An Account of the Celebration by the New York Historical Society of Their Fortieth Anniversary, Wednesday, Nov. 20th, 1844," *Proceedings of the New York Historical Society for the Year 1844* (1845): 65.
123. George Bancroft to NYHS, 18 November 1844, reprinted in *Proceedings of the New York Historical Society for the Year 1844* (1845): 66.
124. Brodhead, *The Final Report of John Romeyn Brodhead*, 2, 26.
125. For the sparse scholarship on O'Callaghan's life, see A. Everett Peterson, "Edmund Bailey O'Callaghan: Editor of New York Historical Records," *New York History* 16, no. 1 (January 1935): 64–74; Francis Shaw Guy, *Edmund Bailey O'Callagh: A Study in American Historiography* (Washington, DC: Catholic University of America, 1934); and Jack Verney, *O'Callaghan: The Making and Unmaking of a Rebel* (Montreal: McGill-Queen's University Press, 1994).
126. "Early History of New York," *Littell's Living Age*, 4 April 1846.
127. John Romeyn Beck to O'Callaghan, 12 May 1845, vol. 1, O'Callaghan Papers, Library of Congress, Washington, DC.

128. Edmund Bailey O'Callaghan to Senator Dix, 28 January 1847, vol. 4, O'Callaghan Papers. For a discussion of the Warehousing Act, see Gautham Rao, "Cities of Ports: The Warehousing Act of 1846 and the Centralization of American Commerce," *Thresholds*, no. 34 (2007): 34–37.
129. Solomon Alofsen to O'Callaghan, 25 October 1850, vol. 5, O'Callaghan Papers.
130. *Newark Daily Advertizer*, 2 August 1848, newspaper cut-out in vol. 3, O'Callaghan Papers.
131. O'Callaghan to Chargé d'affaires of the Netherlands, 11 September 1848, vol. 3, O'Callaghan Papers.
132. Francis Parkman to O'Callaghan, 3 September 1852, vol. 6, O'Callaghan Papers.
133. O'Callaghan to Robert Pruyn, 11 May 1848, vol. 3, O'Callaghan Papers.
134. "An Act to Provide for the Publication of Certain Documents Relating to the Colonial History of this State" is reproduced in Brodhead's "Introduction" to *Documents Relative to the Colonial History of the State of New-York*, xliii.
135. "Report of the Comptroller in Reply to a Resolution of the Assembly Relative to the Printing, &c., the Documentary and Colonial Histories," *Documents of the Assembly of the State of New York*, vol. 2 (New York: 1857), 1–5.
136. O'Callaghan, draft letter to New York State Comptroller, 28 December 1855, vol. 9, O'Callaghan Papers.
137. O'Callaghan, *Documents*, 13.

5. ALL HISTORY IS LOCAL

1. Frances Manwaring Caulkins to James Savage, 25 February 1847, Box 6, James Savage Genealogical Papers, MS N142, Massachusetts Historical Society, Boston.
2. Louis Leonard Tucker, *The Massachusetts Historical Society, A Bicentennial History, 1791–1991* (Boston: Northeastern University Press, 1995), 49, 53. For commentaries on Savage, see "Tribute by the President to James Savage," *Proceedings of the Massachusetts Historical Society, 1871–73* 12 (1873): 433–42; and George S. Hillard, *Memoir of the Hon. James Savage, LL.D., Late President of the Massachusetts Historical Society* (Boston: John Wilson and Son, 1878).
3. James Savage, "Gleanings for New England History," *Collections of the Massachusetts Historical Society*, ser. 3, vol. 8 (1843): 242–43.
4. Henry P. Haven, "Miss Frances Manwaring Caulkins, A Biographical Sketch," *New-England Historical and Genealogical Register* 23 (1869): 402–4.

5. Until recently, Caulkins's accomplishments and significance have been largely neglected. Nancy Steenburg has worked extensively with Caulkins's papers and published the most detailed account of her life and work, from which most of the biographical facts in this chapter are drawn. This includes Nancy Steenburg, "Outside Her Sphere: The Intellectual Adventures of Frances Manwaring Caulkins," *Connecticut History Review* 51, no. 1 (Spring 2012): 40–64; and Steenburg, "How to Build an Archive: Frances Manwaring Caulkins and the Birth of the New London County Historical Society," *Connecticut History Review* 60, no. 1 (Spring 2021): 120–23. A few memorials of Caulkins by her acquaintances and family appeared shortly after her death, such as Rev. G. B. Willcox, *Miss France Manwaring Caulkins, A Sermon, Delivered Feb. 14, 1869* (New London, 1869) and "Miss Frances Manwaring Caulkins. A Biographical Sketch [Communicated by Henry P. Haven, of New-London, Ct.]," *New-England Historical and Genealogical Register and Antiquarian Journal* 23 (1869).
6. Monthly Meeting, March 29, 1849, *Proceedings of the Massachusetts Historical Society, 1835–1855* 2 (1880): 424. Caulkins is the first woman to appear in the comprehensive list of members between 1791 and 1991 in the bicentennial history published by the Massachusetts Historical Society. The next woman to be selected as a member, novelist and historian Esther Forbes, was not nominated until 1967 (Tucker, *Bicentennial History, 1791–1991*, 427, 471–538; Steenburg, "Outside Her Sphere," 58–59).
7. Robert Winthrop, February 1869 meeting, "Death of Miss Frances M. Caulkins," *Proceedings of the Massachusetts Historical Society, 1867–1869* 10 (1869): 473.
8. Cited in Tucker, *Bicentennial History*, 58.
9. In addition to the correspondence with Savage archived at the Massachusetts Historical Society, the majority of her genealogical papers and correspondence is preserved at the New London County Historical Society.
10. Caulkins to Savage, 28 May 1845, Savage Genealogical Papers.
11. Caulkins, "Dedication," in *History of Norwich, Connecticut, from Its Settlement in 1660, to January 1845* (Norwich, CT: Thomas Robinson, 1845), iii.
12. See Nicole Tonkovich, *Domesticity with a Difference: The Nonfiction of Catharine Beecher, Sarah J. Hale, Fanny Fern, Margaret Fuller* (Jackson: University of Mississippi Press, 1997), 53. See also Mary Kelley, *Private Woman, Public Stage: Literary Domesticity in Nineteenth-Century America* (New York: Oxford University Press, 1984).
13. The crucial study of the variety of women's public-facing historical writing in these years is Nina Baym, *American Women Writers and the Work of*

History, 1790–1860 (New Brunswick, NJ: Rutgers University Press, 1995). The household work of historical preservation and writing is explored in Susan M. Stabile, *Memory's Daughters: The Culture of Remembrance in Eighteenth-Century America* (Ithaca, NY: Cornell University Press, 2004). On nineteenth-century historical research and writing gendered as masculine, Bonnie G. Smith, *The Gender of History: Men, Women, and Historical Practice* (Cambridge, MA: Harvard University Press, 1998).

14. Women's role as "stewards of family memory" is discussed in François Weil, *Family Trees: A History of Genealogy in America* (Cambridge, MA: Harvard University Press, 2013), 53–54. The work of women as "custodians of the local past" is described in Julie Des Jardins, *Women and the Historical Enterprise in America: Gender, Race, and the Politics of Memory, 1880–1945* (Chapel Hill: University of North Carolina Press, 2003), 1–3.
15. Caulkins, preface to *History of Norwich*, v–vi.
16. Savage, *Genealogical Dictionary*, vol. 1, viii.
17. Savage, *Genealogical Dictionary*, vol. 1, v–vi.
18. Caulkins to Savage, 10–11 August 1846, James Savage Genealogical Papers.
19. Weil, *Family Trees*, 63–65.
20. Caulkins to Savage, 7 April 1849, James Savage Genealogical Papers.
21. Caulkins, *New London*, 473.
22. Jean M. O'Brien's *Firsting and Lasting: Writing Indians out of Existence in New England* (Minneapolis: University of Minnesota Press, 2010), 35.
23. Caulkins, *Norwich*, 49.
24. Caulkins, *Norwich*, v.
25. Sylvester Judd to Caulkins, 30 December 1852, Frances Manwaring Caulkins Papers, New London County Historical Society. For this tendency among historians and historical societies, see O'Brien, *Firsting and Lasting*.
26. "Address by William Lincoln," *Proceedings of the American Antiquarian Society, 1812–1849* (1912): 315.
27. Christopher Columbus Baldwin, *Diary of Christopher Columbus Baldwin, Librarian of the American Antiquarian Society, 1829–1835* (Worcester, MA: American Antiquarian Society, 1901), 112.
28. Baldwin, *Diary of Christopher Columbus Baldwin*, xiii.
29. Caulkins to Savage, 3 October 1846, James Savage Genealogical Papers.
30. Caulkins to Savage, 3 February 1847, James Savage Genealogical Papers.
31. Haven, "Miss Frances Manwaring Caulkins," 404.
32. David D. Van Tassel, *Recording America's Past: An Interpretation of the Development of Historical Studies in America, 1607–1884* (Chicago: University of Chicago Press, 1960), 122.

33. Caulkins to Savage, 21 October 1846, James Savage Genealogical Papers.
34. Caulkins to Savage, 17 November 1846, James Savage Genealogical Papers.
35. Caulkins to Savage, 4 July 1851, James Savage Genealogical Papers.
36. Caulkins to Savage, 9 July 1845, James Savage Genealogical Papers.
37. Caulkins to Savage, 10–11 August 1846, James Savage Genealogical Papers.
38. Caulkins to Savage, 10–11 August 1846, James Savage Genealogical Papers.
39. Smith, *The Gender of History*, 136–37.
40. Caulkins to Savage, 15 November 1847, James Savage Genealogical Papers.
41. Caulkins to Savage, 25 March 1846, James Savage Genealogical Papers.
42. Caulkins to Savage, 9 July 1850, James Savage Genealogical Papers.
43. Caulkins to Savage, 9 July 1850, James Savage Genealogical Papers.
44. Caulkins, *New London*, 44.
45. Cheng, *Plain and Noble Garb of Truth*, 30–32.
46. O'Brien, *Firsting and Lasting*, xiii.
47. Weil, *Family Trees*, 59–60; Weil, "John Farmer and the Making of American Genealogy," *New England Quarterly* 80, no. 3 (2007): 408–34.
48. Caulkins to Savage, 25 March 1846, James Savage Genealogical Papers.
49. Caulkins to Savage, 15 November 1847, James Savage Genealogical Papers.
50. John J. Babson, *History of the Town of Gloucester, Cape Ann, Including the Town of Rockport* (Gloucester, MA: Procter Brothers, 1860), iii.
51. Caulkins to Savage, 3 October 1846, James Savage Genealogical Papers.
52. Smith, *The Gender of History*, 116–29.
53. James Savage to William Barton Rogers, 11 December 1850, in *Letters of James Savage to His Family*, ed. Emma Savage (Boston, 1906), 131–32.
54. Caulkins to Savage, 28 May 1845, James Savage Genealogical Papers.
55. Scott Caspar, *Constructing American Lives: Biography and Culture in Nineteenth-Century America* (Chapel Hill: University of North Carolina Press, 1999), 159–60.
56. Caulkins to Savage, 15 November 1847, James Savage Genealogical Papers.
57. Caulkins to Savage, 16 March 1848, James Savage Genealogical Papers.
58. Caulkins to Savage March 25, 1846, James Savage Genealogical Papers.
59. Caulkins to Savage, 26 May 1851, James Savage Genealogical Papers.
60. Caulkins to Savage, 10–11 August 1846, James Savage Genealogical Papers.

61. Caulkins to Savage, 3 February 1847, James Savage Genealogical Papers.
62. Caulkins to Savage, 9 July 1845, James Savage Genealogical Papers; Caulkins to Savage, 3 October 1846, James Savage Genealogical Papers.
63. Van Tassel, *Recording America's Past*, 122–23.
64. Richard Frothingham, Jr. to Frances Manwaring Caulkins, 18 May 1848, Frances Manwaring Caulkins Papers.
65. James Savage, *A Genealogical Dictionary of the First Settlers of New England, Showing Three Generations of Those Who Came before May, 1692, on the Basis of Farmer's Register*, vol. 1 (Boston: Little, Brown, 1860), xi.
66. Sylvester Judd to James Savage, Nov 3, 1846, vol. 1, Sylvester Judd Correspondence, James Savage Genealogical Papers.
67. Caulkins to Savage, 24 January 1849, James Savage Genealogical Papers.
68. Caulkins to Savage, 24 January 1849, James Savage Genealogical Papers.
69. Smith, *The Gender of History*, 43.
70. Caulkins to Savage, 19 March 1849, James Savage Genealogical Papers.
71. James Savage, "More Gleanings for New England History," *Collections of the Massachusetts Historical Society*, ser. 4, vol. 1 (1852): 91–101.
72. Tucker speculates that if other members objected to Savage's unprecedented nomination of Caulkins, they may have been fearful to challenge the "strong-minded" president (Tucker, *A Bicentennial History*, 55–57).
73. Caulkins to Savage, 7 April 1849, James Savage Genealogical Papers; A. Lawson to Caulkins, 10 July 1849, Frances Manwaring Caulkins Papers.
74. Payne Kenyon Kilbourn to Caulkins, 1 February 1853, Frances Manwaring Caulkins Papers.
75. Smith, *The Gender of History*, 103–31; Peter Novick, *That Noble Dream: The "Objectivity Question" and the American Historical Profession* (New York: Cambridge University Press, 1998), 47–60.
76. Charles Miner to Caulkins, 3 July 1845, Frances Manwaring Caulkins Papers.
77. Caulkins to Savage, 23 July 1851, James Savage Genealogical Papers.
78. Caulkins to Savage, 16 March 1848, James Savage Genealogical Papers.
79. Smith, *The Gender of History*, 118.
80. Caulkins to Savage, 9 July 1845, James Savage Genealogical Papers; Caulkins, *History of Norwich*, 24.
81. Caulkins to Savage, 9 July 1845, James Savage Genealogical Papers.
82. Based on his research in the town records of Connecticut, Hinman had recently published *A Catalogue of the Names of the First Puritan Settlers of the Colony of Connecticut* (Hartford: R. Gleason, 1846).

83. Caulkins to Savage, 21 August 1848, James Savage Genealogical Papers.
84. Caulkins to Savage, 24 January 1849, James Savage Genealogical Papers.
85. Sylvester Judd to James Savage, Nov 3, 1846, vol. 1, Sylvester Judd correspondence, James Savage Genealogical Papers.
86. Caulkins, *History of Norwich*, vi.
87. Caulkins to Savage, 25 February 1847, James Savage Genealogical Papers.
88. James Savage to Emma Savage, 30 July 1867, in *Letters of James Savage to His Family*, ed. Emma Savage (Boston, 1906), 283.
89. Caulkins to Savage, 21 April 1849, James Savage Genealogical Papers.
90. Weil, *Family Trees*, 62.
91. Caulkins, *New London*, 56.
92. Cheng, *Plain and Noble Garb of Truth*, 105.
93. David Hall and Alan Taylor, "Reassessing the Local History of New England," in *New England: A Bibliography of Its History* (Hanover, NH: University Press of New England, 1989), xxxix.
94. "New Publications," *New England Historical and Genealogical Review* 12 (1853): 95.
95. Des Jardins, *Women and the Historical Enterprise in America*, 20–25; Smith, *The Gender of History*, 103–31.
96. *Collections of the Massachusetts Historical Society*, ser. 4, vol. 1 (1852): x–xi.
97. Alex Young to Caulkins, 26 April 1849, Frances Manwaring Caulkins Papers.
98. Sylvester Judd to Caulkins, 30 December 1852, Frances Manwaring Caulkins Papers.
99. Quoted in Henry P. Haven, *Memoir of Frances Manwaring Caulkins* (New London, CT, 1874), 30.
100. Henry Bond to Caulkins, 24 April 1854, Frances Manwaring Caulkins Papers.
101. E. Oakes Smith to Caulkins, 16 October 1858, Frances Manwaring Caulkins Papers.
102. Charles Bushnell to Caulkins, 9 April 1855, Frances Manwaring Caulkins Papers.
103. Charles Bushnell to Caulkins, from 9 April 1855, Frances Manwaring Caulkins Papers.
104. Weil, *Family Trees*, 58.
105. Such as the footnote to "See the excellent and interesting History of Norwich, by Miss Caulkins" in "Perkins Genealogy," *New England Historical and Genealogical Register* 10 (1856): 215, or in her essay on the "Ancient

Burial Ground at New London, Conn.," *New England Historical and Genealogical Register* 11 (1857): 21–30.
106. Lyman Draper to Caulkins, 6 April 1855, Frances Manwaring Caulkins Papers. After the Civil War, the Buffalo Historical Society also elected her a member. George Armstrong to Caulkins, 15 February 1867, Frances Manwaring Caulkins Papers. "Objects of Collection Desired by the Society," *Collections of the State Historical Society of Wisconsin* 1 (repr., 1903): 146–47.
107. S. Green, 1 April 1856, Frances Manwaring Caulkins Papers.
108. Lorenzo Sabine to Caulkins, 14 October 1861, Frances Manwaring Caulkins Papers.
109. Weil, *Family Trees*, 52–53.
110. Roger Baldwin to Caulkins, August 1845, Frances Manwaring Caulkins Papers.
111. Van Tassel, *Recording America's Past*, 90.
112. J. Rhowdly (?) to Caulkins, 7 September 1849, Frances Manwaring Caulkins Papers.
113. Miss F. M. Caulkins, *Memoir of the Rev. William Adams of Dedham, Mass. and of the Rev. Eliphalet Adams of New London, Conn.* (Cambridge, 1849), 8.
114. Caulkins, *Norwich*, 10–11.
115. Caulkins, *New London*, 15.
116. Buell, *New England Literary Culture*, 308–9; Stephen Nissenbaum, "New England as Region and Nation," in *All Over the Map: Rethinking American Regions* (Baltimore, MD: John Hopkins University Press, 1996), 50. See also Joseph A. Conforti, *Imagining New England: Explorations of Regional Identity from the Pilgrims to the Mid-Twentieth Century* (Chapel Hill: University of North Carolina, 2001), 124.
117. Caulkins, "Old Burial Ground of New London," 5.
118. Savage, *Genealogical Dictionary*, vol. 1, v–vi.
119. Savage, *Genealogical Dictionary*, vol. 1, vi–vii.
120. O'Brien, *Firsting and Lasting*, xiii.
121. Hall and Taylor, "Reassessing the Local History of New England," xxv.
122. Caulkins, *New London*, iii.

CONCLUSION

1. William Willis, "Introductory Address before the Maine Historical Society," *Collections of the Maine Historical Society* 4 (1856): 3–4.
2. Willis, "Introductory Address before the Maine Historical Society," 4.

3. For instance, on the challenges of interpreting silence in the archives of slavery, see Brian Connolly and Marisa Fuentes, "Introduction: From Archives of Slavery to Liberated Futures?" *History of the Present* 6, no. 2 (2016): 105–16; and Fuentes, *Dispossessed Lives: Enslaved Women, Violence, and the Archive* (Philadelphia: University of Pennsylvania Press, 2016).
4. For the classic discussion of this development in the profession, see Peter Novick, *That Noble Dream: The 'Objectivity Question' and the American Historical Profession* (New York: Cambridge University Press, 1988).
5. For the development of the discipline after the Civil War, see Julie Des Jardins, *Women and the Historical Enterprise in America: Gender, Race, and the Politics of Memory, 1880–1945* (Chapel Hill: University of North Carolina Press, 2003).
6. James Louis Petigru, "Oration Delivered on the Third Anniversary of the South-Carolina Historical Society," 27 May 1858, *Collections of the South-Carolina Historical Society* 2 (1858): 21.
7. For the divided historical consciousness and practice of building archives after the Civil War, see David Blight, *Race and Reunion: The Civil War in American Memory* (Cambridge, MA: Harvard University Press, 2002); W. Fitzhugh Brundage, *Southern Past: A Clash of Race and Memory* (Cambridge, MA: Harvard University Press, 2008); and Yael A. Sternhell, "The Afterlives of a Confederate Archive: Civil War Documents and the Making of Sectional Reconciliation," *Journal of American History* 102, no. 4 (March 2016).

➤ INDEX ◄

Aberdeen, Lord (George Hamilton-Gordon, 4th earl of Aberdeen), 140–42, 152
Adams, John, 13, 98, 110
Adams, John Quincy, 2–5, 88–91, 103, 106, 143
Alamán, Lucas, 89–91
American Antiquarian Society (AAS), 11–18, 24–25, 27, 29, 31–32, 37, 54, 87, 159
American Philosophical Society (APS), 16, 24, 31, 46, 54, 121–23
American Revolution, 4, 11–13, 16, 25, 31, 37–38, 41, 48, 85–92, 94–96, 103–14, 117, 176
Anglo-Saxon, 2, 66–67, 178–79
antiquarianism. *See* Sprague, William Buell
Antiquitates Americanae, 43–44, 50–52, 56–61, 68–70, 75–77
archives: and colonialism, 1–2; 18–21, 28, 41–42, 122–24, 126–27, 134–35, 147–49, 162, 177–80; in contemporary debates, 9–10, 183; European contexts, 14–15, 28–29, 33–36, 40–41, 49–50, 80–83, 104–5, 119–20, 132–33, 136, 138–43, 152; and gender, 8, 106–14, 123–24, 152–55; and international exchanges, 7–8, 25, 37–38, 44, 51–52, 56–57, 68–69, 88–93, 104–5, 133, 137–44, 152, 184; and state governments, 119–21, 127–28, 132–33, 135–37, 143–45, 147–50, 181–82
Atwater, Caleb, 27–28. *See also* American Antiquarian Society (AAS)

Baldwin, Christopher Columbus, 11–12, 37–39, 159. *See also* American Antiquarian Society
Bancroft, George, 49, 57, 70, 78, 86, 106–7, 144, 146, 150, 162–63, 174, 178, 184, 212n137
Barber, John Warner, 171
Beck, John Romeyn, 145–46
Belknap, Jeremy, 13–14, 17, 36. *See also* Massachusetts Historical Society (MHS)
Bliss, Leonard, 125–29. *See also* Kentucky Historical Society
Bolívar, Simón, 24–25, 87, 90–91, 94, 206n21
Britain, 13–15, 28, 92, 96, 99, 104–5, 108–12, 119–20, 130, 132–33, 136–46, 152, 154–55, 167
Brodhead, John Romeyn, 5, 36, 137–48, 152

Canada, 48, 74, 130, 139–40, 145, 148
Cass, Lewis, 23, 142

230 INDEX

Caulkins, Frances Manwaring: research methods, 157–62, 182–83; scholarly community, 162–71, 174–76, 184; scholarly identity, 9, 152–56, 164–66, 222n5
Child, Lydia Maria, 66
Civil War, The, 4–5, 131–32, 181, 184
Clay, Henry, 4, 92, 103, 105
Clinton, DeWitt, 135–36, 150
Cole, Thomas, 80–81
Columbus, Christopher, 2–6, 45–50, 56–57, 70, 74–80
Congress of Panama, 90–94
Connecticut, 11, 23, 34, 74, 151–80. See also Caulkins, Frances Manwaring; Connecticut Historical Society (CHS)
Connecticut Historical Society (CHS), 34, 36
consuls. See United States diplomatic and consular officials

Denmark, 46–47, 49, 51–53, 55, 62, 83
diplomacy. See United States diplomatic and consular officials
Dorchester Antiquarian and Historical Society, 32, 40
Draper, Lyman, 41, 175. See also Wisconsin Historical Society (WHS)
Du Ponceau, Pierre-Etienne, 24, 46, 121–22. See also American Philosophical Society (APS)

Ellet, Elizabeth, 165
Emerson, Ralph Waldo, 66
Everett, Alexander Hill, 45, 49, 67, 91–93
Everett, Edward: 35, 54, 63, 70, 75, 80, 86, 106–7, 115–18, 139–42, 152, 219n99

Folsom, George, 65, 77, 131
France, 5, 25, 28, 45, 62, 78, 82–84, 104–5, 119–20, 132–33, 137–38, 142–43, 145, 167

Gallatin, Albert, 119–20, 150
genealogy, 16, 53, 55, 58, 67, 131, 153, 155, 158–59, 163–68, 172, 176
Genius of Oblivion. See Hale, Sarah Josepha
Georgia Historical Society (GHS): 4, 19, 24, 29, 33, 35–36, 54
Guizot, François, 83, 142–43

Hale, Sarah Josepha, 25–28, 101, 184. See also New Hampshire Historical Society (NHHS)
Harvard University, 54, 79, 85, 87, 89, 152, 174
historical discipline, 50, 60–61, 67, 70–71, 76–77, 86, 105, 140–41, 153–54, 182–84, 219n99
historical fiction. See Hale, Sarah Josepha; Sedgwick, Catharine Maria
historical societies: buildings, 23, 29–31; circular letters, 18, 20, 35, 40; and civic life, 6, 16–17, 30–34; commemorations, 5–6, 24, 34, 40, 124, 131–32, 143–44; committees, 1–5, 53–53, 56–57; diplomas, 23–24, 54–55, 174; engagement with women, 25–28, 107, 122–25, 153, 168, 174, 184; and European learned institutions, 11–18, 24–25, 27–28, 40–41, 43–46, 50–62, 68–70, 80–81; membership, 15, 21–42; and patriarchy, 21–24, 28, 30; state support of, 29–30
Historical Society of Pennsylvania (HSP), 16–17, 21, 38, 122–25
Holland. See Netherlands, Kingdom of the

Iceland. See Norse
Indigenous peoples, 2, 5–6, 20–21, 36–37, 49, 56, 71–72, 158–59, 178–80, 181–83
Irving, Washington, 1–2, 6, 45–49, 74–78, 107, 134–35, 138, 140, 146

Jarvis, Edward, 125–29. *See also* Kentucky Historical Society
Jefferson, Thomas, 94–95, 117
Judd, Sylvester, 40, 158, 167, 170–71, 174

Kentucky, 125–29. *See also* Kentucky Historical Society
Kentucky Historical Society (KHS): 33, 125–29, 182–83

Lafayette, Marquis de, 24–25, 38, 86–87, 93, 96–97, 100, 109, 205n16, 205n18
Law, Eliza Parke Custis, 98
Lear, Tobias, 97
Linwoods, The. See Sedgwick, Catharine Maria
local history, 9, 151–78, 182
Logan, Deborah Norris, 122–25, 155, 184, 213n13. *See also* American Philosophical Society (APS); Historical Society of Pennsylvania (HSP)
Logan, George, 122–24
Longfellow, Henry Wadsworth, 54, 57, 69, 73

Madison, Dolley, 117, 214n22
Madison, James, 104, 117
Maine, 30, 37, 39, 120–21, 129–33, 140, 145, 150, 160, 181–82. *See also* Maine Historical Society (MEHS)
Maine Historical Society (MEHS), 30, 35, 37, 39–40, 121, 129–33, 181–83
Marsh, George Perkins, 54, 57–59, 63–65
Marshall, John, 98, 102, 109, 209–10n86
Maryland Historical Society (MDHS): 4, 13, 17, 24, 33, 54
Massachusetts, 13–14, 17, 19, 23, 47, 56–57, 65, 69–70, 84, 86–89, 103, 107, 115, 117, 125, 128–29, 131, 133, 140, 142, 152–53, 158–59, 163–65, 167, 174. *See also* American Antiquarian Society;

Massachusetts Historical Society (MHS)
Massachusetts Historical Society (MHS), 2–5, 13, 17–19, 25, 31, 39, 125–26, 152, 168, 174, 222n6
McLane, Louis, 115–17
Moore, Jacob Bailey, 25–27. *See also* New Hampshire Historical Society (NHHS)
Morris, Gouverneur, 20. *See also* New York Historical Society (NYHS)
Mound Builders, 2, 25–28, 71, 191–92n52. *See also* Indigenous peoples
Mount Vernon, 37, 84, 96–103, 115–17

Netherlands, Kingdom of the, 5, 105, 119–20, 132, 136–39
New Hampshire Historical Society (NHHS), 16, 20, 25–26, 29, 32, 53, 163
New Jersey Historical Society (NJHS): 4, 33, 40
New Netherland, 133–36, 139, 145–49
New York, 5, 9, 11, 18, 36, 78, 108–14, 119–20, 131, 133–50, 152, 154, 174–75, 183. *See also* New York Historical Society (NYHS)
New York Historical Society (NYHS): 9, 15–18, 29–31, 35, 46, 53, 65, 77, 119, 130–31, 134–38, 143, 150 182–83
Norse: American perceptions of, 66–80, 201–2n86; and Iceland, 44, 48, 50–51, 55, 65–66, 75–76, 79–80; Old Icelandic manuscripts, 44, 48, 58–59, 63–67, 134, 198n28; theory of discovery, 43, 47–48, 50–51, 132
North American Review, 47, 49–50, 57, 63–64, 66, 70, 85–93, 106–7, 132, 197–98n20, 204–5n10, 212n137

O'Callaghan, Edmund Bailey, 145–50, 183
Ohio Historical and Philosophical Society, 41–42, 125

oral history, 2, 20, 32, 55, 60–61, 63–64, 66, 82, 95, 125–26, 151, 158–60, 171–72, 177, 179

Parkman, Francis, 78, 148–50.
Penn, William, 18, 121–25. See also Historical Society of Pennsylvania
Pennsylvania, 24, 55, 120–25, 128–29, 145, 150, 169, 174, 183. See also American Philosophical Society; Historical Society of Pennsylvania
Pintard, John, 18, 35. See also New York Historical Society (NYHS)
poetry: depictions of European colonialism, 28, 71–72; depictions of Indigenous civilization, 25–27; depictions of the Norse, 71–74; depictions of Washington, 101
Popham colony, 130–32. See also Maine Historical Society (MEHS)
Prescott, William Hickling, 54, 78, 86–87, 93, 106, 162–63

Rafn, Carl Christian, 43–44, 50–51, 52–57, 62–65, 68–69, 183. See also Royal Society of Northern Antiquaries
Ranke, Leopold von, 164
Restrepo, Jose Manuel, 89–90, 93
Rhode Island Historical Society (RIHS), 16, 21, 29, 32–34, 40, 56, 60, 68–70
Royal Society of Northern Antiquaries, 9, 43–44, 51–62, 65, 67–70, 74–75, 79–80, 83, 104, 118, 182; See also Antiquitates Americanae; Norse; Rafn, Carl Christian

Savage, James, 125–26, 140–42, 151–72, 175, 178–80. See also Massachusetts Historical Society (MHS)
Schoolcraft, Henry Rowe, 64, 70, 76–77
Sedgwick, Catharine Maria, 106–14, 133, 155, 184

Seward, William, 137–38, 142, 150
Sigourney, Lydia, 71–74, 80, 152, 155, 184, 203n99
South Carolina, 96, 184
Spain, 2–3, 45–46, 49, 54, 62, 78, 83, 87, 91, 130, 132, 135
Spanish American republics, 24, 85–95, 206n21
Sparks, Jared: archival collecting, 38–39, 94–96, 100–102, 104–5, 115–17; documentary projects, 9, 38–39, 84, 103–6, 149, 182–83; European correspondents, 83–84, 86–87, 104–6, 142; religious life, 85–86; scholarly network, 106–14, 117–18, 133, 162–63; Spanish American correspondents, 88–93
Sprague, William Buell, 11–12, 37–39, 98, 174

Thomas, Isaiah, 14–15, 31–32. See American Antiquarian Society
Thoreau, Henry David, 79–80
Thornton, John Wingate, 131–32, 174
Ticknor, George, 86–87, 93, 96
Tocqueville, Alexis de, 82–84, 133–34

Unitarianism, 85–86
United States: federal archives, 14, 84, 92, 103, 106, 114–17, 137; foreign perceptions of, 5–6, 24–25, 82–83, 98–100, 144–45; foreign policy, 3, 87–92, 140–41
United States diplomatic and consular officials: Harmanus Bleecker, 138–39, 150; John Romeyn Brodhead, 138; Alexander Hill Everett, 67, 91; Edward Everett, 139–42, 152, 219n99; Washington Irving, 1–2, 45–46; Robert Lowry, 89; Obadiah Rich, 45–46; Joel Poinsett, 89, 92, 206n26; Caesar Rodney, 89; David Bailie Warden, 25, Henry Wheaton, 46–49

Van der Kemp, Francis Adrian, 136
Verplanck, Gulian Crommelin, 135, 150. *See also* New York Historical Society (NYHS)
Virginia, 29, 94, 96, 99, 116
Virginia Historical and Philosophical Society (VHPS), 17, 29

War of 1812, 41, 100
Washington, Bushrod, 96–103, 209–10n86
Washington, George, 4, 9, 37–39, 84, 94–118, 120, 150, 182

Washington, George Corbin, 115–17
Webb, Thomas, 54, 56–58, 68–70. *See also* Rhode Island Historical Society (RIHS)
Webster, Daniel, 86–87, 103, 129, 140
Willis, William, 23–24, 37, 181–83. *See also* Maine Historical Society (MEHS)
Wisconsin Historical Society (WHS), 24, 29–30, 41, 54, 175–76
Woods, Leonard, 132–33. *See also* Maine Historical Society (MEHS)
Writings of George Washington, The. *See* Sparks, Jared; Washington, George

FROM PAMPHLETS TO PODCASTS
An Institute for Thomas Paine Studies Series

This series takes its cue from Thomas Paine, who wrote that "America . . . replenished the world with more useful knowledge and sounder maxims of civil government" than any other society. It is intended to encompass a balanced mix of titles designed to advance a new and innovative approach to scholarship on the contests over knowledge making and the pursuit of informed, democratic citizenship in Thomas Paine's time, and about these processes' relevance to our own. It is open to intellectual histories, projects on Indigenous ways of knowing, scholarship that historicizes concepts of expertise, propaganda, and information, and studies that make transparent the methodologies (including digital) that undergird that work.

www.ingramcontent.com/pod-product-compliance
Lightning Source LLC
Chambersburg PA
CBHW031808220426
43662CB00007B/566